Communications
in Computer and Information Science 1840

Rationale

The CCIS series is devoted to the publication of proceedings of computer science conferences. Its aim is to efficiently disseminate original research results in informatics in printed and electronic form. While the focus is on publication of peer-reviewed full papers presenting mature work, inclusion of reviewed short papers reporting on work in progress is welcome, too. Besides globally relevant meetings with internationally representative program committees guaranteeing a strict peer-reviewing and paper selection process, conferences run by societies or of high regional or national relevance are also considered for publication.

Topics

The topical scope of CCIS spans the entire spectrum of informatics ranging from foundational topics in the theory of computing to information and communications science and technology and a broad variety of interdisciplinary application fields.

Information for Volume Editors and Authors

Publication in CCIS is free of charge. No royalties are paid, however, we offer registered conference participants temporary free access to the online version of the conference proceedings on SpringerLink (http://link.springer.com) by means of an http referrer from the conference website and/or a number of complimentary printed copies, as specified in the official acceptance email of the event.

CCIS proceedings can be published in time for distribution at conferences or as postproceedings, and delivered in the form of printed books and/or electronically as USBs and/or e-content licenses for accessing proceedings at SpringerLink. Furthermore, CCIS proceedings are included in the CCIS electronic book series hosted in the SpringerLink digital library at http://link.springer.com/bookseries/7899. Conferences publishing in CCIS are allowed to use Online Conference Service (OCS) for managing the whole proceedings lifecycle (from submission and reviewing to preparing for publication) free of charge.

Publication process

The language of publication is exclusively English. Authors publishing in CCIS have to sign the Springer CCIS copyright transfer form, however, they are free to use their material published in CCIS for substantially changed, more elaborate subsequent publications elsewhere. For the preparation of the camera-ready papers/files, authors have to strictly adhere to the Springer CCIS Authors' Instructions and are strongly encouraged to use the CCIS LaTeX style files or templates.

Abstracting/Indexing

CCIS is abstracted/indexed in DBLP, Google Scholar, EI-Compendex, Mathematical Reviews, SCImago, Scopus. CCIS volumes are also submitted for the inclusion in ISI Proceedings.

How to start

To start the evaluation of your proposal for inclusion in the CCIS series, please send an e-mail to ccis@springer.com.

Ludovico Boratto · Stefano Faralli ·
Mirko Marras · Giovanni Stilo
Editors

Advances in Bias and Fairness in Information Retrieval

4th International Workshop, BIAS 2023
Dublin, Ireland, April 2, 2023
Revised Selected Papers

 Springer

Editors
Ludovico Boratto ⓘ
University of Cagliari
Cagliari, Italy

Stefano Faralli ⓘ
Sapienza University of Rome
Rome, Italy

Mirko Marras ⓘ
University of Cagliari
Cagliari, Italy

Giovanni Stilo ⓘ
University of L' Aquila
L'Aquila, L'Aquila, Italy

ISSN 1865-0929   ISSN 1865-0937 (electronic)
Communications in Computer and Information Science
ISBN 978-3-031-37248-3   ISBN 978-3-031-37249-0 (eBook)
https://doi.org/10.1007/978-3-031-37249-0

This Springer imprint is published by the registered company Springer Nature Switzerland AG
The registered company address is: Gewerbestrasse 11, 6330 Cham, Switzerland

Advances in Bias and Fairness in Information Retrieval: Preface

The Fourth International Workshop on Algorithmic Bias in Search and Recommendation (BIAS 2023) was held as part of the 45th European Conference on Information Retrieval (ECIR 2023) on April 2, 2023. BIAS 2023 was held in Dublin, Ireland, with support for remote attendance. The workshop was jointly organized by University of Cagliari (Italy), Sapienza University of Rome (Italy), and University of L'Aquila (Italy). It was supported by the ACM Conference on Fairness, Accountability, and Transparency (ACM FAccT) Network.

This year, the workshop counted 36 submissions from different countries. All submissions were double-blind peer-reviewed by at least three internal Program Committee members, ensuring that only high-quality work was then included in the final workshop program. Compared to the previous year, the pool of reviewers has been strengthened, integrating and catching up with both new and accomplished researchers in the field from industry and academia. The final program included 10 full papers and 4 short papers.

The workshop day included interesting paper presentations and a final discussion to highlight open issues and research challenges, and briefly summarize the outcomes of the workshop. The collected novel contributions fell under four main topics. The first topic touched on biases exploration and assessment, studying accuracy, miscalibration and popularity bias in recommendations, measuring bias in multimodal models, and evaluating fairness metrics in different domains. Under the second topic, papers were concerned about mitigation strategies against biases, from user mainstreaminess to intersectional biases, from position bias to system diversity, from biases in texts to team formation. Papers included in the third topic analyzed biases in newly emerging domains of application, including healthcare, Wikipedia and news. Finally, the fourth topic targeted novel perspectives and conceptualizations of biases in the context of generative models and graph neural networks. More than 70 attendees participated.

In addition to the paper presentations, the program also included three keynote talks. As for the first one, Asia Biega from the Max Planck Institute for Security and Privacy (Germany) examined the tensions between fairness and other responsibility principles mandated by data protection laws, demonstrated the role of interface design in the societal outcomes of a ranking platform, and finally reflected on the importance and practical outcomes of normatively grounding fairness metrics. In the second keynote talk, Harrie Oosterhuis from Radboud University (The Netherlands) compared counterfactual estimation for bandit algorithms with methods specifically made for learning to rank; subsequently he described a recently introduced doubly robust method for correcting position-bias in user interactions with rankings. Finally, during the third keynote talk, Henriette Cramer from Spotify (USA) shared lessons learnt from both organizational and technical practice that could be useful for those trying to address ethical challenges in product development, and for those that study algorithmic impact methods academically.

This workshop continues to confirm the success observed in the three previous editions, with an increasing level of engagement thanks to the return to in-presence events. BIAS 2023 strengthened the community working on algorithmic bias and fairness in information retrieval more and more, representing a key event where ideas and solutions for the current challenges were discussed. This success motivates us to organize the fifth edition of the workshop next year. The organizers would like to thank the authors, the reviewers for shaping an interesting program, and the attendees for their participation.

May 2023

Ludovico Boratto
Stefano Faralli
Mirko Marras
Giovanni Stilo

Organization

Workshop Chairs

Ludovico Boratto	University of Cagliari, Italy
Stefano Faralli	Sapienza University of Rome, Italy
Mirko Marras	University of Cagliari, Italy
Giovanni Stilo	University of L'Aquila, Italy

Program Committee

Marcelo Gabriel Armentano	CONICET, Argentina
Ashwathy Ashokan	University of Nebraska Omaha, USA
Ebrahim Bagheri	Ryerson University, Canada
Christine Bauer	Utrecht University, The Netherlands
Alejandro Bellogin	Universidad Autónoma de Madrid, Spain
Jeffrey Chan	RMIT University, Australia
Evgenia Christoforou	CYENS Centre of Excellence, Cyprus
Giordano D'Aloisio	University of L'Aquila, Italy
Andrea D'Angelo	University of L'Aquila, Italy
Yashar Deldjoo	Polytechnic University of Bari, Italy
Danilo Dessí	GESIS, Germany
Francesco Fabbri	Spotify, Spain
Nina Grgic-Hlaca	MPI-SS, Germany
Danila Hettiachchi	RMIT University, Australia
Toshihiro Kamishima	AIST, Japan
Kunal Khadilkar	Adobe, USA
Dominik Kowald	Know-Center, Austria
Emanuel Lacic	Technical University of Graz, Austria
Dana Mckay	RMIT University, Australia
Giacomo Medda	University of Cagliari, Italy
Cataldo Musto	University of Bari, Italy
Julia Neidhardt	Technical University of Wien, Austria
Harrie Oosterhuis	Radboud University, The Netherlands
Panagiotis Papadakos	FORTH-ICS, Greece
Alessandro Sebastian Podda	University of Cagliari, Italy
Simone Paolo Ponzetto	University of Mannheim, Germany
Lorenzo Porcaro	Joint Research Centre EC, Italy

Erasmo Purificato	Otto-von-Guericke Univ. Magdeburg, Germany
Alessandro Raganato	University of Helsinki, Finland
Amifa Raj	Boise State University, USA
Vaijanath Rao	Quicken Inc., USA
Yongli Ren	RMIT University, Australia
Mete Sertkan	Technical University of Wien, Austria
Manel Slokom	Delft University of Technology, The Netherlands
Nasin Sonboli	Tufts University, USA
Tom Sühr	Technische Universität Berlin, Germany
Marko Tkalcic	University of Primorska, Slovenia
Antonela Tommasel	CONICET, Argentina
Christoph Trattner	University of Bergen, Norway
Rohini Uppuluri	Glassdoor, USA
Eva Zangerle	University of Innsbruck, Austria
Arkaitz Zubiaga	Queen Mary University of London, UK

Chairs and program committee members are in alphabetical order by last name.

Contents

A Study on Accuracy, Miscalibration, and Popularity Bias in Recommendations

Dominik Kowald[1,2]([✉]), Gregor Mayr[2], Markus Schedl[3], and Elisabeth Lex[2]

[1] Know-Center GmbH, Graz, Austria
dkowald@know-center.at
[2] Graz University of Technology, Graz, Austria
gregor.mayr@student.tugraz.at, {elisabeth.lex,dominik.kowald}@tugraz.at
[3] Johannes Kepler University & Linz Institute of Technology, Linz, Austria
markus.schedl@jku.at

Abstract. Recent research has suggested different metrics to measure the inconsistency of recommendation performance, including the accuracy difference between user groups, miscalibration, and popularity lift. However, a study that relates miscalibration and popularity lift to recommendation accuracy across different user groups is still missing. Additionally, it is unclear if particular genres contribute to the emergence of inconsistency in recommendation performance across user groups. In this paper, we present an analysis of these three aspects of five well-known recommendation algorithms for user groups that differ in their preference for popular content. Additionally, we study how different genres affect the inconsistency of recommendation performance, and how this is aligned with the popularity of the genres. Using data from Last.fm, MovieLens, and MyAnimeList, we present two key findings. First, we find that users with little interest in popular content receive the worst recommendation accuracy, and that this is aligned with miscalibration and popularity lift. Second, our experiments show that particular genres contribute to a different extent to the inconsistency of recommendation performance, especially in terms of miscalibration in the case of the MyAnimeList dataset.

Keywords: Recommender systems · Popularity bias · Miscalibration · Accuracy · Recommendation inconsistency · Popularity lift

1 Introduction

Recommender systems benefit users by providing personalized suggestions of content such as movies or music. However, we also know from previous research that recommender systems suffer from an inconsistency in recommendation performance across different user groups [2,9]. One example of this inconsistency is the varying recommendation accuracy across different user groups, which could

---

D. Kowald and G. Mayr—Both authors contributed equally to this work.

© The Author(s), under exclusive license to Springer Nature Switzerland AG 2023
L. Boratto et al. (Eds.): BIAS 2023, CCIS 1840, pp. 1–16, 2023.
https://doi.org/10.1007/978-3-031-37249-0_1

lead to unfair treatment of users whose preferences are not in the mainstream of a community [18,19]. Other examples are inconsistencies between the input data of a recommender system and the recommendations generated, which could lead to recommendations that are either too popular and/or do not match the interests of specific user groups [2,9]. Thus, popularity bias can be seen as one particular example of recommendation inconsistencies.

Apart from measuring recommendation accuracy differences across different user groups, related research [2] suggests quantifying the inconsistency of recommendation performance along two metrics, namely miscalibration and popularity lift. Miscalibration quantifies the deviation of a genre spectrum between user profiles and actual recommendations [24,29]. For example, if a user listens to songs belonging to 45% pop, 35% rock, and 20% rap, whereas a calibrated recommendation list should contain the same genre distribution.

Related research also proposes the popularity lift metric to investigate to what extent recommendation algorithms amplify inconsistency in terms of popularity bias [3,4]. This popularity lift metric quantifies the disproportionate amount of recommendations of more popular items in a system. For example, a positive popularity lift indicates that the items recommended are on average more popular than the ones in the user profile. Therefore, in the remainder of this paper, we refer to popularity lift as a metric that measures the popularity bias of recommendation algorithms.

However, a study that relates miscalibration and popularity lift to recommendation accuracy across different user groups is still missing. We believe that the outcomes of such a study could help choose the most suitable recommendation debiasing methods for each user group. Additionally, it is unclear if particular genres contribute to the emergence of inconsistency in recommendation performance across user groups. This knowledge could be helpful, e.g., for enhancing recommendation debiasing methods based on calibration.

The Present Work. In this paper, we contribute with a study on accuracy, miscalibration, and popularity bias of five well-known recommendation algorithms that predict the preference of users for items, i.e., UserItemAvg, UserKNN, UserKNNAvg [12], NMF [25], and Co-Clustering [10] in the domains of music (Last.fm), movies (MovieLens), and animes (MyAnimeList). We split the users in each dataset into three user groups based on the low, medium, and high inclination towards popular content, which we call LowPop, MedPop, and HighPop, respectively. With this, we aim to shed light on the connection between accuracy, miscalibration, and popularity bias in recommendations.

Furthermore, in this paper, we investigate what genres in the user groups are particularly affecting recommendation inconsistency across the algorithms and domains. With this, we aim to understand if particular genres contribute to the emergence of inconsistency in recommendation performance, and if this is aligned with the popularity of the genres.

Findings and Contributions. We find that LowPop consumers consistently receive the lowest recommendation accuracy, and in all investigated datasets, miscalibration is the highest for this user group. In terms of popularity lift, we observe that all algorithms amplify popularity bias.

Concerning our analysis on the level of genres, we find that there are indeed genres that highly contribute to inconsistency, especially in terms of miscalibration in the case of the MyAnimeList dataset. In sum, the contributions of our paper are four-fold:

1. We extend three well-known datasets from the field of recommender systems with genre information to study the inconsistency of recommendation performance.
2. We evaluate five well-known recommendation algorithms for accuracy, miscalibration, and popularity lift.
3. We inspect recommendation inconsistency on the genre level and show that different genres contribute differently to the emergence of inconsistency in recommendation performance.
4. To foster the reproducibility of our work, we share the extended datasets and source code used in our study with the research community.

2   Related Work

Bias in information retrieval and recommender systems is an emerging research trait, and related works have shown multiple ways to quantify different biases in a system [7,22]. One such bias is the popularity bias, which arises due to items with higher popularity getting recommended more often than items with lower popularity. Works [9] have found, that not all users are affected identically, with some user groups receiving more inconsistent recommendations than others. Ekstrand et al. [9,17], for example, found inconsistencies in recommendation accuracy among demographic groups, with groups differing in gender and age showing statistically significant differences in effectiveness in multiple datasets. The authors evaluated different recommendation algorithms and identified varying degrees of utility effects.

Abdollahpouri et al. [2–4] also contributed to this line of research and introduced two metrics to quantify the inconsistency in recommendation performance from the user's perspective. The first one is the miscalibration metric, which quantifies the misalignment between the genre spectrum found in a user profile and the genre spectrum found in this user's recommendations. The second one is the popularity lift metric, which measures to what extent a user is affected by popularity bias, i.e., the unequal distribution of popular items in a user profile and this user's recommendations. In datasets from the movie domain, they found that users that are more affected by popularity bias also receive more miscalibrated results. Similarly, Kowald et al. [19] analyzed popularity bias and accuracy differences across user groups in the music domain. The authors found that the popularity lift metric provided different results in the music domain than in the movie domain due to repeat consumption patterns prevalent in the music-listening behavior of users.

Table 1. Dataset statistics including the number of users $|U|$, items $|I|$, ratings $|R|$, and distinct genres $|C|$ as well as sparsity and rating range R-range.

Dataset	$|U|$	$|I|$	$|R|$	$|C|$	$|R|/|U|$	$|R|/|I|$	Sparsity	R-range
LFM	3,000	131,188	1,417,791	20	473	11	0.996	$[1-1,000]$
ML	3,000	3,667	675,610	18	225	184	0.938	$[1-5]$
MAL	3,000	9,450	649,814	44	216	69	0.977	$[1-10]$

In this paper, we extend these works by connecting miscalibration and popularity lift to recommendation accuracy across different user groups. Additionally, we examine if particular genres contribute to the emergence of recommendation inconsistency across user groups and datasets. With this, we hope to inform research on popularity bias mitigation methods. As an example, [5] has proposed in-processing methods for debiasing recommendations based on calibration. We believe that our findings on which genres contribute to miscalibrated results could be used to enhance these methods. Additionally, related research has proposed post-processing methods to re-rank recommendation lists [1,6]. We believe that our findings for the connection of accuracy and popularity lift for different user groups could help choose the right users for whom such re-ranking should be performed.

3   Method

In this section, we describe the datasets, the experimental setup, and the evaluation metrics used in our study.

3.1   Datasets

We use three different datasets in the domains of music, movies, and animes. Specifically, we use dataset samples from Last.fm (LFM), MovieLens (ML), and MyAnimeList (MAL) provided in our previous work [17][1]. Here, each dataset consists of exactly 3,000 users, which are split into three equally-sized groups with 1,000 users each. We use 1,000 users per user group to be comparable with previous works that also used groups of this size. The groups are created based on the users' inclination toward popular items. Following the definitions given in [17], we define a user u's inclination towards popular items as the fraction of popular items in u's user profile. We define an item i as popular if it is within the top-20% of item popularity scores, i.e., the relative number of users who

---

[1] We do not use the BookCrossing dataset due to the lack of genre information.

have interacted with i. We term the group with the lowest, medium, and highest inclination toward popular items *LowPop*, *MedPop*, and *HighPop*, respectively. In Fig. 1, we show boxplots of the fraction of popular items in the user profiles of the three groups for our three datasets.

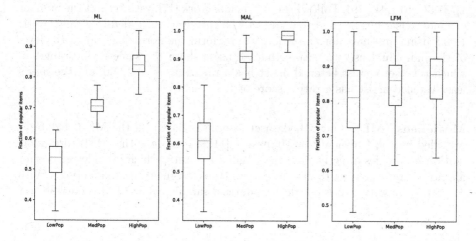

Fig. 1. Boxplots depicting the fraction of popular items in the user profiles for the three user groups and datasets. The LowPop group has the smallest ratio of popular items, compared to MedPop and HighPop. In the LFM dataset, this difference is not as apparent as in the other datasets, due to repeat consumption patterns in music listening behavior.

In Fig. 1, we show boxplots depicting the fraction of popular items in the user profiles for the three user groups and datasets. We see that the LowPop user group has the smallest ratio of popular items, compared to MedPop and HighPop. In the case of the LFM dataset, this difference is not as apparent as in the case of the other datasets, due to repeat consumption patterns in music listening behavior.

Basic statistics of the datasets can be found in Table 1, and we share our dataset samples via Zenodo[2]. In the following, we give more details on these datasets and how we extend them with genre information. Additionally, we analyze the popularity distributions in the datasets on the levels of ratings and users to give context for our study on genre level, which follows later on.

Last.fm (LFM). The LFM dataset sample used in our study is based on the LFM-1b dataset [28] and the subset used in [17]. It contains listening records from the music streaming platform Last.fm. We include only listening records to music artists that contain genre information. Genre is acquired by indexing Last.fm's user-generated tags (assigned to artists) with the 20 main genres from

---

[2] https://doi.org/10.5281/zenodo.7428435.

the AllMusic database (top-3: rock, alternative, pop). When comparing the LFM dataset sample in Table 1 with the one from [17], we notice that the number of artists $|I|$ decreases from 352,805 to 131,188, which means that there is no genre information available in LFM for a large set of the long-tail artists. However, in terms of ratings, this leads to a relatively small reduction in ratings from 1,755,361 to 1,417,791. Following our previous work [17], we interpret the number of times a user has listened to an artist as a rating score, scaled to a range of [1; 1,000] using min-max normalization. We perform the normalization on the level of the individual user to ensure that all users share the same rating range, in which the user's most listened artist has a rating score of 1,000 and the user's least listened artist has a rating score of 1.

MovieLens (ML). Our ML dataset sample is based on the ML-1M dataset provided by the University of Minnesota [11]. Here, we gather the genre information for movies directly from the original dataset[3], which provides genres for all movies and contains 18 distinct genres (top-3: comedy, drama, action). With respect to sparsity, ML is our densest dataset sample, while LFM is our sparsest one.

MyAnimeList (MAL). The MAL dataset used in our study is based on a recommender systems challenge dataset provided by Kaggle. As in the case of ML, the original dataset[4] already provides genre information for each item, which leads to 44 distinct genres (top-3: comedy, action, romance). However, one special characteristic of MAL is that this dataset also contains implicit feedback (i.e., when a user bookmarks an anime). Following [17], we set the implicit feedback to an explicit rating of 5. In terms of the number of ratings, MAL is the smallest dataset used in our study, while LFM is the largest one.

Genre Popularity Distribution. To get a better understanding of the popularity of the individual genres across the three user groups, in Fig. 2, we plot the genre popularity distribution on the levels of ratings and users. The genres are ordered by their overall popularity in terms of ratings across all three user groups, i.e., the most popular genre is the leftmost. On the level of ratings (left plots), we see similar popularity distributions across all user groups. Interestingly, for ML and MAL, the LowPop group has the largest number of ratings across all genres, while for LFM this is the case for the MedPop group.

On the level of users, we identify similar popularity distributions across all user groups for LFM and ML. However, in the case of MAL, we see a prominent drop for the genre "Hentai" when investigating the MedPop and HighPop user groups. This is not the case for the LowPop user group, and thus, the preference for these genres among LowPop users exclusively could lead to an inconsistent recommendation performance for LowPop in the MAL dataset. When relating

---

[3] https://grouplens.org/datasets/movielens/1m/.

[4] https://www.kaggle.com/CooperUnion/anime-recommendations-database.

these results to the rating distributions on the left, we see no drop for the MedPop and HighPop user groups in the case of the "Hentai" genre. However, we see an increase in ratings for LowPop for this genre. This again shows the considerable interest of LowPop users for animes associated with the "Hentai" genre.

Finally, we also investigated the item popularity distributions across genres and user groups, where we did not inspect any noticeable differences when comparing the user groups on the genre level.

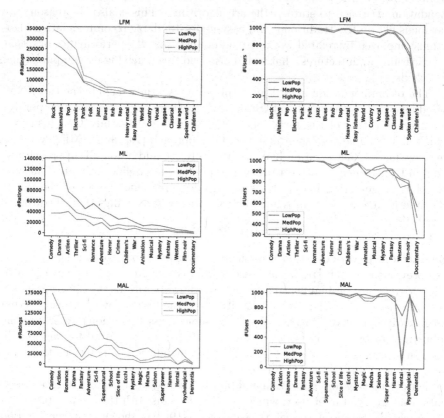

Fig. 2. Genre popularity distribution on the level of ratings (on the left) and on the level of users (on the right) for our three datasets and user groups.

3.2   Experimental Setup

Next, we describe the five recommendation algorithms and the evaluation protocol utilized in our study.

Recommendation Algorithms. Following our previous research [17,19], we formulate the recommendation task as a rating prediction problem by utilizing

the Python-based Surprise framework [12]. Specifically, we use the four collaborative filtering (CF) recommendation algorithms studied in [17]. Since our previous work [17] also uses the same dataset samples as we do in the present work,
we stick to the same hyperparameter settings. Please refer to our source-code
shared via GitHub[5] for the exact parameter settings. We refrain from performing any additional hyperparameter optimization since our main interest lies in
assessing (relative) differences of our evaluation metrics between the three user
groups LowPop, MedPop, and HighPop, and not in comparing a novel recommendation approach to state-of-the-art algorithms. This is also the reason why
our focus lies on five traditional and easy understandable recommendation algorithms employed by related work instead of analyzing the performance of recent
deep learning architectures, that would also lead to a much higher computational
complexity.

The recommendation algorithms utilized in our study include the two KNN-
based algorithms UserKNN and UserKNNAvg, where the latter one incorporates
the average rating of the target user and item. We also study Co-Clustering,
which is a scalable co-clustering-based CF approach [10], and NMF, i.e., non-
negative matrix factorization [25]. Additionally, we add a non-CF approach utilized in [19], namely UserItemAvg, which predicts a baseline estimate using the
overall average rating in the dataset and adds preference biases of the target
user and item, e.g., if a user tends to give more positive ratings than the average
user [14].

Evaluation Protocol. Concerning our evaluation protocol, we again follow
our previous research [17,19] and use a random 80/20 train/test split in a 5-
fold cross-validation manner. Thus, we train our algorithms on the training set
and measure the accuracy of the algorithms on the test set by comparing actual
ratings with predicted ratings. By using 5-fold cross-validation, we ensure the
robustness of our evaluation protocol, and control for potential fluctuations in
the genre proportions or outliers in the recommendation calculations that may
be introduced due to the random train/test splits.

For calculating miscalibration and popularity lift, we use a top-10 recommendation set for the target user, which are the 10 items with the highest predicted
rating scores. Since our previous research [17,19] has shown that the LopPop
user group typically receives the worst recommendation accuracy across all user
groups, we are especially interested in this user group. Therefore, we test for
statistical significance using a t-test between LowPop and MedPop as well as
between LowPop and HighPop. We report average values across all 5 folds for
all metrics and indicate statistical significance only in case it applies for all 5
folds.

3.3   Evaluation Metrics

We quantify the inconsistency of recommendation performance using (i) accuracy differences between user groups, (ii) miscalibration, and (iii) popularity lift:

---

[5] https://github.com/domkowald/FairRecSys.

Accuracy (MAE). We measure accuracy using the well-known mean absolute error (MAE) metric. The MAE of a user u is given by:

$$MAE(u) = \frac{1}{|R_u^{test}|} \sum_{r_{u,i} \in R_u^{test}} |r_{u,i} - R_{u,i}|$$ (1)

Here, the predicted rating score $R_{u,i}$ of user u and item i is compared to the real rating scores $r_{u,i}$ in u's test set R_u^{test}. We favor MAE over the commonly used root mean squared error (RMSE) metric due to several disadvantages of RMSE, especially regarding the comparison of groups with different numbers of observations (i.e., ratings in our case) [30]. We report the MAE of a user group g by averaging the MAE values of all users of g.

To validate our accuracy results in terms of MAE also in top-n recommendation evaluation settings, we also report the well-known Precision and Recall metrics. For this, we classify an item in the test set as relevant if its rating is higher than the average rating in the train set.

Miscalibration (MC). The calibration metric proposed by Steck [29] quantifies the similarity of a genre spectrum between user profiles p and actual recommendations q. This metric was reinterpreted by Lin et al. [24] in the form of miscalibration, i.e., the deviation between p and q. We follow this definition and calculate the deviation using the Kullback-Leibler (KL) divergence between the distribution of genres in p, i.e., $p(c|u)$, and the distribution of genres in q, i.e., $q(c|u)$. This is given by:

$$KL(p||q) = \sum_{c \in C} p(c|u) \log \frac{p(c|u)}{q(c|u)}$$ (2)

Here, C is the set of all genres in a dataset. Therefore, $KL = 0$ means perfect calibration, and higher KL values (i.e., close to 1) mean miscalibrated recommendations. As in the case of MAE, we report the miscalibration values averaged over all users of a group g.

Popularity Lift (PL). The popularity lift metric investigates to what extent recommendation algorithms amplify the popularity bias inherent in the user profiles [3,4]. Thus, it quantifies the disproportionate recommendation of more popular items for a given user group g (i.e., LowPop, MedPop, HighPop). We define the group average popularity $GAP_p(g)$ as the average popularity of the items in the user profiles p of group g. Similarly, $GAP_q(g)$ is the average popularity of the recommended items for all users of the group g. The popularity lift is then given by:

$$PL(g) = \frac{GAP_q(g) - GAP_p(g)}{GAP_p(g)}$$ (3)

Here, $PL(g) > 0$ means that the recommendations for g are too popular, $PL(g) < 0$ means that the recommendations for g are not popular enough, and $PL(g) = 0$ would be the ideal value.

4   Results

In this section, we describe and discuss the results of our study, first on a more general level and then on the level of genres.

Table 2. MAE, MC, and PL results for the LowPop, MedPop, and HighPop user groups. The highest (i.e., worst) results are highlighted in **bold**. Statistical significance according to a t-test between LowPop and MedPop, and LopPop and HighPop is indicated by * for $p < 0.05$. Rating ranges are shown in brackets.

Algorithm	Data Metric	LFM [1-1,000] MAE	MC	PL	ML [1-5] MAE	MC	PL	MAL [1-10] MAE	MC	PL
UserItemAvg	LowPop	48.02*	0.52*	1.28	0.74*	0.78*	0.70*	0.99*	0.95*	1.12*
	MedPop	38.48	0.48	**1.61**	0.71	0.71	0.42	0.96	0.73	0.42
	HighPop	45.24	0.42	1.35	0.69	0.63	0.24	0.97	0.64	0.15
UserKNN	LowPop	54.32*	0.51*	0.52	0.80*	0.75*	0.64*	1.37*	0.92*	0.74*
	MedPop	46.76	0.50	**0.82**	0.75	0.69	0.37	1.34	0.72	0.22
	HighPop	49.75	0.45	0.80	0.72	0.62	0.20	1.31	0.63	0.08
UserKNNAvg	LowPop	50.12*	0.49*	0.35	0.76*	0.78*	0.49*	1.00*	0.90*	0.54*
	MedPop	40.30	0.47	0.61	0.73	0.70	0.33	0.95	0.73	0.24
	HighPop	46.39	0.42	**0.64**	0.70	0.61	0.20	0.95	0.64	0.11
NMF	LowPop	42.47*	0.54*	0.10	0.75*	0.78*	0.57*	1.01*	0.91*	0.87*
	MedPop	34.03	0.52	0.17	0.72	0.71	0.37	0.97	0.72	0.35
	HighPop	41.14	0.48	**0.33**	0.70	0.63	0.22	0.95	0.63	0.13
Co-Clustering	LowPop	52.60*	0.52*	0.68	0.74*	0.77*	0.70*	1.00*	0.90*	1.10*
	MedPop	40.83	0.51	**1.04**	0.71	0.70	0.43	0.96	0.72	0.42
	HighPop	47.03	0.45	0.99	0.68	0.62	0.25	0.98	0.63	0.16

Connection Between Accuracy, Miscalibration and Popularity Bias. Table 2 summarizes our results for the three metrics (MAE, MC, PL) over the three user groups (LowPop, MedPop, HighPop), three datasets (LFM, ML, MAL) and five algorithms (UserItemAvg, UserKNN, UserKNNAvg, NFM, Co-Clustering). The results presented are averaged over all users and all folds. We can see that in the case of ML and MAL, the LowPop user group receive the worst results for MAE, MC, and PL. These results are also statistically significant according to a t-test with $p < 0.05$. For LFM, the LowPop user group also gets the worst results for the MAE and MC metrics.

However, when looking at the PL metric, we observe different results, namely the highest popularity lift for either MedPop or HighPop. This is in line with our previous research [19], which has shown that the PL metric provides different results for LFM than for ML. One potential difference between music and movies (and also animes) is that music is typically consumed repeatedly (i.e., a user listens to the same artist multiple times), while movies are mostly watched only once. The definition of the PL metric [24] does not account for repeat consumption patterns [15], since items are given the same importance regardless of their consumption frequency. This means that items that are consumed for instance 1,000 times by a specific user have the same importance as items that are consumed only once by this user.

Finally, in Table 3, we validate our accuracy results in terms of MAE also in top-n recommendation evaluation settings using the well-known Precision and Recall metrics. To classify relevant items in the test sets, we calculate the average rating in the training sets and treat a test item as relevant if it exceeds this average train rating. We see very similar results as in the case of the MAE metric. This means that in almost all cases, LowPop gets the worst results (i.e., lowest) and HighPop gets the best results (i.e., highest).

Table 3. Accuracy results in terms of Precision and Recall. We tested for statistical significance using a t-test between LowPop and MedPop, and LowPop and HighPop users, which is indicated by * for p < 0.05. The best (i.e., highest) results are highlighted in **bold**. The results are in line with the MAE ones, which means that LowPop receives worst accuracy results, while HighPop receives the best accuracy results.

Algorithm	Data Metric	LFM Precision	Recall	ML Precision	Recall	MAL Precision	Recall
UserItemAvg	LowPop	0.30	0.11	0.78*	0.19*	0.71*	0.15*
	MedPop	0.28	0.08	0.82	0.26	0.80	0.21
	HighPop	**0.39**	**0.14**	**0.83**	**0.36**	**0.80**	**0.33**
UserKNN	LowPop	0.33*	0.16	0.78*	0.18*	0.71*	0.15*
	MedPop	0.38	0.14	0.83	0.25	0.80	0.22
	HighPop	**0.53**	**0.22**	**0.83**	**0.35**	**0.81**	**0.34**
UserKNNAvg	LowPop	0.34	0.16	0.80*	0.20*	0.73*	0.16*
	MedPop	0.34	0.12	0.83	0.27	0.80	0.23
	HighPop	**0.47**	**0.19**	**0.83**	**0.36**	**0.81**	**0.36**
NMF	LowPop	0.34	0.16	0.70*	0.14*	0.67*	0.13*
	MedPop	0.34	0.12	0.79	0.23	0.79	0.21
	HighPop	**0.46**	**0.19**	**0.82**	**0.34**	**0.81**	**0.33**
Co-Clustering	LowPop	0.33	0.16*	0.76*	0.17*	0.69*	0.14*
	MedPop	0.33	0.12	0.83	0.25	0.80	0.22
	HighPop	**0.46**	**0.20**	**0.84**	**0.35**	**0.81**	**0.34**

Influence of Genres on Inconsistency of Recommendations. Furthermore, Fig. 3 visualizes the results of our investigation on what genres in the user groups are particularly affecting inconsistency of recommendation performance in terms of miscalibration for the three datasets. We investigate this study for the miscalibration metric only, since we do not observe any particular differences across the genres for the MAE and popularity lift metrics. To map the users' miscalibration scores to a genre g, we assign the MC score of a user u to all genres listened to u. Then for each genre g, we calculate the average MC scores of all users of a specific user group who listened to g. These values are then plotted in Fig. 3 for both the NMF algorithm and the Co-Clustering algorithm. For better readability, we apply min-max normalization in a range of 0 - 1.

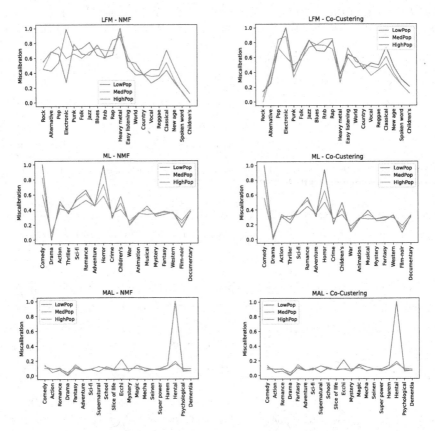

Fig. 3. Influence of different genres on MC for the NMF algorithm (on the left) and Co-Clustering (on the right). We see that some genres highly contribute to inconsistency, especially in case of animes (MAL).

As in the case of Fig. 2, the genres are ordered by their popularity. For the sake of space, we only show the results for NMF and Co-Clustering, which are, in general, inline with results obtained for the other algorithms. However, our

GitHub repository also allows the inspection of the results for the other algorithms. Additionally, for MAL, we exclude 24 genres for which no substantial fluctuations are observed. This leads to 20 shown genres, as in the case of LFM.

For the MAL dataset and the LowPop group, we observe highly miscalibrated results for the "Hentai" genre. In particular, indicated by its position, "Hentai" is an unpopular genre for most of the MAL users. However, as also shown in Fig. 2, for users within the LowPop group (and only for this user group), it is a relevant genre that is underrepresented in their recommendation lists. This demonstrates that there are indeed particular genres that contribute to a large extent to recommendation inconsistency for specific user groups.

5   Conclusion and Future Work

In this paper, we have studied the interconnection between accuracy, miscalibration, and popularity bias for different user groups in three different domains. Here, we measured popularity bias in terms of popularity lift, a metric that compares the popularity of items in recommendation lists to the popularity of items in user profiles. Additionally, we investigated miscalibration, a metric that compares the genre spectrums in user profiles with the ones in recommendation lists. We find that, in general, the inconsistency of recommendations in terms of miscalibration and popularity lift is aligned with lower accuracy performance.

One exception to this is the popularity lift metric in the case of music recommendations; however, this result is in line with our previous work [19], in which repeat consumption settings have been studied. Additionally, we find that different genres contribute differently to miscalibration and popularity lift. That finding is particularly pronounced in the case of anime recommendations for Low-Pop users and for genres that are unpopular among other user groups. Another contribution of our work is that we publicly share our datasets and source code investigated in this study with the research community.

Limitations and Future Work. One limitation of our work is that we have focused solely on datasets from the multimedia/entertainment domains, namely music, movies, and animes. Although we have investigated domains with and without repeat consumption patterns, for future work, we plan to also study other domains with respect to accuracy, miscalibration, and popularity bias. This could include recommendations in online marketplaces [20] or recommendations in social networks [16] and will contribute to the generalizability of our findings. To further strengthen the generalizability of our work, we also plan to conduct further experiments with novel recommendation algorithms employing deep learning-based methods [22].

Another limitation of our work is that we have used MAE, Precision, and Recall as the only metrics to measure the accuracy of recommendations. In the future, we plan to extend this by also investigating ranking-based metrics such as nDCG [13, 21] as well as metrics that measure the novelty and diversity of recommendations [8]. In this respect, we also plan to enhance our evaluation protocol and move from random train/test splits to temporal train/test splits [27]. Finally, we also plan to do experiments with a higher number of user groups with a smaller number of users per group (e.g., 10 groups with 300 users per group). With this, we aim to address a potential limitation with respect to having different popularity tendencies within a group.

As a general path for future work, we plan to build on the findings of this paper to develop strategies to overcome the inconsistency of recommendation performance across different user groups. For example, for particular genres where we find high miscalibration, we aim to research calibration-based debiasing approaches [5]. Another possibility to address popularity bias in the recommender system could be to build models based on concepts from psychology [23]. Finally, we plan to investigate novel metrics to measure popularity lift in repeat consumption settings, e.g., music recommendations. Here, we plan to either introduce a weighted variant of the metric or investigate alternative methods for converting implicit feedback (e.g., play counts) into explicit ratings [26].

Acknowledgements. This research was funded by the "DDAI" COMET Module within the COMET - Competence Centers for Excellent Technologies Programme, funded by the Austrian Federal Ministry for Transport, Innovation and Technology (bmvit), the Austrian Federal Ministry for Digital and Economic Affairs (bmdw), the Austrian Research Promotion Agency (FFG), the province of Styria (SFG) and partners from industry and academia. Additionally, this work was funded by the Austrian Science Fund (FWF): P33526 and DFH-23.

References

1. Abdollahpouri, H., Burke, R., Mobasher, B.: Managing popularity bias in recommender systems with personalized re-ranking. In: The Thirty-second International Flairs Conference (2019)
2. Abdollahpouri, H., Mansoury, M., Burke, R., Mobasher, B.: The impact of popularity bias on fairness and calibration in recommendation. arXiv preprint arXiv:1910.05755 (2019)
3. Abdollahpouri, H., Mansoury, M., Burke, R., Mobasher, B.: The unfairness of popularity Bias in recommendation. arXiv preprint arXiv:1907.13286 (2019)
4. Abdollahpouri, H., Mansoury, M., Burke, R., Mobasher, B.: The connection between popularity bias, calibration, and fairness in recommendation. In: Fourteenth ACM Conference on Recommender Systems, pp. 726–731 (2020)
5. Abdollahpouri, H., Mansoury, M., Burke, R., Mobasher, B., Malthouse, E.: User-centered evaluation of popularity bias in recommender systems. In: Proceedings of the 29th ACM Conference on User Modeling, Adaptation and Personalization, pp. 119–129 (2021)
6. Adomavicius, G., Kwon, Y.: Improving aggregate recommendation diversity using ranking-based techniques. IEEE Trans. Knowl. Data Eng. **24**(5), 896–911 (2011)
7. Baeza-Yates, R.: Bias in search and recommender systems. In: Fourteenth ACM Conference on Recommender Systems, p. 2 (2020)

8. Castells, P., Hurley, N.J., Vargas, S.: Novelty and diversity in recommender systems. In: Ricci, F., Rokach, L., Shapira, B. (eds.) Recommender Systems Handbook, pp. 881–918. Springer, Boston, MA (2015). https://doi.org/10.1007/978-1-4899-7637-6_26

9. Ekstrand, M.D., et al.: All the cool kids, how do they fit in?: Popularity and demographic biases in recommender evaluation and effectiveness. In: Conference on Fairness, Accountability and Transparency, pp. 172–186. PMLR (2018)

10. George, T., Merugu, S.: A scalable collaborative filtering framework based on co-clustering. In: Fifth IEEE International Conference on Data Mining (ICDM2005), p. 4. IEEE (2005)

11. Harper, F.M., Konstan, J.A.: The MovieLens datasets: History and context. ACM Trans. Interact. Intell. Syst. **5**, 1–19 (2015)

12. Hug, N.: Surprise: a python library for recommender systems. J. Open Source Soft. **5**(52), 2174 (2020)

13. Järvelin, K., Kekäläinen, J.: Cumulated gain-based evaluation of IR techniques. ACM Trans. Inf. Syst. (TOIS) **20**(4), 422–446 (2002)

14. Koren, Y.: Factor in the neighbors: scalable and accurate collaborative filtering. ACM Trans. Knowl. Discov. Data (TKDD) **4**(1), 1–24 (2010)

15. Kotzias, D., Lichman, M., Smyth, P.: Predicting consumption patterns with repeated and novel events. IEEE Trans. Knowl. Data Eng. **31**(2), 371–384 (2018)

16. Kowald, D., Dennerlein, S., Theiler, D., Walk, S., Trattner, C.: The social semantic server: a framework to provide services on social semantic network data. In: 9th International Conference on Semantic Systems, I-SEMANTICS 2013, pp. 50–54. CEUR (2013)

17. Kowald, D., Lacic, E.: Popularity Bias in collaborative filtering-based multimedia recommender systems. In: Boratto, L., Faralli, S., Marras, M., Stilo, G. (eds.) Advances in Bias and Fairness in Information Retrieval. BIAS 2022. Communications in Computer and Information Science, vol. 1610, pp. 1–11. Springer, Cham (2022). https://doi.org/10.1007/978-3-031-09316-6_1

18. Kowald, D., Muellner, P., Zangerle, E., Bauer, C., Schedl, M., Lex, E.: Support the underground: characteristics of beyond-mainstream music listeners. EPJ Data Sci. **10**(1), 1–26 (2021). https://doi.org/10.1140/epjds/s13688-021-00268-9

19. Kowald, D., Schedl, M., Lex, E.: The unfairness of popularity bias in music recommendation: a reproducibility study. In: Jose, J.M., et al. (eds.) ECIR 2020. LNCS, vol. 12036, pp. 35–42. Springer, Cham (2020). https://doi.org/10.1007/978-3-030-45442-5_5

20. Lacic, E., Kowald, D., Parra, D., Kahr, M., Trattner, C.: Towards a scalable social recommender engine for online marketplaces: the case of apache solr. In: Proceedings of the 23rd International Conference on World Wide Web, pp. 817–822 (2014)

21. Lacic, E., Kowald, D., Traub, M., Luzhnica, G., Simon, J.P., Lex, E.: Tackling cold-start users in recommender systems with indoor positioning systems. In: Poster Proceedings of the 9th {ACM} Conference on Recommender Systems. ACM (2015)

22. Lesota, O., et al.: Analyzing item popularity bias of music recommender systems: are different genders equally affected? In: Proceedings of the 15th ACM Conference on Recommender Systems, pp. 601–606 (2021)

23. Lex, E., Kowald, D., Seitlinger, P., Tran, T.N.T., Felfernig, A., Schedl, M., et al.: Psychology-informed recommender systems. Found. Trends® Inf. Retrieval **15**(2), 134–242 (2021)

24. Lin, K., Sonboli, N., Mobasher, B., Burke, R.: Calibration in collaborative filtering recommender systems: a user-centered analysis. In: Proceedings of the 31st ACM Conference on Hypertext and Social Media, pp. 197–206. HT 2020, Association for Computing Machinery, New York, NY, USA (2020)
25. Luo, X., Zhou, M., Xia, Y., Zhu, Q.: An efficient non-negative matrix-factorization-based approach to collaborative filtering for recommender systems. IEEE Trans. Industr. Inf. **10**(2), 1273–1284 (2014)
26. Pacula, M.: A matrix factorization algorithm for music recommendation using implicit user feedback. Maciej Pacula (2009)
27. Quadrana, M., Cremonesi, P., Jannach, D.: Sequence-aware recommender systems. ACM Comput. Surv. (CSUR) **51**(4), 1–36 (2018)
28. Schedl, M.: The LFM-1b dataset for music retrieval and recommendation. In: Proceedings of the 2016 ACM on International Conference on Multimedia Retrieval, pp. 103–110 (2016)
29. Steck, H.: Calibrated recommendations. In: Proceedings of the 12th ACM Conference on Recommender Systems, pp. 154–162. RecSys 2018, Association for Computing Machinery, New York, NY, USA (2018)
30. Willmott, C.J., Matsuura, K.: Advantages of the mean absolute error (mae) over the root mean square error (rmse) in assessing average model performance. Climate Res. **30**(1), 79–82 (2005)

Measuring Bias in Multimodal Models: Multimodal Composite Association Score

Abhishek Mandal[1]([✉])(iD), Susan Leavy[2](iD), and Suzanne Little[1](iD)

[1] Insight SFI Research Centre for Data Analytics, School of Computing, Dublin City University, Dublin, Ireland
abhishek.mandal2@mail.dcu.ie, suzanne.little@dcu.ie
[2] Insight SFI Research Centre for Data Analytics, School of Information and Communication Studies, University College Dublin, Dublin, Ireland
susan.leavy@ucd.ie

Abstract. Generative multimodal models based on diffusion models have seen tremendous growth and advances in recent years and are being used for information search and retrieval along with traditional search engines. Models such as DALL-E and Stable Diffusion have become increasingly popular, however, they can reflect social biases embedded in training data which is often crawled from the internet. Research into bias measurement and quantification has generally focused on small single-stage models working on a single modality. Thus the emergence of multi-stage multimodal models requires a different approach. In this paper, we propose Multimodal Composite Association Score (MCAS) as a new method of measuring bias in multimodal generative models and using this method, uncover gender bias in DALL-E 2 and Stable Diffusion. We propose MCAS as an accessible and scalable method of quantifying potential bias for models with different modalities and a range of potential biases.

Keywords: Bias · Multimodal Models · Generative Models

1 Introduction

Social biases and their potential consequences, such as those pertaining to gender [1,2], race [3], ethnicity and geography [4,5], found in deep neural networks used in computer vision models have been well documented. Most current methods auditing bias in vision models generally use two types of techniques: (1) measuring associations in the learning representations [1,6,7] and (2) analysing the predictions [3,8]. Most of these techniques [1,3,6,7] are designed for predictive models, mainly Convolutional Neural Networks (CNNs). Recent advances in deep learning, however, have given rise to multi-stage, multimodal models with DALL-E and Stable Diffusion being two of the most popular models.

Generative multimodal models based on diffusion models are easier to train than GANs and have higher variability in image generation that enables them to

L. Boratto et al. (Eds.): BIAS 2023, CCIS 1840, pp. 17–30, 2023.
https://doi.org/10.1007/978-3-031-37249-0_2

model complex multimodal distributions. This allows them to generate images using abstract ideas with less tight bounding than GANs [10,11]. The easier training regimen allows developers to train these models on very large datasets. This has led to models being trained on increasingly large datasets, often crawled from the Internet. These datasets are generally unfiltered, leading to the models inheriting social biases prevalent on the web [17]. These models therefore, require new approaches to detecting bias.

Models such as DALL-E [10], Stable Diffusion [11] and Contrastive Language and Image Pre-training (CLIP) [9] operate on multiple modalities, such as text and images. These models have numerous applications ranging from content creation to image understanding and image and video search [12]. They also combine multiple different models using outputs to form inputs to another model. CLIP uses Vision Transformer or ResNet for image encoding and a text encoder for text encoding. DALL-E and Stable Diffusion use CLIP for their first stage involving generating text embeddings and a diffusion model (unCLIP for DALL-E and Latent Diffusion for Stable Diffusion) to generate images. This multi-stage multi-model approach also carries the risk of bias amplification, where one model amplifies the bias of another model [2].

With the increasing popularity of generative models, an increasing volume of internet content may be AI generated and this content, comprising both images and text may be indexed by search engines and appear in search results. Apart from concerns arising from privacy and copyright law, biased and harmful generated content can further exacerbate social issues already present in search engine results [5,16]. As data from the internet (often using web scraping using search engines) is used for training generative models [5,16], this may create a loop that further amplifies social biases. The integration of generative AI and search engines, which is currently being developed may complicate these issues further.

We propose the *Multimodal Composite Association Score (MCAS)* to measure associations between concepts in both text and image embeddings as well as internal bias amplification. This work builds on work by Caliskan et al. [13] who developed the Word Embeddings Association Test (WEAT). The objective was to provide the ability to measure bias at the internal component level and provide insights into the extent and source model for observable bias. MCAS generates a numerical value signifying the type and magnitude of associations. While validation experiments that are presented within this paper focus on uncovering evidence of stereotypical concepts of men and women this approach to evaluating bias using MCAS is designed to be scalable to include a range of genders or evaluate further concepts such as representations of race.

The remainder of this paper summarises related work in the field of gender bias for computer vision models and the emergence of generative models. The formula for MCAS is defined and the calculation of the component scores is described. MCAS is demonstrated on four concept categories with high potential for gender bias and assessed using DALL-E 2 and Stable Diffusion queries.

2   Related Work

Authors of multimodal general purpose models have highlighted the prevalence of gender bias in their models. Radford et al. [9] found that CLIP assigns words related to physical appearance such as 'blonde' more frequently to women and those related to high paying occupations such as 'executive' and 'doctor' to men. Occupations more frequently associated with women included 'newscaster', 'television presenter' and 'newsreader' despite the gender neutral terms. The DALL-E 2 model card [14] acknowledges gender bias in the generative model. Inputs with terms such as 'lawyer' and 'CEO' predominantly produce images of people with visual features commonly associated with men whereas images generated for 'nurse' and 'personal assistant' present images of people with features associated with women.

In a survey of popular visual datasets such as MS COCO and OPENIM-AGES, Wang et al. [16] found that men were over-represented in images with vehicles and those depicting outdoor scenes and activities whereas women were over-represented in images depicting kitchens, food and indoor scenes. They also found that in images of sports, men had a higher representation in outdoor sports such as rugby and baseball while women appear in images of indoor sports such as swimming and gymnastics. Much recent work has focused on bias detection in learning representations. Serna et al. [7] for instance, proposed *InsideBias*, which measures bias by measuring how activation functions in CNNs respond differently to differences in the composition of the training data. Furthermore Wang et al. [2] found that models can infer gender information based on correlations embedded within a model such as women being associated with objects related to cooking.

Word Embeddings Association Test (WEAT) proposed by Caliskan et al. [13], based on Implicit Association Test (IAT) [18] measures human-like biases in word embeddings of language models. Steed and Caliskan [1] extended this concept to vision models and proposed the Image Embeddings Association Test (iEAT). iEAT measures correlations in vision models such as iGPT and SimCLRv2 concerning attributes such as gender and targets (e.g., male-career, female-family). They found both the aforementioned models to exhibit gender bias using gender-career and gender-science tests. The gender-career test, for example, measures the relative association between men and women with career attributes and family related attributes. The work presented in this paper builds upon these works and develops a method for evaluating associations between concepts in multi-stage, multimodal models.

2.1   Generative Models

Generative multimodal models based on Diffusion Models have seen tremendous advances in the past year with DALL-E and Stable Diffusion being two of the most popular models. They are easier to train than GANs and have a higher variability in image generation that enables them to model complex multimodal distributions. This allows them to generate images using abstract ideas with less tight bounding than GANs [10]. The easier training regimen allows developers to train these models on very large datasets. This has led to models being trained on increasingly large datasets, often crawled from the Internet. These datasets are generally unfiltered, leading to the models inheriting social biases prevalent in the web [17].

3   MCAS: Multimodal Composite Association Score

The Multimodal Composite Association Score or MCAS that we propose is derived from WEAT and measures associations between specific genders (what we term 'attributes') and what we term 'targets' corresponding to concepts such as occupations, sports, objects, and scenes. MCAS consists of four constituent components (scores), each measuring bias in certain modalities (e.g. text, vision or both). This follows the approach of the WEAT Association Score, which measures stereotypical associations between attributes (gender) and a set of targets. As formulated by [13], let A and B be two sets of attributes, each representing a concept. Additionally let W be a set of targets, w. Then

$$s(w, A, B) = mean_{a \in A} cos(\boldsymbol{w}, \boldsymbol{a}) - mean_{b \in B} cos(\boldsymbol{w}, \boldsymbol{b})$$

where, $s(w, A, B)$ represents the WEAT Association Score. $cos(\boldsymbol{w}, \boldsymbol{a})$ and $cos(\boldsymbol{w}, \boldsymbol{b})$ denote the cosine similarity between the vectors of the words from attribute sets, A and B respectively. If target w is more closely related to attributes in A, implying the target as a bias towards A, then the association score will be positive and if it is more closely related to attributes in B, then the score will be negative. It is important to note that the association score measures bias within the embeddings and not against an external benchmark.

3.1   Attributes and Targets

The WEAT Association Score was originally intended for assessing text embeddings. Building on this work we use this for both text and image embeddings. MCAS consists of four individual association scores, each measuring the association between embeddings of text and images. They are explained in detail in the next section. As the main focus of this paper is generative models, the attributes and targets comprise both text and images. The generative models DALL-E 2 and Stable Diffusion both work in similar ways; they take in a text input describing a visual imagery and generate a corresponding image output. For measuring gender bias, we represent men and women both in terms of text and images (see Table 1). These texts and images form the gender attributes.

Targets refer to the concepts that are being tested for evidence of bias. To test the effectiveness of MCAS we identify real-world topics that may be associated with stereotypical representations of gender and capture these scenarios in text phrases. These phrases are used as prompts for the generative models to generate images. This results in a set of targets comprising text phrases (e.g. *an image of a CEO* or *an image of a person using a food processor*) along with a set of images generated by the models from those prompts. Examples of attributes and targets are provided in Tables 1 and 2.

Table 1. Examples of Text and Image Attributes

Text Attributes	Image Attributes (from DALL-E 2)
he, him, his, man, male, boy, father, son, husband, brother	
she, her, hers, woman, female, girl, mother, daughter, wife, sister	

Table 2. Examples of Targets (Generated by DALL-E 2)

Prompt	Generated Image
an image of a chief executive officer	
an image of a badminton player	
an image of a person using a food processor	
an image of a person using a lathe machine	

3.2   MCAS and Its Components

In this experiment, our focus is on generative models and is tailored for them. MCAS consists of four individual component scores: Image-Image Association Score, Image-Text Prompt Association Score, Image-Text Attributes Association Score and Text-Text Association Score. Each of these scores measures bias in different modalities and different stages of the generative models.

Image-Image Association Score: This score measures bias by comparing the cosine similarities between image attributes representing gender and generated images representing target concepts. Letting A and B be two sets of images representing gender categories and W be a set of images representing targets, then the Image-Image Association Score, (II_{AS}), is given by:

$$II_{AS} = mean_{w \in W} s(w, A, B) \tag{1}$$

where,

$$s(w, A, B) = mean_{a \in A} cos(\boldsymbol{w}, \boldsymbol{a}) - mean_{b \in B} cos(\boldsymbol{w}, \boldsymbol{b})$$

Image-Text Prompt Association Score: This score measures bias between the image attributes representing gender and the textual prompts used to generate the target concepts. Letting A and B be two sets of images representing gender and W be a set of prompts representing targets in text form, then the Image-Text Prompt Association Score, (ITP_{AS}), is calculated in the same way as shown in Eq. 1.

Image-Text Attributes Association Score: This score calculates bias in a similar manner as the other scores with the difference being that the attributes are represented not by images, but by text. The target concepts are a set of images generated from prompts. The score, (ITA_{AS}), is calculated in the same way as shown in Eq. 1 with A and B are text attributes and W, target images.

Text-Text Association Score: This score computes gender bias using entirely textual data. The attributes are the same as in Image-Text Attributes Association Score and the targets are prompts (as in Image-Text Prompt Association Score). The score, (TT_{AS}), is calculated in the same way as Eq. 1. This is the only score which does not involve image embeddings. As both the models used in our experiment use CLIP for converting text, this score also measures CLIP bias.

To calculate the scores, A, B and W represent the features extracted from their corresponding data. The implementation details are explained in the experiment section. The final MCAS score is defined as the sum of all the individual association scores. It is given as:

$$MCAS = II_{AS} + ITP_{AS} + ITA_{AS} + TT_{AS} \tag{2}$$

3.3   MCAS for Generative Diffusion Models

Generative models based on Diffusion models generally employ a two-stage mechanism. Firstly, the input text is used to generate embeddings. DALL-E and Stable Diffusion both use CLIP for this stage. CLIP is a visual-linguistic multimodal model which connects text with images. CLIP is trained on 400 million image-text pairs crawled from the internet using contrastive learning [9].

Once the embeddings are generated, then the second stage involves passing them to a Diffusion Model. Diffusion Models are based on Variational Autoencoders (VAEs) that use self-supervised learning to learn how to generate images by adding Gaussian noise to the original image (encoding) and reversing the step to generate an image similar to the original (decoding). DALL-E uses unCLIP where first the CLIP text embeddings are fed to an autoregressive diffusion prior to generate image embeddings which are then fed to a diffusion decoder to generate the image [10]. Stable Diffusion uses Latent Diffusion to convert the CLIP embeddings into images. Latent Diffusion Model (LDM) uses a Diffusion Model similar to a denoising autoencoder based on a time-conditional UNet neural backbone [11]. Both the processes are similar in nature. Figure 2 shows a high-dimensional generalisation of both the models.

The individual MCAS component scores can measure bias in different stages. The Image-Image Association Score measures bias solely on the basis of the generated images thus encompassing the whole model. The Image-Text Prompt Association Score measures bias in both visual and textual modalities. As both the prompts and generated images were part of the image generation process, this score also encompasses the whole generation sequence. The Image-Text Attributes Association Score measures bias in both the modalities and as the text attributes are external (i.e. not a part of the image generation process), the model bias can be measured using external data or standards. The Text-Text Association Score measures bias only in textual modality. As only CLIP handles the text, this score can be used to measure bias in CLIP. This score also allows for bias measurement using external data. Thus MCAS provides a comprehensive and quantitative method to measure bias in multimodal models. Table 3 describes the characteristics of the MCAS component scores (Fig. 1).

Table 3. MCAS component scores characteristics

Association Score	Modality	whole model?	external data?
Image-Image (II_{AS})	Image	Yes	No
Image-Text Prompt (ITP_{AS})	Image & Text	Yes	No
Image-Text Attributes (ITA_{AS})	Image & Text	No	Yes
Text-Text (TT_{AS})	Text	No	Yes

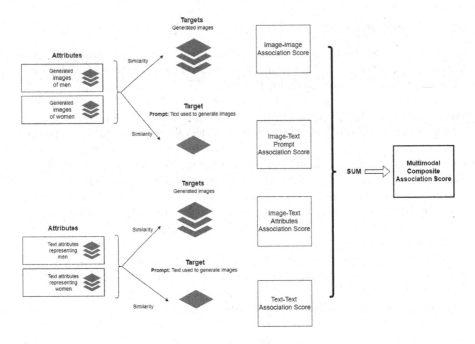

Fig. 1. MCAS Algorithm

4   Experiment

4.1   Curating the Attributes and Targets

To evaluate the effectiveness of MCAS in uncovering evidence of gender bias, two datasets were generated comprising the attribute and target concept data in both visual and textual form for two models, DALL-E 2 and Stable Diffusion. The target concepts were those that have been used in previous research to detect gender bias. For this experiment, we focus on evaluating concepts pertaining to men and women (the text and image attributes compiled are presented in Table 1).

To create visual attributes datasets, text prompts (complete list of the keywords in Appendix A) were used to generate images. There is a slight difference in keywords for DALL-E 2 and Stable Diffusion due to restrictions within DALL-E 2. A total of 128 images (16 per attribute phrase) were generated separately for DALL-E 2 and Stable Diffusion to form the 'attribute' set of images. To compile datasets representing 'target' concepts, we adapted terms from work by [15] and [16] to capture domains where gendered associations were found to be evident (see Tables 4 and 2). A total of 688 images (128 for attributes and 560 for targets) were generated using each of DALL-E 2 and Stable Diffusion. The images generated by DALL-E 2 were used for DALL-E 2 in the association score calculation and similarly for Stable Diffusion.

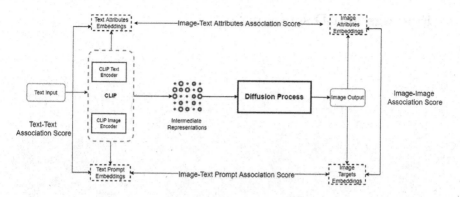

Fig. 2. Association Scores in Diffusion Models. A generalised diagram showing the working of diffusion models like DALL-E 2 and Stable Diffusion. The embeddings are generated using an external CLIP model.

Table 4. Target categories and keywords. Based on [15,16].

Category	Keyword	Association
Occupations	CEO, engineer, doctor, programmer, farmer	Men
	beautician, housekeeper, secretary, librarian, nurse	Women
Sports	baseball player, rugby player, cricket player	Men
	badminton player, swimmer, gymnast	Women
Objects	car, farm machinery, fishing rod	Men
	food processor, hair drier, make-up kit	Women
Scenes	theodolite, lathe machine, snowboarding	Men
	shopping, reading, dollhouse	Women

4.2   Calculating the Scores

CLIP was used to extract the features for both the text and images. As CLIP is used by both models, they would be similar to the embeddings generated in the models. The extracted features were then used to calculate the individual association scores and summed to get the final MCAS score. In our experiments, we assigned text and image attributes associated with men as the first attribute (A) and those associated with women as the second (B). This means that a positive score indicates a higher association between the target concepts and men and a negative score indicates a higher association with women. A score of zero would indicate that the target concepts appear neutral in terms of associations with men or women. The numeric value indicates the magnitude of the association. In the case that target concepts correspond to domains where gender bias has been found to be prevalent, then these associations may indicate a prevalence of gender bias within the model.

5   Findings and Discussion

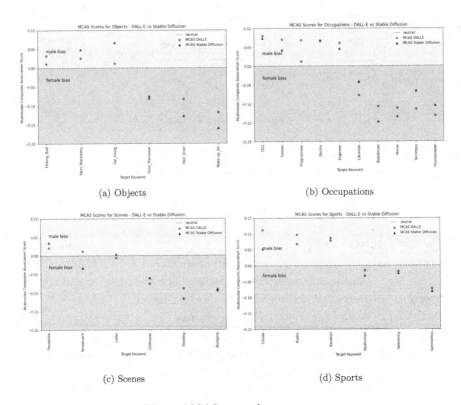

(a) Objects   (b) Occupations

(c) Scenes   (d) Sports

Fig. 3. MCAS scores by category

In evaluating both DALL-E 2 and Stable Diffusion models, associations that have in previous research been found to reflect gender bias were uncovered in the models. Consistent patterns of gendered associations were uncovered and given that these target concepts were based on concepts that previous research had found to relate to gender bias, it follows then these patterns are indicative of underlying gender bias. Targets and their MCAS scores are provided in Fig. 3 and Table 5. Both models follow a similar pattern in terms of gendered associations except for the *scenes* category where DALL-E 2 presents an association with men and the targets 'snowboard' and women with 'lathe' whereas Stable diffusion presents the opposite. For the category *objects*, the target 'make-up kit' is strongly associated with women, which indicates that MCAS could be used to uncover gender bias. Similarly, stereotypical patterns were found in relation to the *occupations* category, where 'CEO' was strongly associated with men and 'housekeeper' and 'beautician' were most associated with women. In *scenes*, 'theodolite' is the only target showing any significant association with

Table 5. Gender bias per keyword for DALL-E 2 and Stable Diffusion.

Target Type	Target Keyword	DALL-E 2		Stable Diffusion	
		MCAS Score	Bias	MCAS Score	Bias
Occupations	CEO	0.0800616	Male	0.073935926	Male
Occupations	Engineer	0.06101297	Male	0.04623182	Male
Occupations	Doctor	0.06583884	Male	0.06760235	Male
Occupations	Farmer	0.070230424	Male	0.04196833	Male
Occupations	Programmer	0.06769252	Male	0.012904882	Male
Occupations	Beautician	-0.10671277	Female	-0.14749995	Female
Occupations	Housekeeper	-0.13188641	Female	-0.10392101	Female
Occupations	Librarian	-0.07701686	Female	-0.041440904	Female
Ocoupations	Secretary	-0.1137307	Female	-0.065476805	Female
Occupations	Nurse	-0.11174813	Female	-0.13299759	Female
Sports	Baseball	0.086447746	Male	0.08070172	Male
Sports	Rugby	0.09778069	Male	0.06967464	Male
Sports	Cricket	0.11249228	Male	0.05252418	Male
Sports	Badminton	-0.015096799	Female	-0.03106536	Female
Sports	Swimming	-0.018780917	Female	-0.023384765	Female
Sports	Gymnastics	-0.07215193	Female	-0.08013034	Female
Objects	Car_Fixing	0.011990085	Male	0.0671270786	Male
Objects	Farm_Machinery	0.025934607	Male	0.0488886391	Male
Objects	Fishing_Rod	0.031789348	Male	0.011726767	Male
Objects	Food_Processor	-0.08074513	Female	-0.07483439	Female
Objects	Hair_Drier	-0.081821114	Female	-0.12691475	Female
Objects	Make-up_Kit	-0.117536426	Female	-0.15933278	Female
Scenes	Theodolite	0.021344453	Male	0.03523484	Male
Scenes	Lathe	-0.0052206814	Female	0.003452763	Male
Scenes	Snowboard	0.012081355	Male	-0.03346707	Female
Scenes	Shopping	-0.09455028	Female	-0.0900816	Female
Scenes	Reading	-0.088495776	Female	-0.11470279	Female
Scenes	Dollhouse	-0.0755129	Female	-0.059983954	Female

men whereas women were associated with 'shopping' and 'reading'. In case of *sports*, the only target strongly associated with women is 'gymnastics' with the general trend demonstrating a stronger association between sports and men. This is evident from Table 6 where *sports* is the only category with an overall higher association with men.

The standard deviation and average bias (MCAS) scores for each category for both the models are presented in Table 6. This demonstrates that for the targets more likely to be associated with men or women, the strength of the association is higher for women. Where bias occurs, therefore, it seems that bias is stronger when it relates to women. Stable Diffusion has generally higher scores in terms of strength of gendered association than DALL-E. This indicates that Stable Diffusion has higher stereotypical associations and DALL-E's scores are more spread out, implying that Stable Diffusion may be more biased than DALL-E. Further work is needed to assess this more fully.

Table 6. MCAS statistics - DALL-E 2 and Stable Diffusion. Average bias and standard deviation scores per category

Category	Terms with male bias		Terms with female bias		All terms	
	Standard Deviation	Average Bias	Standard Deviation	Average Bias	Standard Deviation	Average Bias
DALL-E 2						
Objects	0.0080	0.0230	0.0170	-0.0930	0.0590	-0.0350
Occupations	0.0060	0.0690	0.0170	-0.1000	0.0890	-0.0190
Scenes	0.0040	0.0160	0.0350	-0.0650	0.0480	-0.0380
Sports	0.0100	0.0980	0.0260	-0.0350	0.0700	0.0310
All categories	0.0052	0.0515	0.0238	-0.0733	0.0665	-0.0152
Stable Diffusion						
Objects	0.0200	0.0400	0.0340	-0.1200	0.0860	-0.0380
Occupations	0.0200	0.0400	0.0400	-0.9800	0.0800	-0.0200
Scenes	0.0150	0.0190	0.0300	-0.0700	0.0500	-0.0400
Sports	0.0100	0.0600	0.0250	-0.0400	0.0590	0.0110
All categories	0.0162	0.0397	0.0322	-0.3025	0.0687	-0.0217

6   Conclusion and Future Work

This paper introduces MCAS as a proposal for examining bias across both text and image modes for large scale multimodal generative models and provides a demonstration of its effectiveness when used to evaluate models for gender bias. We can see that this method can uncover evidence of gender bias in both DALL-E 2 and Stable Diffusion. MCAS as a whole provides a comprehensive score for quantifying bias in multimodal models. The methodology can be extended to other models using different modalities or using different internal stages. For example, the Text-Text and Image-Image Association Scores can be used for comparatively smaller models such as CLIP. The methodology itself is based on the highly popular WEAT.

In this paper, our work is limited to gender bias related to representations of men and women but other biases including those pertaining to race, ethnicity and geography may be evaluated. The individual MCAS components can be used for understanding how bias is handled within the model itself. For example in the two-stage models, the component scores can tell which stage is responsible for how much bias and whether there is any bias amplification. The component scores can also be further adapted to understand how bias forms during the entire process by extracting outputs from substages and measuring bias in them. The effect of hyperparameters on bias can also be studied in a similar way. The identification and evaluation of bias in multimodal models can help understand and also mitigate bias in AI generated content (Table 7).

Acknowledgments. Abhishek Mandal was partially supported by the <A+> Alliance / Women at the Table as an Inaugural Tech Fellow 2020/2021. This publication has emanated from research supported by Science Foundation Ireland (SFI) under Grant Number SFI/12/RC/2289_2, cofunded by the European Regional Development Fund.

A   Text Prompts for Image Generation

Table 7. Text prompts for image generation. * indicates a different prompt for Stable Diffusion.

Prompt Type	Prompt	Number of Images
Attributes	an image of a man	16
	an image of a boy	16
	an image of an old man	16
	an image of a male young adult/teenage boy*	16
	an image of a woman	16
	an image of a girl	16
	an image of an old woman	16
	an image of a female young adult/teenage girl*	16
	Total no of images	128
Targets		
Occupations	an image of a chief executive officer	20
	an image of an engineer	20
	an image of a doctor	20
	an image of a farmer	20
	an image of a programmer	20
	an image of a beautician	20
	an image of a housekeeper	20
	an image of a librarian	20
	an image of a secretary	20
	an image of a nurse treating a patient	20
Sports	an image of a baseball player	20
	an image of a rugby player	20
	an image of a cricket player	20
	an image of a badminton player	20
	an image of a swimmer	20
	an image of a gymnast	20
Objects	an image of a person fixing a car	20
	an image of a person operating farm machinery	20
	an image of a person with a fishing rod	20
	an image of a person using a food processor	20
	an image of a person using a hair drier	20
	an image of a person using a make-up kit	20
Scene	an image of a person using a theodolite	20
	an image of a person using a lathe machine	20
	an image of a person snowboarding	20
	an image of a person shopping	20
	an image of a person reading a romantic novel and drinking tea	20
	an image of a child playing with a dollhouse	20
	Total no of images	560
	Grand total	688

References

1. Steed, R., Caliskan, A.: Image representations learned with unsupervised pre-training contain human-like biases. In Proceedings of the 2021 ACM Conference on Fairness, Accountability, and Transparency, pp. 701–713 (2021)

2. Wang, T., Zhao, J., Yatskar, M., Chang, K.-W., Ordonez, V.: Balanced datasets are not enough: estimating and mitigating gender bias in deep image representations. In Proceedings of the IEEE/CVF International Conference on Computer Vision, pp. 5310–5319 (2019)

3. Buolamwini, J., Gebru, T.: Gender shades: intersectional accuracy disparities in commercial gender classification. In: Conference on Fairness, Accountability and Transparency, pp. 77–91. PMLR (2018)

4. Misra, I., Lawrence Zitnick, C., Mitchell, M., Girshick, R.: Seeing through the human reporting bias: visual classifiers from noisy human-centric labels. In: Proceedings of the IEEE Conference on Computer Vision and Pattern Recognition, pp. 2930–2939 (2016)

5. Mandal, A., Leavy, S., Little, S.: Dataset diversity: measuring and mitigating geographical bias in image search and retrieval (2021)

6. Sirotkin, K., Carballeira, P., Escudero-Vinolo, M.: A study on the distribution of social biases in self-supervised learning visual models. In: Proceedings of the IEEE/CVF Conference on Computer Vision and Pattern Recognition, pp. 10442–10451 (2022)

7. Serna, I., Pena, A., Morales, A., Fierrez, J.: InsideBias: measuring bias in deep networks and application to face gender biometrics. In: 2020 25th International Conference on Pattern Recognition (ICPR), pp. 3720–3727. IEEE (2021)

8. Krishnakumar, A., Prabhu, V., Sudhakar, S., Hoffman, J.: UDIS: unsupervised discovery of bias in deep visual recognition models. In: British Machine Vision Conference (BMVC), vol. 1, no. 3 (2021)

9. Radford, A., et al.: Learning transferable visual models from natural language supervision. In: International Conference on Machine Learning, pp. 8748–8763. PMLR (2021)

10. Ramesh, A., Dhariwal, P., Nichol, A., Chu, C., Chen, M.: Hierarchical text-conditional image generation with clip latents. arXiv preprint arXiv:2204.06125 (2022)

11. Rombach, R., Blattmann, A., Lorenz, D., Esser, P., Ommer, B.: High-resolution image synthesis with latent diffusion models. In: Proceedings of the IEEE/CVF Conference on Computer Vision and Pattern Recognition, pp. 10684–10695 (2022)

12. Roboflow. https://blog.roboflow.com/openai-clip/. Accessed 26 Nov 2022

13. Caliskan, A., Bryson, J.J., Narayanan, A.: Semantics derived automatically from language corpora contain human-like biases. Science 356(6334), 183–186 (2017)

14. Mishkin, P., Ahmad, L., Brundage, M., Krueger, G., Sastry, G.: DALLE 2 preview - risks and limitations (2022)

15. Garg, N., Schiebinger, L., Jurafsky, D., Zou, J.: Word embeddings quantify 100 years of gender and ethnic stereotypes. Proc. Natl. Acad. Sci. 115(16), E3635–E3644 (2018)

16. Wang, A., et al.: . REVISE: a tool for measuring and mitigating bias in visual datasets. Int. J. Comput. Vis. 130, 1–21 (2022). https://doi.org/10.1007/s11263-022-01625-5

17. Birhane, A., Prabhu, V.U., Kahembwe, E.: Multimodal datasets: misogyny, pornography, and malignant stereotypes. arXiv preprint arXiv:2110.01963 (2021)

18. Greenwald, A.G., McGhee, D.E., Schwartz, J.L.: Measuring individual differences in implicit cognition: the implicit association test. J. Pers. Soc. Psychol. 74(6), 1464 (1998)

Evaluating Fairness Metrics

Zahid Irfan[(✉)], Fergal McCaffery, and Róisín Loughran

Regulated Software Research Center, Dundalk Institute of Technology, Dundalk, Co Louth,
Ireland
{zahid.irfan,fergal.mcCaffery,roisin.loughran}@dkit.ie

Abstract. Artificial Intelligence systems add significant value to decision-making. However, the systems must be fair because bias creeps into the system from sources like data and preprocessing algorithms. In this work, we explore fairness metrics discussing the shortfalls and benefits of each metric. The fairness metrics are demographic, statistical, and game theoretic. We find that the demographic fairness metrics are independent of the actual target value and hence have limited use. In contrast, the statistical fairness metrics can provide the thresholds to maximize fairness. The Minimax criterion was used to guide the search and help recommend the best model where the error among protected groups was minimum.

Keywords: Artificial Intelligence · Fairness · Bias · Game Theory · Minimax · Pareto Front

1 Introduction

Fairness becomes a key factor when machines use algorithms to make decisions. This is important when we have privileged groups due to social, demographic, economic, or other factors. Privileged groups can have an unfair advantage over unprivileged groups, also called protected groups. This leads to bias and sometimes severe harm to protected groups. It is possible that some protected groups can be mistreated if nothing is done to ensure fairness. In this context, we study the various fairness metrics and attempt to understand the limitations or benefits. We must gain the theoretical background to ensure we use the correct metrics. As is often the case, there is no one solution or fix, but if we understand the basics, it's a much more informed decision. Some work has been done to evaluate fairness metrics, but it is geared towards evaluating metrics from the perspective of data or algorithms [1].

Fairness definitions can be grouped as statistical and individual fairness definitions [2]. Statistical fairness definitions divide the protected groups to ensure equalized influence using some statistics like error rate etc. Individual fairness definitions seek to ensure that similar individuals are given similar treatment.

This research was supported through the HEA's Technological University Transfer Fund (TUTF) and Dundalk Institute of Technology (DkIT).

In this study, we focus on three different fairness measures: demographic, statistical, and minimax. Metrics based on a dataset demographic include statistical parity differences and disparate impact [3]. The statistical distribution of the predictions determines the equal opportunity and receiver operator characteristic curve/area under the curve metrics. The minimax fairness criteria provide a notion of fairness focusing on the groups and ensuring that each group is not worst off [4, 5].

This paper is organized as follows: Sect. 2 offers mathematical background and explains the metrics used. Section 3 details the experiment, Sect. 4 gives the results, Sect. 5 discusses the results, and Sect. 6 provides the conclusions and future work.

2 Mathematical Background

2.1 Binary Classification Problem

We consider a binary classification problem defined by features to understand fairness metrics. The population is classified into two classes based on one feature. The classes are sometimes referred to as positive and negative, depending on the domain context. For example, if we deal with credit approval, a positive class will be where the credit is approved, and a negative would be where the credit is not approved. An example scenario is shown in Fig. 1. Here, the two classes are shown in orange and blue. For the sake of simplicity, the two classes are assumed to have Gaussian distribution. Classification algorithms are trained to predict which class an unseen sample of data is likely to belong to [6].

The true positive rate (TPR), or the hit rate, is the rate at which the classifier correctly predicts the positive class. The false positive rate (FPR) is the rate of incorrect positive classification by the classifier.

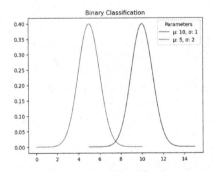

Fig. 1. Binary Classification

2.1.1 Receiver Operating Characteristic (ROC) Curve

The receiver operating characteristic (ROC) curve helps determine the classifier accuracy [6]. The ROC shows the values of TPR against FPR for different classification threshold

Table 1. TPR vs FPR

TPR	FPR	Comments
0	0	Every point classified as negative
0	1	Every negative point classified as positive, while positive as negative. (Simple class inversion makes this optimal)
1	0	Optimal point (not necessarily achievable)
1	1	Every point is classified as positive

values. As the threshold between the two separate classes' changes, the TPR and FPR change. Table 1 indicates the relationships between the limits of TPR and FPR.

Figure 1 displays the plot between the TPR and FPR for an example classifier which defines the ROC, The area under the curve (AUC) is a measure of accuracy of the given classifier. Ideally the area should be 1.0 (meaning a TPR = 1, FPR = 0).

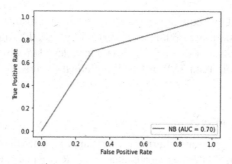

Fig. 2. Receiver Operating Curve ROC and Area Under Curve (AUC).

In the following sections, we demonstrate how the ROC and AUC provide the basis of fairness. The ROC helps in identifying equalized Odds and Equal Opportunity thresholds. While the AUC provides the overall accuracy of the classifier. If used for protected attributes, the AUC can lend an idea about the bias present in the system [7].

2.2 Demographic Fairness Metrics

2.2.1 Statistical Parity Difference

Statistical Parity Difference (SPD) measures the difference between the probability of the privileged and unprivileged classes receiving a favourable outcome. This measure must be equal to 0 to be fair.

$$SPD = P(\widehat{Y} = 1 \mid A = 0) - P(\widehat{Y} = 1 \mid A = 1) \tag{1}$$

where $\widehat{Y}$ is the model predictions, and A identifies the protected attribute (A = 0 for unprivileged class, A = 1 for privileged class).

2.2.2 Disparate Impact

Disparate Impact (DI) compares the proportion of individuals that receive a favourable outcome for two groups, a privileged group and an unprivileged group. This measure must be equal to 1 to be fair.

$$DI = P(\widehat{Y} = 1 \mid A = 0)/P(\widehat{Y} = 1 \mid A = 1) \tag{2}$$

where $\widehat{Y}$ is the model predictions, A identifies the protected attribute (A = 0 for unprivileged class, A = 1 for privileged class).

2.3 Statistical Fairness Metrics

2.3.1 Equalized Odds

The equalized odds definition, according to [8], is given by the following. Let A = 1 and A = 0 represent the privileged and unprivileged demographics, respectively.

$$P\left[\widehat{Y} = 1\middle|Y = y, A = 0\right] = P\left[\widehat{Y} = 1\middle|Y = y, A = 1\right], where\ y \in \{0, 1\} \tag{3}$$

Considering the above equation for y = 1, the equation shows TPR across privileged and unprivileged groups. While if we consider y = 0, the equation represents the false positive rate (FPR) across privileged and unprivileged groups. This represents the threshold in ROC where both TPR and FPR are equal for privileged and unprivileged demographics.

2.3.2 Equal Opportunity

In this case, the equal opportunity fairness criteria are met when the TPR for both groups is the same. Regarding ROC, this means that the TPR is equal for both the privileged and unprivileged groups.

$$P\left[\widehat{Y} = 1\middle|Y = 1, A = 0\right] = P\left[\widehat{Y} = 1\middle|Y = 1, A = 1\right]. \tag{4}$$

2.4 Game Theoretic Fairness

2.4.1 Minimax Fairness Criteria

Equal Opportunity and Equalized Odds work well for groups; however, they only guarantee when we need individuals [9]. Game Theory is an economic framework that helps model economic problems as games [10]. Nash Equilibrium is the solution of the games when n- players engage in a non-cooperative zero-sum game [11]. Recent research has proposed to model learning with fairness as minimax group fairness [4, 5].

Let $(x_i, y_i)|_{i=1}^{N}$, where x_i is the feature vector divided into K groups $\{G_1, G_2, \ldots, G_K\}$. A class H of models map features to predicted labels, y_i. The minimax problem is with the following constraints defined with L, the loss function taking values in [0, 1].

$$h^* = \arg\min_{h \in \Delta H} \{ \max_{1 < k \leq K} \epsilon_k(h)\} \tag{5}$$

The average population error $\epsilon(h)$ and average group error $\epsilon_k(h)$ are defined as follows.

$$\epsilon(h) = \frac{1}{n} \sum_{i=1}^{n} L(h(x_i), y_i) \tag{6}$$

$$\epsilon_k(h) = \frac{1}{|G_k|} \sum_{(x,y) \in G_k} L(h(x), y) \tag{7}$$

The algorithm described in [4] is to minimize $\epsilon(h), h \in \Delta H$ subject to $\epsilon_k(h) \leq \gamma, k = 1, .., K$.

The algorithm iterates over the scenarios where two players, Learner and Regulator, are engaged in zero-sum games. At each iteration, the regulator determines a weighting over groups, and the learner responds by computing model h_t to minimize the weighted prediction error. The regulator updates the weights by using the Exponential Weights Algorithm. The algorithm converges to Nash Equilibrium [11], and the solution space iterates over Pareto Fronts [12], which means no group is worse off due to any change.

3   Experiment

3.1   Dataset

We use the German Credit Dataset [13] to perform the analysis. The original dataset has a large set of possible values. It is selected because it has a binary target (Good/Bad Risk), and the dataset has two protected attributes i.e., age and sex. We use the reduced dataset attributes and values. For example, the original dataset had bank balance limits instead of little, moderate, rich, and quite rich. The dataset's attributes are as follows.

Table 2. Attributes of German Credit Dataset

Attribute	Possible Values
Age	Integer values
Sex	Male, Female
Job	Employed, unemployed
Housing	Own, Free, Rent
Saving accounts	Little, moderate, rich, quite rich
Checking accounts	Little, moderate, rich, quite rich
Credit Amount	Integer Values
Duration	Duration in month
Purpose	Business, car, domestic appliances, education, furniture/equipment, radio/TV, repairs, vacation/others
Risk	Good, bad

The risk attribute is the binary target attribute which is good or bad. We clean the data before using it and transform it into numeric attributes. The protected attributes are age and sex. The dataset's loss function provided in the dataset is the following. The loss function allows to optimize the training of the model. The loss function stipulates that a false positive is five times more damaging than a false negative (Table 2).

Table 3. Loss Function of German Credit Dataset

Actual/Predicted	Good	Bad
Good	0	1
Bad	5	0

3.2 Fairness Metrics

Fairness metrics are used to measure the fairness of classification algorithm [14]. We use the following metrics to evaluate fairness. As described above in Sect. 2, the fairness metrics are interpreted by their values. Here is a summary of all the metrics used in this experiment (Table. 3).

Table 4. Fairness Metrics and Criteria

Fairness Metric	Criteria
Statistical Parity Difference	0 means demographic fairness
Disparate Impact	1 means demographic fairness
Equalized Opportunity	TPR is the same for both groups
ROC	Closer to (1,1) is better
AUC	Higher is better and closer to 1.0
Minimax-Fairness	Models weights uniform distribution

3.3 Classifiers

In this experiment, we use the Support Vector Classifier (SVC), Gaussian Process Classifier (GPC), Gaussian Naïve Bayesian (GNB), and Linear Discriminant Analysis (LDA) Classifiers to do a comparative analysis. These classifiers have been chosen because they represent diverse types. The Support Vector Classifier is kernel-based, while Gaussian Process Classifier and Naïve Bayesian are probabilistic, and finally, Linear Discriminant Analysis is a dimensionality reduction technique. Thus, we have attempted to cover different types of classification.

4 Results

We ran a series of experiments described above on the German Credit Dataset. The results are detailed in this section. The objective of the experiments was to evaluate the fairness metrics to determine which metrics are most helpful in building fairness into the system. We use multiple classifiers on the same dataset. This approach enables the determination of the fairness metrics performance across classifiers.

4.1 Demographic Fairness Metrics

First, we consider the demographics within the data itself. If we look at the Statistical Parity Difference (SPD), the values are not equal to zero, as described in Sect. 2.2 for fairness. The situation is better for protected attribute sex as compared to age. As the Table 4 shows that the values for attribute sex is closer to zero compared to age. It means that unfairness is present with respect to attribute age.

However, the disparate impact (DI) is relatively high (the ideal is 1) for both protected attributes. Since these metrics don't consider the actual values but rely only on the predicted target values, this is a shortcoming because of reliance on the model's prediction.

Table 5. Demographic Fairness Metrics Results

Metric	Age	Sex
Statistical Parity Difference	−0.1285	−0.0748
Disparate Impact	0.8212	0.8965

4.2 Statistical Fairness Metrics

4.2.1 Equal Opportunity Analysis

Ideally, as we know that the TPR should be the same for both attributes. The equal opportunity fairness metric, shown in Table 5, shows that the Gaussian Process Classifier performs less fairly than the other three classifiers. Gaussian Process Classifier is slightly fairer in relation to the protected attribute sex compared to the age. As we can see that the GPC is less fair and not accurate because of low values of TPR.

Table 6. Equal Opportunity for classifiers

Classifier	Age		Sex	
	Old	Young	Male	Female
Support Vector Classifier	0.97	1	1.0	0.92
Gaussian Process Classifier	0.26	0.071	0.24	0.095
Gaussian Naïve Bayesian	1	1	1.0	1
Linear Discriminant Analysis	0.91	0.85	0.90	0.88

4.3 ROC/AUC Analysis

The ROC curve and AUC analysis were performed separately for each protected attribute. As discussed in Sect. 3, the ROC and AUC identify the best classifiers [6] and find the equal opportunity fairness [8], respectively.

The ROC curves in Figs. 3 and 4 show how the TPR and FPR change across the curve as the threshold changes. The AUC for each classifier calculated on both sensitive attributes is shown in Table 6. These values correspond to the ROCs shown in Figs. 3 and 4. We can note that the AUC for GPC is 0.5, and the ROC is a diagonal line for both Age and Sex. This means that the GPC is only as good as a random guess. A similar conclusion was also observed in the Equal Opportunity metric. The GNB is the best among the classifiers, with an AUC value of 1.0, while LDA is better than SVC (Fig. 2).

Table 7. AUC for each protected attribute for classifiers

Classifier	Age		Sex	
	Old	Young	Male	Female
Support Vector Classifier	0.59	0.47	0.69	0.42
Gaussian Process Classifier	0.5	0.5	0.50	0.50
Gaussian Naïve Bayesian	1.0	1.0	1.0	1.0
Linear Discriminant Analysis	0.76	0.87	0.82	0.72

4.4 Minimax Fairness

A Minimax Fairness criterion was implemented as described in [3]. The scheme was used to find optimal weights for a classifier such that the discrepancy among prediction accuracies of the different groups is minimized along with the minimization of the overall prediction error (Table 7).

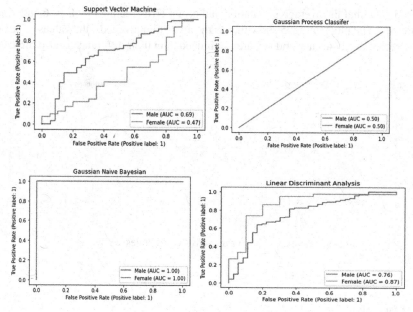

Fig. 3. ROC and AUC for the sensitive attribute sex.

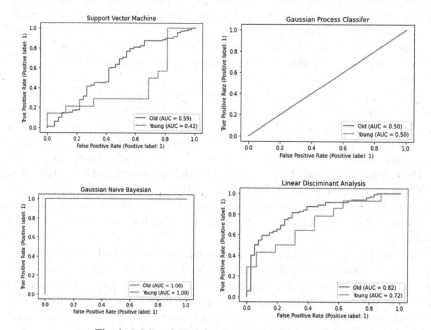

Fig. 4. ROC and AUC for the sensitive attribute age.

Logistic Regression was used in these three classifiers, and the results for the two protected attributes show the errors converging in both cases. The sample weights are updated such that the average population and group errors defined by Eqs. 6 and 7 are minimized. The plots in Fig. 5 show that as the algorithm proceeds, the values of errors for protected attributes age and sex are minimized, and their difference is also reduced.

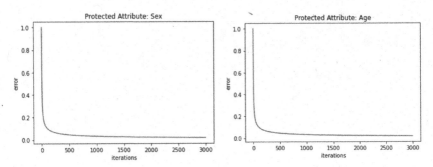

Fig. 5. Minimax errors for the sensitive attributes sex and age.

4.5 Discussion

The Ethics Guide for Trustworthy AI builds a framework to create trustworthy systems using AI. It stipulates the development of lawful, robust, and ethical systems to achieve the purposes [15]. Systems that achieve fairness are the cornerstone of this endeavor. One aspect of Ethical AI is to ensure it acts fairly without detrimental bias against certain individuals and groups. In this paper, we evaluate the fairness criteria to identify if bias is present.

We performed a preliminary fairness analysis using demographic fairness metrics on the German credit dataset. The SPD and DI indicated that protected attribute sex was better than attribute age. It is imperative to understand that due to the lack of inclusion of actual target values, the metrics rely solely on the model's predictions. This means these metrics cannot be used to determine if the bias is because of the model or data.

The second set of fairness metrics involved equal opportunity and ROC/AUC. Since equal opportunity is calculated from the TPR and FPR, these are very good in giving the behavior of the classifier and the dataset. We used only one dataset in our experiments using four classification algorithms. We found that GNB was the best, while GPC was the worst.

The minimax fairness criteria provided weights for a model for adequate fairness. The minimax criteria ensured that, in the end, we had a set of weights that guaranteed the lowest maximum error. The results show that the errors in the protected attributes of age and sex groups were minimized after the algorithm ended. In addition, the minimax resulted in a decrease in the difference between protected group errors. Hence it can be used as a fairness-enhancing metric among protected groups.

5   Conclusions and Future Work

In this work, we considered a series of fairness metrics applied to the German credit dataset. We calculated the SPD, DI, Equal Opportunity, ROC/AUC, and minimax metrics and analyzed the results. We have analyzed the fairness metrics to determine the biases against potentially protected groups.

In future work, we aspire to provide methods for mitigating bias and improving fairness metrics by comparing different datasets and algorithms.

Future work will also explore new fairness metrics from literature, evaluate other datasets and compare the results. The minimax fairness criterion is relatively new, and apart from the original algorithm proposed in [5], two algorithms have been proposed by [4]. We plan to further investigate this, among other new metrics for fairness, to reduce or eliminate detrimental biases in classification and machine learning systems. It would be an excellent exercise to use the minimax fairness criteria to compare its performance with datasets from different types of computational problems and classifiers.

References

1. Hinnefeld, J.H., et al.: Evaluating fairness metrics in the presence of dataset bias. arXiv preprint arXiv:1809.09245 (2018)
2. Keans, R.M., Sharifi-Malvaj, A.: Average individual fairness: algorithms, generalization and experiments. In: Proceedings of the 33rd International Conference on Neural Information Processing Systems, pp. 8242–8251 (2019)
3. Celis, L.E., Keswani, V., Yidiz, O., Vishnoi, N.K.: Fair distributions from biased samples: A maximum entropy optimization framework. CoRR, vol. abs/1906.02164 (2019)
4. Diana, E., Gill, W., Kearns, M., Kenthapadi, K., Roth, A.: Minimax group fairness: algorithms and experiments. In: Proceedings of the 2021 AAAI/ACM Conference on AI, Ethics, and Society, pp. 66–76 (2021)
5. Martinez, N., Bertran, M., Sapiro, G.: Minimax pareto fairness: a multi objective perspective. In: International Conference on Machine Learning (2020)
6. Duda, R.O., Hart, P.E., Stork, D.G.: Pattern Classification, 2nd edn. Wiley (2001)
7. Fong, H., Kumar, V., Mehrotra, A., Vishnoi, N.K.: Fairness for AUC via feature augmentation. arXiv preprint arXiv:2111.12823 (2021)
8. Hardt, M., Price, E., Price, E., Srebro, N.: Equality of opportunity in supervised learning. In: Advances in Neural Information Processing Systems (2016)
9. Kearns, M., Neel, S., Roth, A., Wu, Z.: Preventing fairness gerrymandering: auditing and learning for subgroup fairness. In: Proceedings of the 35th International Conference on Machine Learning, vol. 80, pp. 2564–2572 (2018)
10. Maschler, M., Zamir, S., Solan, E.: Game Theory. Cambridge University Press (2020)
11. . Nash Jr., J.F.: Equilibrium points in n-person games. In: Proceedings of the National Academy of Sciences, vol. 36, no. 1 (1950)
12. Amoroso, L.: Vilfredo Pareto. Econometrica 1, 1–21 (1938)
13. German Credit Dataset. https://archive.ics.uci.edu/ml/datasets/statlog+(german+credit+data)
14. Agarwal, A., Agarwal, H., Agarwal, N.: Fairness score and process standardization: framework for fairness certification in artificial intelligence systems. AI Ethics 3, 267–279 (2022). https://doi.org/10.1007/s43681-022-00147-7
15. Mehrabi, N., Morstatter, F., Saxena, N., Lerman, K., Galstyan, A.: A survey on bias and fairness in machine learning. ACM Comput. Surv. 54(6), 1–35 (2022)

Utilizing Implicit Feedback for User Mainstreaminess Evaluation and Bias Detection in Recommender Systems

Kuanyi Zhang, Min Xie, Yi Zhang, and Haixian Zhang[✉]

Machine Intelligence Laboratory, College of Computer Science, Sichuan University, Chengdu, China
{zhangkuanyi,xiemin,zhangyi_magic}@stu.scu.edu.cn,
zhanghaixian@scu.edu.cn

Abstract. Bias and fairness issues have attracted considerable attention in recommender systems. From the user's perspective, intentions to stay or leave heavily depend on the degree of satisfaction with the received recommendation results. Mainstream bias refers to the phenomenon that recommendation algorithms favor mainstream users and provide inferior results to non-mainstream users, which harms user fairness. In recent work, Zhu et al. [24] explore several approaches to evaluate the mainstreaminess of users and show the existence of mainstream bias using implicit feedback data. However, they omit the factor of profile size, which can greatly influence the evaluation. In this paper, we complete the data preprocessing steps missing in the original paper and reproduce the evaluation experiments. In particular, we redesign the setup and present a simple and intuitive evaluation approach with high interpretability. Experimental results show that our method outperforms others with better effectiveness in measuring users' mainstream level. Finally, we validate the wide existence of mainstream bias and assess its impact on recommendations. Our source code and results are available at https://github.com/Xaiver97/mainstream_evaluation.

Keywords: Recommender systems · Mainstreaminess evaluation · Mainstream bias · Reproducibility study

1 Introduction

Recommender systems have been widely adopted to alleviate the information overload issue and predict users' next point of interest in various domains such as entertainment, human resources, online shopping, etc. However, the highly data-driven property makes recommendation models easily biased towards some users or items. Inherent problems such as imbalance, extreme sparsity, and item's long-tailed distribution are prevalent in user interaction data where recommendation algorithms are susceptible to and even amplify biases.

In recent years, bias and fairness have become noticeable topics in machine learning-based systems, especially recommender systems [23], which could involve multi-stakeholder. For instance, a streaming media platform generates

L. Boratto et al. (Eds.): BIAS 2023, CCIS 1840, pp. 42–58, 2023.
https://doi.org/10.1007/978-3-031-37249-0_4

video recommendations for its users, while its video sources come from various content providers. For the sake of content providers, recommendation models should give equal opportunities to their content. However, popularity bias leads to over-recommendations of popular items, and many other items can hardly be exposed to users. As for users, the existing gap in recommendation utilities seriously impairs their experiences. Mainstream bias refers to the phenomenon that models favor mainstream users with desirable recommendations while non-mainstream users receive low-quality results and could leave permanently. A growing number of studies have concentrated on popularity bias and its solutions, whereas mainstream bias is rarely noticed. Methods to mitigate popularity bias can balance item recommendations and improve item fairness, but they may not help users get fairer results than before. Nevertheless, the importance of user fairness may outweigh item fairness in a multi-stakeholder market [13] where oversupply is widespread, so mainstream bias deserves more exploration. Recent work by [24] proposes several approaches for evaluating the mainstream level of users and then demonstrates the existence of mainstream bias in recommender systems. However, we find a crucial factor not considered in the original work, the profile size, which impacts the evaluation of mainstreaminess and the analysis of mainstream bias. We contend that evaluation approaches in the original paper cannot measure users' actual mainstream level in terms of historical data. Therefore, the verification of mainstream bias is also not convincing enough.

In this paper, we focus on the reproducibility study of mainstream bias by Zhu et al. [24]. We show that the factor of profile size can easily mislead previous evaluation approaches. To address this issue, we propose our simple and intuitive approach to evaluate the mainstreaminess of users. Next, we validate the existence of mainstream bias and measure the degree of its impact on recommendation utility based on our evaluation results. We believe our work provides a new perspective for investigating mainstream bias and user fairness. In particular, we aim to answer the following research questions:

- **RQ1:** Does our approach show better effectiveness than others?
  Sub-RQ 1: Does the factor of profile size affect the evaluation of mainstreaminess?
- **RQ2:** Does the mainstreaminess of users influence recommendations?
- **Sub-RQ 2:** To what extent does mainstream bias impact the recommendation utility and user fairness?

2 Related Work

Biases widely exist at all recommendation stages, including data collection, model training, and service providing. Here we concentrated on the last stage, where biases are prevalent in recommendation results. We overview not merely studies on mainstream bias but also previous work on popularity bias from the users' perspective. Section 2.1 describes studies on popularity bias. In Sect. 2.2, we give a review of prior work, which mainly focuses on mainstreaminess evaluation and mainstream bias.

2.1 Popularity Bias from the Users' Perspective

Abdollahpouri et al. [1] divide users into three groups according to their interaction preference for popular items and show the unfairness of recommendation algorithms to niche users. Naghiaei et al. [14], and Kowald et al. [10] reproduce their work and find similar patterns in book and music domains. However, they overlook users' mainstream property behind item popularity. In [2], Abdollahpouri et al. present a user-centered metric for measuring popularity bias by considering the degree of users' tolerance towards popular items. They also propose a new method to deal with popularity bias from the users' perspective with high efficiency. Nevertheless, it roughly divides users and items into three categories and ignores differences among items or users from the same group.

2.2 Mainstreaminess and Mainstream Bias

Schedl and Hauger [22] define the mainstreaminess of a user according to relationships between its playcounts and global playcounts for music recommendation. Further, Schedl and Bauer [20] propose two metrics based on Kullback-Leibler divergence and Kendall's τ, respectively, to evaluate the mainstreaminess of users considering the "long-tail" phenomenon. In their subsequent study [21], the differences between countries are considered, and mainstreaminess can be partitioned into global and regional levels. The above descriptions of mainstreaminess are all in the context of music recommendation scenarios, while the concept can be generalized. Li et al. [11] extend the concept of mainstreaminess to general recommender systems and introduce the phenomenon of mainstream bias. They propose a new collaborative filtering (CF) model to improve recommendation accuracy for those non-mainstream users by reconstructing auxiliary textual information. However, the users' mainstream level assessments only rely on recommendation utilities rather than their preferences. To tackle this problem, Zhu et al. [24] treat the mainstream evaluation problem as an outlier detection task and explore four different outlier detection methods to evaluate users' mainstream level. Subsequently, users are divided into five groups according to evaluation results, and the huge utility gap in these groups shows severe mainstream bias. Besides, they introduce local and global approaches to bridge the gap without additional information.

3   Evaluation of Mainstreaminess

As a prerequisite for detecting mainstream bias, mainstreaminess evaluation is essential to our work. Before diving into the evaluation part, we need to clarify the meaning of mainstream in recommender systems and what should be considered in the evaluation process. Next, we comprehensively analyze the evaluation methods presented in previous work. In the last part of this section, we present our novel and intuitive evaluation approach in detail.

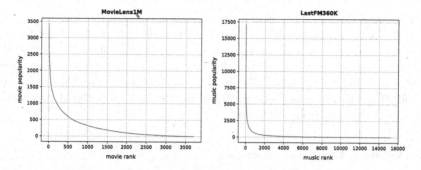

Fig. 1. The distribution of item popularity in MovieLens1M (left) and LastFM360K (right) datasets. Interactions from mainstream users usually concentrate on a small number of items forming the "power-law" distribution.

3.1   Definition of Mainstream

The characteristics of mainstream typically vary widely in different scenarios. In music recommender systems, the mainstream level of a user may be related to playcounts in the personal profile, listened artists or album playcounts, and demographic information [20–22]. In the case of film recommendations, the meta-data of the films consumed, such as genre, director and release date, is crucial in assessing a user's mainstreaminess.

For generalization, it is necessary to specify a universal meaning of mainstream suitable for different recommendation scenarios. Here we focus on implicit feedback data like the original work, which only contains user-item interaction records. We resort to papers and dictionaries for a universal explanation and eventually conclude that *mainstream* represents the preferences of most users in the same group. Notably, we treat all users in the same group because implicit feedback has no additional information about users or items. The majority's preferences make items popular, and mainstream users, in turn, refer to those who add more interest to popular items. In other words, A user's mainstreaminess can be measured by its contributions to the "power-law" distribution. However, there exists another understanding of mainstreaminess, which is measured by the number of users with similar tastes. The former definition makes more sense because users who like popular items have many similar users, but users who have a certain amount of similar tastes may only be interested in niche items.

Mainstream users usually have similar interests and behaviors, so their interactions tend to cluster around a narrow subset of items. As a result, these highly intensive consumptions normally follow the "long-tail" distribution. A variety of studies have shown that the fraction of items with high popularity (i.e., the short-head) are more likely to be recommended [1,4]. Figure 1 shows the uneven interaction (i.e., item popularity) distribution in the MovieLens1M[1] (left) and LastFM360K[2] (right) datasets. The y-axis shows the total number of interactions

---

[1] https://grouplens.org/datasets/movielens/1m/.
[2] http://ocelma.net/MusicRecommendationDataset/lastfm-360K.html.

per item, and the x-axis represents the ranking of items in the whole sequence. A similar pattern can be observed on these two datasets where a great number of users consume a small proportion of items (i.e., the short-head), and the remaining large part of items (i.e., the long-tail) only have a few consumers. More specifically, in the LastFM360K dataset, 3,118 out of 15,263 pieces (i.e., around 20% of the total) account for 80% of interactions, while the MovieLens1M dataset is in an analogous situation.

3.2   Existing Evaluation Methods

For user fairness and bias studies, it is common to group users by specific attributes such as age, gender, etc [15]. In the previous section, we present the universal definition of *mainstream* and the characteristics of mainstream users. However, simply identifying a user as mainstream or not mainstream is insufficient, as differences between individuals cannot be ignored. The mainstreaminess evaluation process can assess the mainstream level of users based on the interactions of their profiles and provide finer results. In the following paragraphs, we analyze different approaches to mainstreaminess evaluation.

The methods of Schedl et al. [20–22] consider domain-specific knowledge for mainstreaminess evaluation in music recommender systems. We skip them because only implicit feedback records are available here. As for the method of Li et al. [11], a user's mainstream level solely relies on the utility of a particular recommendation model. In other words, it is very likely that a user will be assigned a different mainstream level by different models. We argue that users' mainstream levels are reflected by their interactions and will not be affected by recommendation algorithms. Therefore, we do not take this into account as well.

In [24], Zhu et al. insist that users' mainstreaminess should only depend on their intrinsic preferences. To quantify users' mainstreaminess, they use the mainstream score to describe each user's mainstream level. A greater mainstream score means a higher mainstream level. The authors employ several outlier detection methods for the evaluation task. We will now briefly analyze each method proposed in their paper. The first is the *similarity-based* approach, which calculates the average Jaccard similarity between a user and other users as one's mainstream score. The mainstream score of a user u:

$$MS_u^{sim} = \sum_{v \in \mathcal{U} \backslash u} J_{u,v} / (|\mathcal{U}| - 1) \tag{1}$$

where $J_{u,v}$ stands for the Jaccard similarity between the user u and v. This method works because mainstream users have a large group of similar users. However, suppose there is no overlap between items consumed by two mainstream users. In this case, the similarity score between them will be zero, which is unreasonable since these items are very likely to be similar or homogeneous. The second method, named *density-based*, employs the Local Outlier Factor

(LOF) algorithm [5] and takes negative local outlier factor values as mainstream scores:

$$MS_u^{den} = -LOF(u) \tag{2}$$

Its effectiveness has not been proven, and we doubt that it works with the original user-item interaction matrix as input. In addition, even if it does work, the evaluation quality is highly dependent on the hyperparameter k, which determines the number of neighbors for clustering. The next is the *distribution-based* approach, which creates a distribution vector $\mathbf{d}$ to represent the average probability of each item being interacted. The mainstream score can be easily calculated as the cosine similarity between the vector $\mathbf{d}$ and a user's interaction vector $\mathbf{O}_u$:

$$MS_u^{dis} = \cos(\mathbf{O}_u, \mathbf{d}) \tag{3}$$

It seems suitable for implicit feedback data. In practice, however, this method tends to overestimate the mainstream scores of some non-mainstream users due to the overly high probabilities of the "short-head" items. Lastly, based on deep learning, the *DeepSVDD-based* approach employs the structure of DeepSVDD [18], which is adapted for recommender systems. This method maps users into several hyperspaces with multiple hypersphere centers and takes the negative distance from users' representations to the center $\mathbf{c}$ as the mainstream scores:

$$MS_u^{deep} = -\|DeepSVDD(\mathbf{O}_u) - \mathbf{c}\|_F \tag{4}$$

where $DeepSVDD(\mathbf{O}_u)$ denotes the representation of user u. The design of multicenter and mapping functions makes it more likely to capture features of mainstreaminess. Nevertheless, the number of hypersphere centers is still a hyperparameter that should be tuned manually to accommodate different scenarios and datasets.

3.3   Our Evaluation Approach

Similar to the original work, we aim to quantify the mainstream level of users based on interaction records. We consider using the feature of item popularity since it reflects the connection between a user and the majority. However, as seen in Fig. 1, the magnitude of popularity varies significantly from the "short-head" to the "long-tail" items in real-world datasets. Directly using item popularity to compute mainstream scores leads to overestimation for some low-mainstream users, considering the case where a low-mainstream user has few interaction records with popular items due to ubiquitous clickbaits [17]. The mainstream level of this user will be overestimated due to these unintentional interactions. To solve this problem, we scale the magnitude of the item popularity within a reasonable range while preventing mainstream users from being affected. Furthermore, unlike ratings data, we assume that each unique user-item interaction contributes equally to its mainstream level, so we use a user's profile size to average the cumulative value and obtain the final mainstream score.

Formally, we denote $\mathcal{U} = \{u_1, u_2, \ldots, u_m\}$ as a set of m users and $\mathcal{V} = \{v_1, v_2, \ldots, v_n\}$ as a set of n items in a implicit feedback dataset. Each record of this dataset consists of tuple (u, v), representing an interaction between a user u and an item v. Duplicate tuples are removed until only one remains. $\mathcal{L}_u$ indicates the profile of a user u, which includes all interaction records relevant to the user. We use $Pop(v)$ to refer to the popularity (i.e., the total number of interactions) of item v. For a user u, we calculate the mainstream score by considering both the user's interactions and the overall popularity distribution:

$$MS_u = \frac{1}{|\mathcal{L}_u|} \sum_{(u,v) \in \mathcal{L}_u} \log_\alpha(Pop(v) + 1) \tag{5}$$

where $\log_\alpha$ is employed to suppress the magnitude of item popularity, and the base α is a hyperparameter that controls the logarithmic curve. We shift the function one unit to the right to prevent this term from being 0.

4   Experimental Setup

4.1   Datasets

In the original work, Zhu et al. [24] validate their approaches on a synthetic dataset because there is no dataset with ground-truth labels for mainstream users. Figure 2 represents the basic setup of the synthetic dataset. First, two popular item groups and two non-popular item groups are created, each containing 250 items. Then they create two mainstream user groups of size 800 and two non-mainstream user groups of size 200. Each group of mainstream users can only consume popular items in one group. In addition, each group of non-popular items is assigned to a group of non-mainstream users. 100-dimension embedding is randomly generated by different Gaussian distribution parameters for each item. User embeddings can be computed from the item embeddings in the corresponding group. Finally, they form the dataset by randomly sampling the user-item interaction data. However, there are evident distinctions between the synthetic and real-world situations. We argue that the synthetic dataset cannot be used to test evaluation approaches. In the following part, we outline the main differences and present our choices.

The predetermination of user groups does not reflect differences between mainstream and non-mainstream users because randomly sampled interactions cannot ensure that the preferences of the majority match the preferences of mainstream users. Furthermore, there are many discrepancies between the synthetic dataset and the real situation. In real-world datasets, the quantities of the "long-tail" items are much more significant than the quantities of "short-head" items. Thus the ratio of popular to non-popular items in the setup is inappropriate. Furthermore, such access restrictions are also inconsistent with the fact that mainstream users could have several interactions with non-popular items in their records, and non-mainstream users may consume popular items due to clickbaits or their curiosity.

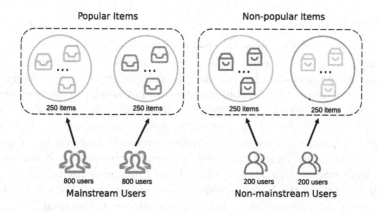

Fig. 2. illustration of the setup for the synthetic dataset.

We choose to conduct experiments on real-world datasets, including Movie-Lens 1M (ML1M), Epinions[3], and Yelp[4], which were adopted in the original work. Moreover, we consider more widely-used public datasets in different domains or with larger scales: BookCrossing[5], LastFM360K (LFM360K), and MovieLens 20M[6] (ML20M). The LFM360K dataset contains more than 17 million listening events from 359,347 users, collected from the Last.fm music community. We select the BookCrossing dataset for its extreme sparsity in book recommendations. As for the ML20M dataset, we consider it as a contrast to the ML1M since both were released by the same research team, and the former is newer with a larger scale. Table 1 summarizes the statistics of these datasets. We keep the splitting strategy that all datasets are divided into training, validation, and testing set in the ratio of 7:1:2.

Table 1. Characteristics of 6 publicly available datasets after preprocessing.

Dataset name	#Users	#Items	#Interactions	$\frac{\#Interactions}{\#Users}$	$\frac{\#Interactions}{\#Items}$	Density
ML1M	6,040	3,706	1,000,209	165.59	269.88	4.46%
ML20M	55,845	8,783	7,995,742	143.17	910.36	1.63%
Yelp	13,991	10,437	467,847	33.43	44.82	0.32%
Epinions	8,521	6,941	188,594	22.13	27.17	0.31%
BookCrossing	5,107	6,515	95,400	18.68	14.64	0.28%
LFM360K	52,966	15,263	2,883,457	54.43	188.91	0.35%

[3] http://www.trustlet.org/epinions.html.
[4] http://www.yelp.com/dataset_challenge/.
[5] http://www2.informatik.uni-freiburg.de/~cziegler/BX/.
[6] https://grouplens.org/datasets/movielens/20M/.

4.2   Preprocessing

For better reproducibility, we reuse the code[7] of the original work and complete the preprocessing part for each dataset, where records are transformed into the format of implicit user-item interaction. The detailed steps are described below.

First, we eliminate several columns that are not needed in this experiment, such as *timestamp*, *gender*, and *age*. The remaining columns include *itemid*, *userid*, and *rating* (if present). In particular, *playcounts* replaces for *rating* in the LFM360K dataset. Then we remove duplicate records where tuples of (*userid*, *itemid*) are the same. To screen for reliable records, we retain only interactions with a rating greater than 3 in the ML20M and Epinions datasets. Records with an implicit rating in the BookCrossing dataset are dropped. For the LFM360K dataset, we discard interactions with personal playcounts less than 20.

After that, the column of *rating (playcounts)* is also removed. Next, we calculate the sum of interactions for each user and item. In the last step, users with only a few records in their profile and too long-tail items are removed for better recommendations. To this end, we set up minimum thresholds for users and items on each dataset except the ML1M dataset, which is consistent with the original work. The thresholds for each dataset are shown in Table 2.

Table 2. Thresholds for user and item in preprocessing.

Threshold	Dataset name					
	ML1M	ML20M	Yelp	Epinions	BookCrossing	LFM360K
For user	-	25	13	9	6	15
For item	-	50	13	9	6	50

4.3   Methods and Metrics

We use our approach ($\alpha = 2$) to evaluate mainstreaminess and adopt four approaches proposed by Zhu et al. [24] as baselines. All users will be divided equally into five subgroups denoted as 'high,' 'med-high,' 'med,' 'med-low,' and 'low' by descending order of mainstream scores, which remains the same as the original.

Without ground-truth labels of mainstream users or mainstream scores, we cannot measure the accuracy of these approaches. Our research goal is to detect the mainstream bias and measure its impact, so we do not need completely accurate results. Inspired by the definition of mainstream, the ratio of popular items in one's profile can be approximated as one's preference for those items, and users with high ratios can be regarded as mainstream users. Thus, we could generate pseudo labels to verify these approaches. This experiment examines the ability to distinguish mainstream users, but how do these approaches perform for all users? Taking this into account, we also expect the evaluation results to

---

[7] https://github.com/Zziwei/Measuring-Mitigating-Mainstream-Bias.

conform to mainstream levels' characteristics, and one of the most conspicuous characteristics is the relationship between profile size and mainstreaminess [1, 9, 10, 14].

To overcome sparsity problems, we require a recommendation model available to provide accurate results to as many users as possible. Therefore, we compare several recommendation models, including MF [8], BPR [16], NCF [7], and VAECF [12]. Our results show that VAECF outperforms other models on almost all datasets, and similar results have been found in another study [6]. So we select VAECF as the base recommendation model in the next section, with the model's hyperparameters remaining unchanged from the original work. We use truncated normalized discounted cumulative gain (nDCG@K) and Precision (Precision@K) to evaluate the recommendation utility. The rank position K of each metric is set to 1, 5, 10, and 20 by considering the different characteristics of these datasets.

5   Experimental Results

For each dataset, we select items with the top 20% interaction records as popular items and label users with the top 20% ratios of popular items in their profiles as mainstream users. We then compute mainstream scores for each user using different approaches, and users with the top 20% mainstream scores are treated as predictions of each approach. Since we do not differentiate the degree of popularity for popular items, we use Recall instead of nDCG as the performance metric to evaluate these approaches.

To further investigate how these approaches work for all users, we divide them into five subgroups based on their mainstream scores. Next, we train the VAECF model and generate recommendations on real-world datasets. Due to space limitations, we only present the results of nDCG@20 in this section, which make the patterns as obvious as possible. Other metrics show consistent trends, and full results can be found in our code.

Table 3. Performance comparisons of different evaluation approaches. We use Recall as the metric and our approach achieves the best performance on all datasets.

Dataset	Evaluation approach				
	Similarity	Density	Distribution	DeepSVDD	Our approach
ML1M	0.149	0.004	0.090	0.039	**0.763**
ML20M	0.398	0.026	0.339	0.180	**0.716**
Yelp	0.620	0.064	0.550	0.358	**0.789**
Epinions	0.394	0.119	0.370	0.274	**0.627**
BookCrossing	0.351	0.081	0.296	0.233	**0.610**
LFM360K	0.548	0.066	0.547	0.262	**0.705**

5.1   RQ1: Analysis of Mainstreaminess Evaluation

Table 3 reports the performance of different approaches in distinguishing main-stream users. Our evaluation approach achieves the best performance with the highest Recall on all these datasets. As the best baseline, the *similarity-based* approach gets a Recall of 14.9% on the ML1M dataset, while ours gets a high value of 76.3%. Notably, the variance of our approach's results (≈ 0.004) is relatively low, indicating better robustness in different scenarios. Next, we analyze the evaluation results for all users.

Figure 3 shows the average recommendation utility (y-axis) of each group (x-axis) plotted as tiny dots or rectangles. For comparison, we connect them with lines in colors representing different evaluation approaches. The results of previous approaches show similar patterns on almost all datasets, where subgroups with higher mainstream levels are better served with more accurate recommendations. As the mainstream level increases, the average utility also increases. Notably, on the ML1M dataset, other approaches show nearly identical patterns, while our approach performs differently. By our approach, the 'high' group gets the lowest value of nDCG@20, whereas the utilities for the 'low' and 'med-low' groups are relatively high. It shows great discrepancies in evaluations between ours and other approaches. Moreover, almost all approaches show the same trend on the Yelp dataset, but the composition of these groups could be completely different. These phenomena suggest that we should consider more factors and find out what influenced the evaluation.

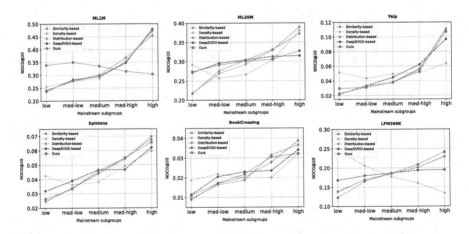

Fig. 3. Relationship between user subgroups in different mainstream levels and the average recommendation utility (nDCG@20). Solid red lines represent the results of our approach and dotted lines in different colors show the results of other approaches. (Color figure online)

In collaborative filtering, profile size can primarily affect recommendation utility. A user with a larger profile usually receives more desirable recommendations

[19, 25]. Moreover, previous studies revealed a strong negative correlation between profile size and the ratio of popular items in the profile [1, 9, 10, 14], which means we can roughly evaluate these approaches by matching previous conclusions. We sort all users by mainstream score from low to high and split them into five groups evenly. To see the correlations, we compute the percentage of overlap for all subgroups divided by profile size and mainstream score. The results on two typical datasets are shown in Fig. 4a and Fig. 4b.

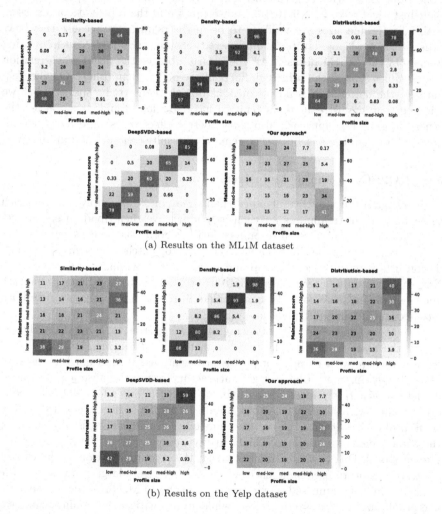

(a) Results on the ML1M dataset

(b) Results on the Yelp dataset

Fig. 4. Matrix of overlap percentages between profile size subgroups and mainstream score subgroups. Names of subgroups indicate increasing order of value corresponding to the label along each axis.

The results show a remarkably similar pattern for all approaches except ours: the positive correlation between profile size and mainstream level, contrary to previous conclusions. As can be seen, the values around counter diagonals are obviously larger than others, especially the *density-based* approach, which implies that the approaches in the original paper are vulnerable to profile size and incorrectly take it as one of the features of mainstreaminess. In contrast, many studies show that users with few interactions prefer to consume popular items. At the same time, those with large profiles generally have many non-popular items in their historical records [1,9,10,14]. As we can see in the top-right corner, users with large profile sizes are unlikely to be mainstream users because they may exhaust the most popular items and have to consume other niche but interesting items. On the ML1M dataset, we can clearly observe the negative correlation where values around the principal diagonal are higher than others. On the Yelp dataset, the correlation is not as obvious due to the extreme sparsity, but we still see that mainstream users tend to have smaller profile sizes. As for the other datasets, our approach also shows better effectiveness and more reasonable results than the baselines. The remaining results can be found in our code.

5.2   RQ2: Detection of Mainstream Bias

To investigate the influence of users' mainstreaminess, we apply our approach to evaluate mainstreaminess for each individual. We then divide users by recommendation utility to see if recommendation algorithms favor users with high mainstream scores. We filter out users with zero matches in their recommendation lists to form a 'zero' group and mark their total share as a percentage. Next, the remaining users are split into five groups, as before. Since profile size and mainstream score could be confounders in recommendations, we take both into account in our subsequent analysis.

The results and properties of each group are reported in Table 4. Profile size is still the main reason for the increase in utility on the ML1M and ML20M datasets, where we see apparent positive correlations. With a much larger profile, a low-mainstream user can get satisfactory results because a well-trained model can accurately identify its preference. On the other four datasets, however, groups with large profile sizes obtain the worst utilities, and users with small profile sizes receive the best recommendations, which seems confusing. At the same time, we notice that 'high' utility groups achieve the highest mainstream scores. Due to the extreme sparsity, the recommendation model cannot accurately capture user preferences even with relatively large profiles, and the impact of mainstreamness becomes notable. In the LFM360K dataset, the average profile size of each group is close, while groups with higher mainstreaminess scores get significantly better results. These results lead us to believe that mainstreaminess affects the recommendation utility, and the model favors mainstream users.

To see how mainstreaminess impacts the recommendation utility, we perform a correlation analysis between mainstream score and recommendation utility. We group users with close profile sizes to eliminate the effect on recommendation utility. Then, we calculate the Spearman coefficient between the two variables with statistical significance tests for each group. As shown in Table 4, the average correlation coefficients on these datasets are all positive (with p-value < 0.02), which indicates various degrees of mainstream bias exist, and a larger value shows a more significant impact on recommendation utility. On these overly sparse datasets, mainstreaminess plays a more critical role in recommendation than profile size. Additionally, we find that both the profile size and the mainstream score of the 'zero' group are virtually smaller than any other in almost all datasets, implying that cold start users with low mainstreaminess tend to receive the most unfair results.

Table 4. Experimental results and properties of each subgroup.

Metric	Dataset (Correlation)	Recommendation utility					
		zero (pct.)	low	med-low	med	med-high	high
nDCG@20	ML1M	0 (5.4%)	0.125	0.241	0.335	0.438	0.597
PF size	(0.242)	25.16↓	59.51	83.07	101.46	141.51	**220.23**
MS score		8.79↓	8.85	8.90	**8.91**	8.88	8.75
nDCG@20	ML20M	0 (2.8%)	0.109	0.216	0.300	0.388	0.528
PF size	(0.288)	54.66↓	72.96	86.44	96.81	108.91	**142.58**
MS score		11.00↓	11.36	11.49	11.56	**11.60**	11.58
nDCG@20	Yelp	0 (69.7%)	0.057	0.093	0.132	0.196	0.377
PF size	(0.310)	18.66↓	**51.17**	30.00	30.81	29.96	27.68
MS score		5.61↓	5.71	5.96	6.01	6.10	**6.32**
nDCG@20	Epinions	0 (76.0%)	0.066	0.106	0.148	0.220	0.402
PF size	(0.254)	13.25↓	**33.38**	21.17	19.63	19.35	14.60
MS score		4.94↓	5.00	5.15	5.20	5.17	**5.21**
nDCG@20	BookCrossing	0 (87.6%)	0.055	0.093	0.134	0.212	0.409
PF size	(0.375)	10.99	**44.04**	23.67	16.16	29.68	10.57↓
MS score		4.01↓	4.03	4.14	4.24	4.21	**4.27**
nDCG@20	LFM360K	0 (15.8%)	0.065	0.126	0.196	0.281	0.430
PF size	(0.344)	**39.06**	38.31	38.13	37.80	37.77	37.61↓
MS score		8.51↓	8.79	8.97	9.08	9.17	**9.35**

6   Discussion and Conclusions

In this paper, we replicate and improve experiments on evaluating mainstreaminess and detecting mainstream bias using implicit feedback. Based on prior work, we introduce a universal definition of *mainstream* and analyze previous evaluation approaches in detail. We then redesign the experimental setup to adapt to real-world situations and propose an intuitive, explainable approach. Extensive experiments and analysis show that our approach is capable of evaluating mainstreaminess, which exhibits better robustness to profile size. Furthermore, we verify that mainstream bias exists extensively in various domains and measure its impact on different real-world datasets.

Previous work mainly focused on explicit demographic attributes like age, race, and gender to investigate the unfairness behind them. Our work suggests that mainstreaminess as an implicit attribute is also relevant to fairness issues. However, our study has some limitations that we intend to address in the future. One of the limitations is that we have not yet considered the influence of duplicate consumptions. In some scenes, users tend to consume some items repeatedly [3], which may reflect particular preferences and affect mainstreaminess evaluations to some extent. In addition, the mainstreaminess of users could be dynamic as the popularity of items varies over time. Overall, we hope our work provides a new perspective for studying and promoting user fairness.

Acknowledgement. We thank all reviewers for their sagacious comments and our colleagues' great efforts. This work is supported by the Science and Technology Department of Sichuan Province under Grant No. 2021YFS0399 and the Grid Planning and Research Center of Guangdong Power Grid Co. under Grant No. 037700KK52220042 (GDKJXM20220906).

References

1. Abdollahpouri, H., Mansoury, M., Burke, R., Mobasher, B.: The unfairness of popularity bias in recommendation. In: RecSys Workshop on Recommendation in Multistakeholder Environments (RMSE) (2019)
2. Abdollahpouri, H., Mansoury, M., Burke, R., Mobasher, B., Malthouse, E.: User-centered evaluation of popularity bias in recommender systems. In: Proceedings of the 29th ACM Conference on User Modeling, Adaptation and Personalization. p. 119–129. UMAP '21, Association for Computing Machinery, New York, NY, USA (2021). https://doi.org/10.1145/3450613.3456821
3. Anderson, A., Kumar, R., Tomkins, A., Vassilvitskii, S.: The dynamics of repeat consumption. In: Proceedings of the 23rd International Conference on World Wide Web. p. 419–430. WWW '14, Association for Computing Machinery, New York, NY, USA (2014). https://doi.org/10.1145/2566486.2568018
4. Borges, R., Stefanidis, K.: On measuring popularity bias in collaborative filtering data. In: Proceedings of the Workshops of the EDBT/ICDT 2020 Joint Conference. CEUR Workshop Proceedings, vol. 2578. CEUR-WS.org (2020), jufoid=53269; EDBT/ICDT Workshops; Conference date: 01-01-2020
5. Breunig, M.M., Kriegel, H.P., Ng, R.T., Sander, J.: LOF: identifying density-based local outliers. SIGMOD Rec. **29**(2), 93–104 (2000). https://doi.org/10.1145/335191.335388
6. Ferrari Dacrema, M., Cremonesi, P., Jannach, D.: Are we really making much progress? a worrying analysis of recent neural recommendation approaches. In: Proceedings of the 13th ACM Conference on Recommender Systems. p. 101–109. RecSys '19, Association for Computing Machinery, New York, NY, USA (2019). https://doi.org/10.1145/3298689.3347058
7. He, X., Liao, L., Zhang, H., Nie, L., Hu, X., Chua, T.S.: Neural collaborative filtering. In: Proceedings of the 26th International Conference on World Wide Web. p. 173–182. WWW '17, International World Wide Web Conferences Steering Committee, Republic and Canton of Geneva, CHE (2017). https://doi.org/10.1145/3038912.3052569

8. Koren, Y., Bell, R., Volinsky, C.: Matrix factorization techniques for recommender systems. Computer **42**(8), 30–37 (2009). https://doi.org/10.1109/MC.2009.263

9. Kowald, D., Lacic, E.: Popularity bias in collaborative filtering-based multimedia recommender systems. In: Boratto, L., Faralli, S., Marras, M., Stilo, G. (eds.) Advances in Bias and Fairness in Information Retrieval, pp. 1–11. Springer International Publishing, Cham (2022)

10. Kowald, D., Schedl, M., Lex, E.: The unfairness of popularity bias in music recommendation: A reproducibility study. In: Jose, J.M., Yilmaz, E., Magalhães, J., Castells, P., Ferro, N., Silva, M.J., Martins, F. (eds.) Advances in Information Retrieval, pp. 35–42. Springer International Publishing, Cham (2020)

11. Li, R.Z., Urbano, J., Hanjalic, A.: Leave no user behind: Towards improving the utility of recommender systems for non-mainstream users. In: Proceedings of the 14th ACM International Conference on Web Search and Data Mining. p. 103–111. WSDM '21, Association for Computing Machinery, New York, NY, USA (2021). https://doi.org/10.1145/3437963.3441769

12. Liang, D., Krishnan, R.G., Hoffman, M.D., Jebara, T.: Variational autoencoders for collaborative filtering. In: Proceedings of the 2018 World Wide Web Conference. p. 689–698. WWW '18, International World Wide Web Conferences Steering Committee, Republic and Canton of Geneva, CHE (2018). https://doi.org/10.1145/3178876.3186150

13. Mehrotra, R., McInerney, J., Bouchard, H., Lalmas, M., Diaz, F.: Towards a fair marketplace: Counterfactual evaluation of the trade-off between relevance, fairness & satisfaction in recommendation systems. In: Proceedings of the 27th ACM International Conference on Information and Knowledge Management. p. 2243–2251. CIKM '18, Association for Computing Machinery, New York, NY, USA (2018). https://doi.org/10.1145/3269206.3272027

14. Naghiaei, M., Rahmani, H.A., Dehghan, M.: The unfairness of popularity bias in book recommendation. In: Boratto, L., Faralli, S., Marras, M., Stilo, G. (eds.) Advances in Bias and Fairness in Information Retrieval, pp. 69–81. Springer International Publishing, Cham (2022)

15. Neophytou, N., Mitra, B., Stinson, C.: Revisiting popularity and demographic biases in recommender evaluation and effectiveness. In: Hagen, M., et al. (eds.) Advances in Information Retrieval, pp. 641–654. Springer International Publishing, Cham (2022)

16. Rendle, S., Freudenthaler, C., Gantner, Z., Schmidt-Thieme, L.: Bpr: Bayesian personalized ranking from implicit feedback. In: Proceedings of the Twenty-Fifth Conference on Uncertainty in Artificial Intelligence. p. 452–461. UAI '09, AUAI Press, Arlington, Virginia, USA (2009)

17. Rony, M.M.U., Hassan, N., Yousuf, M.: Diving deep into Clickbaits: Who use them to what extents in which topics with what effects? In: Proceedings of the 2017 IEEE/ACM International Conference on Advances in Social Networks Analysis and Mining 2017. p. 232–239. ASONAM '17, Association for Computing Machinery, New York, NY, USA (2017). https://doi.org/10.1145/3110025.3110054

18. Ruff, L., Vandermeulen, R., et al.: Deep one-class classification. In: Dy, J., Krause, A. (eds.) Proceedings of the 35th International Conference on Machine Learning. Proceedings of Machine Learning Research, vol. 80, pp. 4393–4402. PMLR (2018). https://proceedings.mlr.press/v80/ruff18a.html

19. Sahebi, S., Brusilovsky, P.: Cross-domain collaborative recommendation in a cold-start context: The impact of user profile size on the quality of recommendation. In: Carberry, S., Weibelzahl, S., Micarelli, A., Semeraro, G. (eds.) User Modeling, Adaptation, and Personalization, pp. 289–295. Springer, Berlin Heidelberg, Berlin, Heidelberg (2013)

20. Schedl, M., Bauer, C.: Distance- and rank-based music mainstreaminess measurement. In: Adjunct Publication of the 25th Conference on User Modeling, Adaptation and Personalization. p. 364–367. UMAP '17, Association for Computing Machinery, New York, NY, USA (2017). https://doi.org/10.1145/3099023.3099098

21. Schedl, M., Bauer, C.: An analysis of global and regional mainstreaminess for personalized music recommender systems. J. Mobile Multimed. **14**, 95–122 (2018)

22. Schedl, M., Hauger, D.: Tailoring music recommendations to users by considering diversity, mainstreaminess, and novelty. In: Proceedings of the 38th International ACM SIGIR Conference on Research and Development in Information Retrieval. p. 947–950. SIGIR '15, Association for Computing Machinery, New York, NY, USA (2015). https://doi.org/10.1145/2766462.2767763

23. Yao, S., Huang, B.: Beyond parity: Fairness objectives for collaborative filtering. In: Proceedings of the 31st International Conference on Neural Information Processing Systems. p. 2925–2934. NIPS'17, Curran Associates Inc., Red Hook, NY, USA (2017)

24. Zhu, Z., Caverlee, J.: Fighting mainstream bias in recommender systems via local fine tuning. In: Proceedings of the Fifteenth ACM International Conference on Web Search and Data Mining. p. 1497–1506. WSDM '22, Association for Computing Machinery, New York, NY, USA (2022). https://doi.org/10.1145/3488560.3498427

25. Zou, L., Xia, L., Gu, Y., Zhao, X., Liu, W., Huang, J.X., Yin, D.: Neural interactive collaborative filtering. In: Proceedings of the 43rd International ACM SIGIR Conference on Research and Development in Information Retrieval. p. 749–758. SIGIR '20, Association for Computing Machinery, New York, NY, USA (2020). https://doi.org/10.1145/3397271.3401181

Preserving Utility in Fair Top-k Ranking with Intersectional Bias

Nicola Alimonda[1], Alessandro Castelnovo[2,3(✉)], Riccardo Crupi[3], Fabio Mercorio[1], and Mario Mezzanzanica[1]

[1] Department of Statistics and Quantitative Methods, University of Milan-Bicocca, Milan, Italy
[2] Department of Informatics, Systems and Communication, University of Milan-Bicocca, Milan, Italy
[3] Intesa Sanpaolo S.p.A, Milan, Italy
a.castelnovo5@campus.unimib.it

Abstract. Ranking is required for many real applications, such as search, personalisation, recommendation, and filtering. Recent research has focused on developing reliable ranking algorithms that maintain fairness in their outcomes. However, only a few consider multiple protected groups since this extension introduces significant challenges. While useful in the research sector, considering only one binary sensitive feature for handling fairness is inappropriate when the algorithm must be deployed responsibly in real-world applications.

Our work is built on top of Multinomial FA*IR, a Fair Top-k ranking with multiple protected groups, which we extend to provide users the option to balance fairness and utility, adapting the final ranking accordingly. Our experimental results show that alternative better solutions overlooked by Multinomial FA*IR may be found through our approach without violating fairness boundaries. The code of the implemented solution and the experiments are publicly available to the community as a GitHub repository.

Keywords: Fair ranking system · Intersectional Bias · Post-processing Fairness Mitigation

1 Introduction

The ranking-based proposition has become part of everyday life; it is now commonplace to choose movies, travel, or clothes after seeing sorted tips. The Probability Ranking Principle (PRP) [22] is one of the primary technical principles underlying ranking system optimization. It states that the best ranking should organize items in decreasing order of likelihood of relevance for the user. This is because the position of an item in a ranking influences its perception, which affects its eventual selection [13]. Indeed, the main information that ranking systems assign is the items' exposure to users, which is largely determined by the position in the ranking [23].

L. Boratto et al. (Eds.): BIAS 2023, CCIS 1840, pp. 59–73, 2023.
https://doi.org/10.1007/978-3-031-37249-0_5

This scenario becomes delicate, especially when the items to be sorted are people and the rank results from systems based on AI. There is an increasing awareness that data-driven decision-making algorithms may lead to human rights violations or undermine the effective enjoyment of these human rights [9]. Indeed, under certain conditions, AI can systematically make unfair decisions against certain population groups[1] with specific races or gender due to the inherited biases encoded in the data [6,7]. Not surprisingly, the European Commission recently published a proposal for legislation on AI systems, classifying many domains as *high risk*, such as creditworthiness or hiring [25], where ranking systems are typically adopted. Moreover, the European Commission published a communication on fostering a European approach to AI, highlighting that *"AI-generated improvements need to be based on rules that safeguard the functioning of markets and the public sector, and people's safety and fundamental rights"* [11,12].

To ensure trust and adoption of rank systems also in *high risk* domains, the related literature has proposed a number of works aimed at proposing rankings that correctly place appropriate individuals in the top positions while avoiding that members of protected groups could be systematically ranked in low positions [1,27,29].

However, for technical and computational simplicity reasons, only a few are devoted to mitigating fairness considering multiple classes of protected groups [2]. This simplification will not suffice when the systems must be deployed in real-world scenarios. For instance, in loan granting, it is easy to expect that the loan will be granted based on multiple sensitive attributes [4], such as gender, age, and citizenship. This concept, which derives from the sociological concept of *intersectionality*, is known in the literature as *intersectional bias*. [10] is one of the first works to introduce the notion of intersectionality by citing a court case in which black women were subjected to unjust discrimination due to a task intended to handle both racial and gender discrimination separately.

Machine learning can support tackling the problem of intersectionality by enforcing equality in any subset of protected groups. When considering several sensitive features, a typical approach is to construct all possible combinations of the sensitive feature values (for example, man citizen and woman not citizen) and add restrictions for each combination independently. This approach is also known as *fairness-gerrymandering* [15].

In this direction, the work of [21,28] deserve significant credit for developing post-processing [5,14] techniques that enable rank fairness in the presence of multiple sensitive classes. [21] considered the combination of the impact of multiple users' sensitive attributes to generate a less biased ranking in the reputation scores. [28] proposed an algorithm – Multinomial FA*IR – for producing a fair top-K ranking that can be used when more than one protected group is present. Our work builds upon Multinomial FA*IR.

---

[1] In this work we shall use the terms "protected" and "sensitive" group interchangeably to refer to a set of personal attributes, typically "disadvantaged", that must be considered when dealing with fairness and discrimination issues.

Multinomial FA*IR in a Nutshell. Given a set of minimum proportions, one per each sensitive membership group, that the final ranking has to respect to be consider fair, Multinomial FA*IR propose a statistical test based on multinomial binomial distribution to check if these minority groups are fairly represented. This statistical test not only provides an idea of what are the minimum proportions of protected groups that the ranking has to respect in order to achieve fairness but it manages even in which position the individuals will be placed.

This approach aim to reach a re-ranking that ensures a fair representation according to the parameters passed to multinomial distribution, while preserving a certain level of utility, gradually adding individuals for each position that ensure the fairest rank. In [28] is defined also an alternative approach with the aim of prioritizing the individuals with the best relevance value that respect minimum criteria of fairness (instead of choosing the fairest one among fair individuals).

Contribution. In this work, we propose and investigate a novel ranking method that builds upon [28] to manage the level of utility preserving fairness in presence of multiple sensitive population subgroups.

Our contribution allows users to choose their preferred trade-off between fairness and utility, which will be reflected in the final ranking. In particular, we formalize a continuous function that: maximizes fairness – *preserving as much utility as possible* – on the one hand and maximizes utility – *remaining within fairness boundaries* – on the other, in its two extremes configurations.

In our experiment, we show that there can be other optimal solutions between these two extreme solutions without violating fairness boundaries. Moreover, our approach allows for identifying fair optimal solutions in terms of utility metrics other than the Discounted Cumulative Gain (DCG) adopted in Multinomial FA*IR.

The source code of Multinomial FA*IR [28], on which we base our extension, is available at github.com/MilkaLichtblau/BA_Hyerim, while the code of our extension and experiments at github.com/Nicola-Alimonda/MultinomialFair.

2 Background

In this section, we introduce the fair re-ranking problem to set the stage for the discussions and experiments presented in later sections. For the sake of clarity, we will utilize the example of selecting candidates for a company job interview to illustrate our setup.

Let $D = \{d_1, \ldots, d_n\}$ be a set of n individuals to be ranked. Each individual is identified by a set of relevant attributes for performing a specific task $X_i = (X_i^1, \ldots, X_i^p)$. We denote with $G_i \in \{0, 1, \ldots, g\}$ the categorical variable containing the membership information of d_i. We label $\mathcal{G}^a$ the members of the group a, which is a composition of personal attributes. We assume that the group $\mathcal{G}^0$, corresponds to the only non-protected group, while all the other g groups denote protected groups.

In our running example, D is the set of candidates, X is their skills, and G is their personal information.

The goal of a ranking is to associate to each item d_i a score Y_i to create a permutation π of all the elements in D. By $j = \pi_i$ we denote the item in D at rank j where $j = 1, 2, ..., n$.

A better position in the rank denotes a better *utility* of the item for the user [23]. In typical ranking applications, users are interested in a sub-ranking containing the best $k < n$ items of π. In our example, the hiring manager is interested in sorting candidates based on their suitability for the vacant position and choosing the best k to interview, where k depends on the time and resources he can use to conduct the hiring process.

Finally, we must verify that the rank π is fair in respect of G. The fair re-rank problem is necessary whenever π is unfair. Assuming that π is the rank with the highest level of utility without regard for any fairness constraint, i.e. color-blind ranking, the goal is to calculate a new rank ω [28] such that (i) should fairly represent all the protected groups G and (ii) preserve as much utility as possible from the original rank π.

For the sake of clarity, we provide table 1 containing all the information regarding the notation used in this paper.

Table 1. A summary of the notations used in this work.

D	Set of n individual to be ranked
g	Integer denoting the number of protected groups
$\mathcal{G}^a$	Set of individuals which belong to protected population groups a. $\mathcal{G}^a = \{d_i \in D \mid G_i = a\}$
$\mathcal{G}^0$	Set of individuals which belong to unprotected group 0. $\mathcal{G}^0 = \{d_i \notin \mathcal{G}^a \mid a \in \{1, \ldots, g\}\}$.
G_i	d_n individual that belongs to g group; $G_i \in \{0, 1, \ldots, g\}$
Y_i	Score associated to individual d_i
π	Permutation of elements in D in decreasing order by Score Y_i
π_i	The position j in the rank π of the individual i from D
ω	New rank that fairly represent protected groups G_i
ω_p	Counter of individuals in ω per each protected group
$F(\omega_p, j, p)$	Cumulative distribution function F
α_c	Value of cumulative distribution function F
α_t	Threshold value used to determine which items should be included to create the new fair rank ω

2.1   Utility Metrics in Ranking

In this work, we assume π as the rank with the highest level of utility for the user. We'll also refer to it as colour blind·ranking to emphasize that it doesn't consider fairness. Any other potential rank other than it will result in a loss of utility. In our context, where we require to compute a new fair rank ω it is important to define a utility metric to quantify the distance from π and preserve this measure as high as possible.

We consider as utility metrics *individual exposure* [23], *discounted cumulative gain* [23] and *Kendall-τ* [16].

Individual Exposure. This metric aims to weigh more individuals at the top of a ranking, assuming that they provide greater utility. It is calculated considering only the position j in the rank [23]:

$$Exposure(j) = \frac{1}{ln(2 + j)}. \tag{1}$$

This expression can be considered as a discount factor that avoids most utility loss due to the increase in the position of the elements belonging to the protected groups and with lower relevance values.

Due to these characteristics, exposure is often implemented as a discount factor in information retrieval systems to assign more importance to the elements more relevant to the research.

Discounted Cumulative Gain (DCG). This metric is conceptually similar to individual exposure but also consider the score Y_i of each individual in his formula:

$$DCG(j, y) = \frac{y}{ln(2 + j)}. \tag{2}$$

This metric heavily penalizes elements that are at the bottom of the rank. Generally, for a ranking, we can define this utility measure also as:

$$DCG(\pi_i, Y_i) = \frac{Y_i}{ln(2 + \pi_i)} \tag{3}$$

for an individual, and

$$DCG_{tot}(\pi, Y) = \frac{1}{k} \sum_{i=1}^{k} DCG(\pi_i, Y_i) \tag{4}$$

for all the ranks.

Kendall-τ. Kendall-τ distribution is a widely used ranking correlation measure that calculates the similarity between an initial rank π where items are ordered descending based on the Y_i values and another rank ω, which lay within fairness boundaries [26].

The Kendall-τ coefficient is a statistic used to measure the ordinal association between two measured quantities [16]. It's even possible to implement a test for statistical dependence based on the τ coefficient.

This measure calculates the similarity between the original rank and the fair re-rank: the more similar they are, the more utility the new rank has.

2.2 Fairness Metrics in Ranking

In ranking applications, maximising group fairness typically means ensuring that the given minimum proportions p of the protected groups are respected for each k. Group fairness metrics considered in this work are *average exposure* [28], *disparate treatment ratio* [27] and *cumulative distribution function* [28].

Average Exposure. This fairness measure is used to compare the exposure between different sensible groups:

$$AvgExposure(\pi, a) = \sum_{\{d_i \in \mathcal{G}^a\}} \frac{Exposure(\pi_i)}{|\mathcal{G}^a|}. \tag{5}$$

Indeed, if the average exposure of each protected group is similar to the exposure of the unprotected one, the system can be considered fair. However, since the score is based on a mean, this method of assessing fairness is not aware of possible biases.

Disparate Treatment Ratio (DTR). The DTR consider a measure of exposure and a measure of utility, such as the DCG, to quantify the difference in terms of presence in the ranking of individuals of a protected group $\mathcal{G}^a$ with respect to the unprotected group $\mathcal{G}^0$ in the ranking:

$$DTR^{(a,b)}(\pi, Y) = \frac{AvgExposure(\pi, a)}{U^a(\pi, Y)} \frac{U^b(\pi, Y))}{AvgExposure(\pi, b)} \tag{6}$$

$$U^a(\pi, Y) = \frac{1}{|\mathcal{G}^a|} \sum_{\{d_i : d_i \in \mathcal{G}^a\}} U(\pi_i, Y_i) \tag{7}$$

given a utility measure U a rank is considered fair for two groups ($\mathcal{G}^a$, $\mathcal{G}^b$) when the DTR is close to 1. In a multiple protected group case, the DTR is possible to calculate for each group in respect of the unprotected group $\mathcal{G}^0$.

Cumulative Distribution Function for a Binomial Distribution. Another way to check if a rank fairly represents protected groups is given by a statistical test based on cumulative distribution function for a binomial distribution (which for multiple protected groups is extended to the multinomial binomial distribution function) [27]. This test is suitable when fairness is defined as a set of proportions that must be respected for each protected group. To perform this evaluation, it is appropriate to utilize the multinomial binomial distribution function, which provides a distribution of an event (in our case, the inclusion of an individual from a protected group $\mathcal{G}^a$ in the ranking) based on given proportions. When the distribution of individuals belonging to $\mathcal{G}^a$ is similar to a multinomial binomial distribution function, the rank is assumed to be fair.

This distribution's value is calculated with the following statistical discrete probability distribution:

$$\alpha_c = F(\omega_p, j, p), \tag{8}$$

where ω_p is the counter list[2] of protected groups at position j this latter is the rank position which has to be evaluated in terms of fairness, p is the minimum target proportion for each group(s). After configuring a conservative α_t (often equal to 0.1) is possible to implement a statistical test with null hypothesis H_0 such that the rank is fair for a given combination of individuals ω_p at position j. The α_t value in this application represents the probability of rejecting a fair ranking (i.e. larger α_t values correspond to a higher probability to reject a fair rank) [27].

3 Proposed Approach

Our approach aims to create a new fair rank ω that minimises the drop of utility in respect of the original unfair rank π. The utility can be computed by using any desirable metric, such as the Kendall-τ, whereas we consider a rank to be *fair* when it complies with a fairness criterion, such as average exposure. Our method builds upon the algorithm proposed in [28].

The algorithm proposed in [28], called *multinomial Inverse Cumulative Distribution Function (ICDF) continuous* allow us to obtain a pre-computed data structure to verify rank group fairness.

It consists on iterate from 1 to k, at each step j is computed the distribution $\alpha_c = F(\omega_{candidate}, j, p)$, where $\omega_{candidate}$ can be ω_p, of the previous step, or the updated one increasing by one the counter of a group a. If $\alpha_c > \alpha_t$ for the ω_p of the previous step, in position j it is added the best score individual. Otherwise, for g possible $\omega_{candidate}$ it is chosen the one that maximizes α_c, and satisfy $\alpha_c > \alpha_t$. In position j it is added the best score individual of the group is with the increased counter.

Hence, with reference to Fig. 1, we denote starting point as $\omega_p = [0, 0]$, then the algorithm create the $\omega_{candidate}$ $[0, 0]$, $[1, 0]$ or $[0, 1]$ for choosing which individual put in first position. It is calculated $\alpha_c = F(\omega_{candidate}, j, p)$; if $\alpha_c = F([0, 0], 1, p)$ is higher than the designed threshold α_t, this mean that the best score individual (with higher y) is placed at position 1. Otherwise, it

---

[2] E.g. for two protected groups, at position $j = 6$, $\omega_p = [3, 2]$ means that there are three individuals from $\mathcal{G}^1$, two from $\mathcal{G}^2$ and the remaining from the non-protected group $\mathcal{G}^0$.

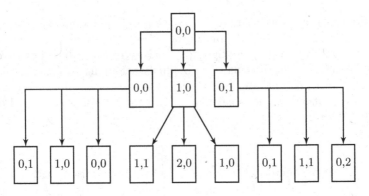

Fig. 1. Example of a Multinomial ICDF continuous mTree generation with p = [1/3, 1/3, 1/3].

chooses the $\omega_{candidate}$ with the higher α_c. Then the algorithm updates ω_p with the chosen $\omega_{candidate}$ and continues to the next iteration $j = 2$ and so on.

We designed an ad-hoc function called *childGenerator*, described by the Algorithm 1, to consider at each position j all the nodes that respect fairness boundaries, defined by α_t.

Algorithm 1. childGenerator

Input $k \in \{1,\ldots,n\}$, $p = [\,p_1,\ldots,\,p_g]$, $\alpha_t \in\ ]0,1[$, $g \geq 1$, $\omega_p = [\omega^1,\ldots,\omega^g]$
Output omegaList

Ensure: $\sum_1^g p_a = 1$
  $gList \leftarrow$ emptyList
  $\alpha_c = F(\omega_p, j, p)$
  if $\alpha_c \geq \alpha_t$ **then**
    $omegaList \leftarrow \omega_p$
    return $omegaList$
  else if $\alpha_c \leq \alpha_t$ **then**
    for all idx in $1 : g$ **do**
      $\omega_{candidate}[idx] = \omega_p[idx] + 1$
      $\alpha_c \rightarrow F(j, p, \omega_{candidate})$
      if $\alpha_c \geq \alpha_t$ **then**
        $omegaList \leftarrow \omega_{candidate}$
        $gList \leftarrow idx$
  return $omegaList, gList$

Then, among the fair nodes, we place in the j position the individuals that maximize a certain utility function. Basically, we are forced to add an individual of the protected group a to respect the minimum proportions p_a at each position j, even if the utility U_i is low. In Algorithm 2, we describe the proposed re-rank process.

Algorithm 2. Generate Re Rank process

Input $k \in \{1,\ldots,n\}$, $p = [\ p_1,\ldots,\ p_g]$, $G = [\ G_0,\ldots,\ G_n]$, $Y = [\ Y_0,\ldots,\ Y_n]$, $\alpha_t \in]0,1[$, $L \in]0,1[$, $g \geq 1$, $\omega_p = [\omega^1,\ldots,\omega^g]$
    Output ω
Ensure: $\sum_1^g p_a = 1$
  $\omega = emptyList$
  for all j in k **do**
    $omegaList, gList \rightarrow childGenerator(j, p, \alpha_t, \omega_p)$
    if $omegaList = \{\omega_p\}$ **then**
      ω.append($\text{argmax}_{i \notin \omega}(Y_i)$)
    else
      $UList = emptyList$
      for all $\omega_{candidate}$ in $omegaList$ **do**
        $UList$.append($U_L(j, Y_i, \omega_{candidate})$)
      $idx = argmax_{U_L \in UList}$
      ω.append($\text{argmax}_{i \notin \omega, G_i = gList[idx]}(Y_i)$)
  return ω

In our application we defined utility as follow:

$$U_L(\pi_i, Y_i, \omega_p) = U(\pi_i, Y_i, L, \omega_p) = \frac{Y_i}{ln(2 + \pi_i)} * L + \alpha_c(\omega_p, \pi_i, p) * (1 - L) \quad (9)$$

$$U_L^a(\pi, Y, \omega_p) = U^a(\pi, Y, L, \omega_p) = \sum_{\{d_i \in \mathcal{G}^a\}} \frac{U_L(\pi_i, Y_i, \omega_p)}{|\mathcal{G}^a|} \quad (10)$$

when minimum targets change, iterating on all possible $\omega_{candidate}$ that respect $\alpha_c > \alpha_t$. Setting the L parameter to his extremes replicates the configurations described in [28]: (i) preserving as much fairness as possible, when $L = 0$; and (ii) maximising utility remaining within fairness boundaries when $L = 1$. Thank our method, the user can directly intervene and optimize the trade-off between fairness and utility.

4 Experiments

Experiments Overview. The post-processing algorithm described in the previous section works by design in any context with at least a initial rank π based on a relevance value y, that is unfair in regard to a set of minimum proportions p that must be guaranteed to multiple sensitive groups membership $\mathcal{G}^a$. As an advantage over previous methods, our approach allows users to choose which utility metric to consider and deal on the trade-off between this metric and fairness, by appropriately setting the L parameter.

In our experiment, we suppose that we want to maximize utility as expressed in terms of $Kendall\text{-}\tau$. Under this assumption, our research questions are:

- Could there be solutions that maximize *Kendall-τ* that satisfy the fairness boundaries, that are not covered by Multinomial FA*IR? In other terms, can the value of L that maximizes *Kendall-τ* be different from 1 and 0?
- What is the relation between *Kendall-τ* and L? Is this relation consistent with the relation between L and other utility metrics, such as the DCG? Moreover, is the relation between *Kendall-τ* and L consistent using different values of α_t?

The experiments are performed using the German Credit[3] benchmark dataset. It is composed of samples of bank customers. The dataset is commonly used for risk assessment prediction or determining whether or not it is risky to offer credit to a person.

In large banks, the credit granting process is typically slow due to the huge number of requests that credit specialists have to manage. In this context, an automatic ranking system that allows the bank to prioritize reliable customers in order to accelerate their loan granting is extremely useful. However, this prioritization process may increase the disparity in the amount of loans granted to minority groups of the population, necessitating the incorporation of fairness constraints into the ranking system. Although this application is specific to the credit field, the approach can be generalized to other datasets of interest in the search and recommendation field.

In our experiments, we are focusing on the financial relevance value y, the position in the rank j, as determined by the financial relevance value order, and the sensitive group membership $\mathcal{G}^a$ to investigate and mitigate intersectional bias. We consider in $\mathcal{G}^a$ the four following intersectional categories: 0-*male-single*, 1-*male-married/widowed*, 2-*male-divorced/separated* and 3-*female-divorced/separated/married*.

Figures 2a and b represent just the differences in ranking between not applying and applying the fairness constraints, respectively.

Through Fig. 2a we show that a rank that maximises solely the *selection utility* and that considers the first $k = 50$ elements is unbalanced in favour of group $\mathcal{G}^0$, while the groups $\mathcal{G}^2$ and $\mathcal{G}^3$ are both underrepresented and structurally positioned in lower positions, even in respect of the group $\mathcal{G}^1$. Figure 2b represents the fair re-rank that solves this unfair situation according to the Multinomial FA*IR algorithm using $p = [0.4, 0.3, 0.2, 0.1]$ as the set of minimum targets proportions and $\alpha_t = 0.1$ a threshold value.

Given this configuration, we apply our approach varying α_t and L, in order to show the existence of other solutions that produce higher utility values in terms of *Kendall-τ*, within the fairness boundaries.

Experiments Evidence. To answer our research questions, we leverage our approach to investigate the utility level via a sensitivity analysis on the L parameter and the α_t and L parameters together.

---

[3] Dataset available at https://archive.ics.uci.edu/ml/datasets/statlog+(german+cred it+data).

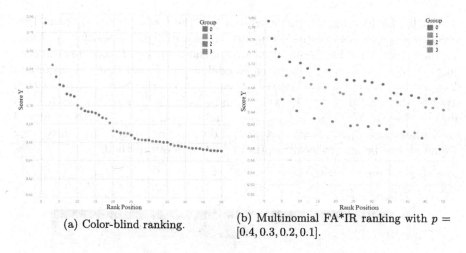

(a) Color-blind ranking.

(b) Multinomial FA*IR ranking with $p = [0.4, 0.3, 0.2, 0.1]$.

Fig. 2. x

In Fig. 3 we show the changing in Kendall-τ and average exposure at L variation. As expected, increasing the L-parameter raises average exposure for groups with higher levels of the score Y_i, such as $\mathcal{G}^0$ and $\mathcal{G}^1$, while the other protected groups tend to be less represented.

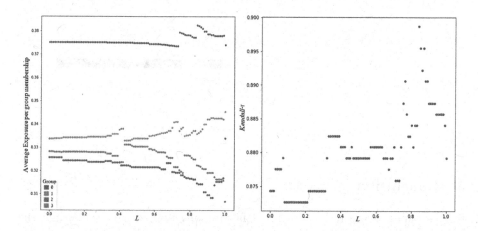

Fig. 3. L vs Average Exposure (on the left) and L vs Kendall-τ (on the right).

In terms of utility, the graph clearly shows a non-linear relationship between L and Kendall-τ. In particular, we observe that in this case the optimal Kendall-τ is achieved when L is near 0.85. This result demonstrates that there may be superior solutions, with configuration not covered by the previous method in the literature. Another conclusion is that the utility metrics do not have the same maximum, in fact, the DCG does when L=1.

Finally, for investigating the consistency of these results with different fairness requirements, we iteratively repeated the sensitivity analysis of L by changing the value of α_t. The resulting heatmap, shown in Fig. 4, confirms the nonlinearity of the relationship between Kendall-τ and L and that the maximum does not lay for $L = 1$. As expected, when $\alpha_t = 0$, i.e. there are no fairness constraints, there is no change between π and ω and so the optimal Kendall-τ is always achieved. While an increase in α_t, and thus an increase in the severity of the fairness constraints, leads to a general decrease in utility. This utility, even if limited, can be always locally optimized through our method.

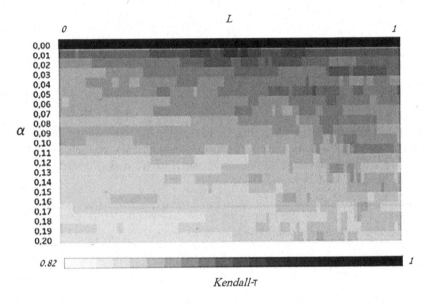

Fig. 4. Kendall-Tau (intensity of gray) at α_t and L variation.

5 Conclusion

In this paper, we introduced a novel fair-ranking approach for managing the level of utility while maintaining fairness, considering the intersectional bias that occurs from considering multiple protected groups.

The proposed method builds upon [28], providing as a contribution the flexibility to choose the preferred trade-off between fairness and utility. Moreover, our approach allows for identifying fair optimal solutions in terms of utility metrics other than DCG. We showed this evidence using the Kendall-τ, but our approach can also be performed using other utility metrics. In particular, we illustrated that when $0 < L < 1$, i.e. with configurations not covered by [28] it is possible to obtain better utility values while still meeting the fairness constraint.

Another finding is that optimal configurations are not consistent among utility metrics, therefore the user's sensitivity in choosing the most appropriate metric for his context remains crucial. In this sense, the proposition of methods like ours that provide the user with sufficient flexibility remains needed.

The complete `python` code to reproduce the experiments is publicly available at github.com/Nicola-Alimonda/MultinomialFair.

In future work, we plan to extend our approach and evidence to other fairness evaluation methods in the literature, such as *Disparate Reputation* [20]. It would be interesting to investigate if our method could be configured to ensure multi-attribute reputation independence [21] and how much it would cost the utility.

Another future direction will be to link fair ranking systems with the fields of works on eXplainable AI aimed to move towards natural language interaction with humans (see, e.g. [3,17,24]) as well as to assess the coherence of the results over multiple retraining phases to observe if the structural utility of sensitive subgroups is increasing over time [8,18,19].

References

1. Boratto, L., Marras, M.: Advances in bias-aware recommendation on the web. In: Proceedings of the 14th ACM International Conference on Web Search and Data Mining, pp. 1147–1149 (2021)
2. Buolamwini, J., Gebru, T.: Gender shades: intersectional accuracy disparities in commercial gender classification. In: FAT, pp. 77–91. PMLR (2018)
3. Cambria, E., Malandri, L., Mercorio, F., Mezzanzanica, M., Nobani, N.: A survey on XAI and natural language explanations. Inf. Process. Manag. **60**(1), 103111 (2023). https://doi.org/10.1016/j.ipm.2022.103111
4. Castelnovo, A., Cosentini, A., Malandri, L., Mercorio, F., Mezzanzanica, M.: FFTree: a flexible tree to handle multiple fairness criteria. Inf. Process. Manag. **59**(6), 103099 (2022)
5. Castelnovo, A., et al.: BeFair: addressing fairness in the banking sector. In: 2020 IEEE International Conference on Big Data (Big Data), pp. 3652–3661. IEEE (2020)
6. Castelnovo, A., Crupi, R., Greco, G., Regoli, D., Penco, I.G., Cosentini, A.C.: A clarification of the nuances in the fairness metrics landscape. Sci. Rep. **12**(1), 1–21 (2022)
7. Castelnovo, A., Crupi, R., Inverardi, N., Regoli, D., Cosentini, A.: Investigating bias with a synthetic data generator: empirical evidence and philosophical interpretation. arXiv preprint arXiv:2209.05889 (2022)
8. Castelnovo, A., Malandri, L., Mercorio, F., Mezzanzanica, M., Cosentini, A.: Towards fairness through time. In: Machine Learning and Principles and Practice of Knowledge Discovery in Databases. ECML PKDD 2021. Communications in Computer and Information Science, vol. 1524, pp. 647–663. Springer (2021). https://doi.org/10.1007/978-3-030-93736-2_46
9. Council of Europe, committee of experts on Internet MSI-NET: study on the human rights dimensions of automated data processing techniques and possible regulatory implications (2017)

10. Crenshaw, K.: Demarginalizing the intersection of race and sex: a black feminist critique of antidiscrimination doctrine, feminist theory and antiracist politics. In: Feminist legal theories, pp. 23–51. Routledge (2013)

11. Crupi, R., Castelnovo, A., Regoli, D., San Miguel Gonzalez, B.: Counterfactual explanations as interventions in latent space. Data Mining and Knowledge Discovery, pp. 1–37 (2022). https://doi.org/10.1007/s10618-022-00889-2

12. European Commission: communication on fostering a European approach to AI. https://ec.europa.eu/newsroom/dae/redirection/document/75790 (2021)

13. Gupta, A., et al.: Online post-processing in rankings for fair utility maximization. In: Proceedings of the 14th ACM International Conference on Web Search and Data Mining, pp. 454–462 (2021)

14. Hardt, M., Price, E., Srebro, N.: Equality of opportunity in supervised learning. In: Advances in Neural Information Processing Systems 29 (2016)

15. Kearns, M., Neel, S., Roth, A., Wu, Z.S.: Preventing fairness gerrymandering: auditing and learning for subgroup fairness. In: ICML, pp. 2564–2572. PMLR (2018)

16. Kendall, M.G.: A new measure of rank correlation. Biometrika **30**(1/2), 81–93 (1938)

17. Malandri, L., Mercorio, F., Mezzanzanica, M., Nobani, N.: ConvXAI: a system for multimodal interaction with any black-box explainer. Cogn. Comput. **15**, 1–32 (2022). https://doi.org/10.1007/s12559-022-10067-7

18. Malandri, L., Mercorio, F., Mezzanzanica, M., Nobani, N., Seveso, A.: ContrXT: generating contrastive explanations from any text classifier. Inf. Fusion **81**, 103–115 (2022). https://doi.org/10.1016/j.inffus.2021.11.016

19. Malandri, L., Mercorio, F., Mezzanzanica, M., Nobani, N., Seveso, A.: The good, the bad, and the explainer: a tool for contrastive explanations of text classifiers. In: Raedt, L.D. (ed.) Proceedings of the Thirty-First International Joint Conference on Artificial Intelligence, IJCAI 2022, Vienna, Austria, 23–29 July 2022, pp. 5936–5939. ijcai.org (2022). https://doi.org/10.24963/ijcai.2022/858

20. Ramos, G., Boratto, L.: Reputation (in) dependence in ranking systems: demographics influence over output disparities. In: Proceedings of the 43rd international ACM SIGIR conference on Research and Development in Information Retrieval, pp. 2061–2064 (2020)

21. Ramos, G., Boratto, L., Marras, M.: Robust reputation independence in ranking systems for multiple sensitive attributes. Mach. Learn. **111**(10), 3769–3796 (2022)

22. Robertson, S.E.: The probability ranking principle in IR. J. Document. **33**, 294–304 (1977)

23. Singh, A., Joachims, T.: Fairness of exposure in rankings. In: Proceedings of the 24th ACM SIGKDD ICKDDM, pp. 2219–2228 (2018)

24. Taesiri, M.R., Nguyen, G., Nguyen, A.: Visual correspondence-based explanations improve AI robustness and human-AI team accuracy. In: Advances in Neural Information Processing Systems (2022)

25. The European Commission: proposal for a Regulation of the European Parliament laying down harmonised rules on AI (AI Act) (2021). https://digital-strategy.ec.europa.eu/en/library/proposal-regulation-laying-down-harmonised-rules-artificial-intelligence

26. Yang, K., Stoyanovich, J.: Measuring fairness in ranked outputs. In: Proceedings of the 29th International Conference on Scientific and Statistical Database Management (2017)

27. Zehlike, M., Bonchi, F., Castillo, C., Hajian, S., Megahed, M., Baeza-Yates, R.: Fa*ir: a fair top-k ranking algorithm. In: Proceedings of the 2017 ACM on Conference on Information and Knowledge Management (2017)
28. Zehlike, M., Sühr, T., Baeza-Yates, R., Bonchi, F., Castillo, C., Hajian, S.: Fair top-k ranking with multiple protected groups. IPM **59**(1), 102707 (2022)
29. Zehlike, M., Yang, K., Stoyanovich, J.: Fairness in ranking, part ii: learning-to-rank and recommender systems. ACM Comput. Surv. (CSUR) **55**, 3533380 (2022)

Mitigating Position Bias in Hotels Recommender Systems

Yinxiao Li[✉]

Meta Platforms, Cambridge, USA
liyinxiao1227@gmail.com

Abstract. Nowadays, search ranking and recommendation systems rely on a lot of data to train machine learning models such as Learning-to-Rank (LTR) models to rank results for a given query, and implicit user feedback (e.g. click data) have become the dominant source of data collection due to its abundance and low cost, especially for major Internet companies. However, a drawback of this data collection approach is the data could be highly biased, and one of the most significant biases is the position bias, where users are biased towards clicking on higher ranked results. In this work, we will investigate the marginal importance of properly mitigating the position bias in an online test environment in Tripadvisor Hotels recommender systems. We propose an empirically effective method of mitigating the position bias that fully leverages the user action data. We take advantage of the fact that when a user clicks a result, they have almost certainly observed all the results above, and the propensities of the results below the clicked result will be estimated by a simple but effective position bias model. The online A/B test results show that this method leads to an improved recommendation model.

Keywords: position bias · recommender systems · learning to rank · unbiased learning · implicit feedback

1 Introduction

With an increasing presence of machine learning in search ranking and recommendation systems, there is a larger demand for data than ever before. Implicit user feedback, such as clicks, conversion and dwell time [38], are cheap and abundant compared with explicit human judgements, especially for large Internet companies. Thus, it has become the dominant source of data collection to solve/improve search ranking and recommendation problems. However, a well-known challenge of implicit user feedback is its inherent bias [8].

Implicit user feedback typically include four types of biases: position bias [20, 29, 37], presentation bias [39], exposure bias [30, 36] and quality-of-context bias [17, 19, 42]. Position bias is that users are biased towards clicking on higher

---

Y. Li—Work performed while at Tripadvisor, USA.

ⓒ The Author(s), under exclusive license to Springer Nature Switzerland AG 2023
L. Boratto et al. (Eds.): BIAS 2023, CCIS 1840, pp. 74–84, 2023.
https://doi.org/10.1007/978-3-031-37249-0_6

ranked results, either due to laziness [20,37] or due to trust to the search site (trust bias) [1,19,29]. Presentation bias describes an effect where users tend to click on results with seemingly more attractive summaries, which inflates the perceived relevance. Exposure bias occurs as users are only exposed to a part of specific items so that the click data used to learn a ranking function are undersampled and thus biased. The quality-of-context bias refers to the fact that users make click decisions not only by the relevance of the clicked result, but also by the contextual information, such as the overall quality of the results in the list, and their cross-positional interactions. Among the four biases, the position bias has the strongest effect on what users click [21]. Therefore, there is a stronger need to debias it in order to fully leverage the power of implicit user feedback data.

In this work, we will focus on the position bias due to laziness, where users may not have evaluated the whole list before making a click. This is especially true for long lists such as Tripadvisor Hotels recommendation, where a maximum of 30 hotels are displayed on a certain page. We assume that the user has evaluated all the hotels above the lowest ranked hotel that they clicked on. For hotels below that, we will estimate their propensities through a position bias model. We then apply propensity sampling to generate the training data, which is used to train a pairwise model to serve live-site traffic. The effectiveness of this model will be verified by online A/B testing.

2   Related Work

2.1   Position Bias

To use implicit user data for model training, researchers have adopted three primary approaches of dealing with the position bias. The first approach is to keep all the results in the training data and neglect this position bias. This approach assumes that user has evaluated all the options [9,15,35], and it is only acceptable for a relatively short list such as Facebook ad recommendation [15]. The second approach is to only keep results up to the last result user clicked on [12]. This approach assumes that the user sequentially views the results from top to bottom, and will click the first relevant result as they are scrolling down and stop (similar to Cascade model [10]). This works reasonably well for a relatively long list such as Airbnb search ranking [12]. However, it has been argued that this approach is systematically biased and will lead to a ranking model that tends to reverse the existing order [18,21].

The third commonly adopted approach is to keep all the results in the training data, but use the propensities as weights in the loss function [5,21,37]. Compared with the previous two approaches, this approach aims at debiasing the training data by taking propensities into account. They have shown that this method leads to an unbiased loss function and thus an unbiased model, and referred to this framework as unbiased Learning-to-Rank [5,21,37]. However, this approach has not yet fully leveraged the user feedback data (e.g. when a user clicks on result N, this user has almost certainly evaluated result 1 to result N-1). Besides, this approach requires propensity estimation, which is another challenging task. In our work, we will incorporate the key ideas from both the second and third approaches for mitigating position bias, and provide propensity estimations by fully leveraging the user actions.

2.2 Propensity Estimation

There has been numerous research on unbiased click propensity estimation, and position bias model [34,37] is one of the most classical methods. The position bias model assumes that the probability of a click on a given result is the product of the probability of evaluating the result and the probability of clicking the result given that it has been evaluated:

$$P(C = 1|i, u, k) = P(E = 1|k) \cdot P(R = 1|i, u) \tag{1}$$

where C represents whether a result is clicked, E represents whether a result is examined, R represents whether a result is relevant, i and u are the item and user (or their feature representation), and k is the position. This model in general requires result randomization experiments which degrade the user experience [21,36], although many efforts have been spent on minimizing this degradation effect [31].

To fully remove the degradation effect, Wang et al. proposed a method without result randomization, to estimate position bias from regular clicks [37]. This method uses a regression-based Expectation Maximization (EM) algorithm to extract the position bias and result relevance simultaneously. After that, Ai et al. proposed a dual learning method to jointly learn an unbiased ranker and a propensity model [4]. Hu et al. further developed a general framework for jointly estimating the position bias and training a pairwise ranker from click data [16]. However, we argue that this type of method tends to assign relevance based on how relevant a result is compared with other results at the same position k, potentially overlooking the fact that results appearing at top ranks are generally better than those appearing at the bottom.

Later, Aslanyan et al. proposed a method to estimate click propensities without any intervention in the live search results. This method takes advantage of the fact that the same query-document pair may naturally change ranks over time in eCommerce search, and uses query-document pairs that appear at different ranks to estimate propensities [5,6]. Similarly, Agarwal et al. proposed an estimating method that also requires no intervention, which uses query-document pairs from different ranking functions [2,3]. Both methods assume that a document will not change much over time and propensities are estimated based on the CTR of the same document at different positions. However, although documents in search engines are relatively static, the price of a hotel is very dynamic and is one of the key factors to consider when users make click/booking decisions, which makes pair generation very difficult for Hotels search.

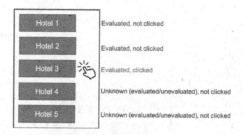

Fig. 1. Demonstration of implicit user click feedback.

3   Method

3.1   Position Bias Mitigation

In this work, we propose to incorporate two of the existing approaches on position bias mitigation (i.e. second and third approaches in Sect. 2.1), to build an unbiased training dataset for recommender systems in Tripadvisor Hotels. Consider an example of implicit user feedback, as shown in Fig. 1, where there are five hotel impressions in the list, and the user makes a click on Hotel 3. Since the user clicks on Hotel 3, Hotel 3 has been evaluated, and we assume Hotel 1 and Hotel 2 are also evaluated [18,19], while Hotel 4 and Hotel 5 are in an unknown state of being evaluated or not. The sampling rate of each hotel impression is equal to its propensity of being observed, which will be discussed in Sect. 3.2.

Specifically, while constructing the training examples, our approach first discards all the search logs where no click/booking happened, and for the remaining searches, we divide the list based on the lowest hotel position that was clicked/booked by the user: the hotel impressions on or above the lowest clicked/booked position will be kept in the training dataset without sampling, while hotel impressions below that will be sampled based on their estimated propensities. Then, the hotel impressions that remain will be used to create training pairs, as shown in Fig. 2. It is noted that since this approach mitigates the position bias via debiasing the training dataset, it does not require any change on the model training/serving infrastructure or impact the complexity of the model.

3.2   Propensity Estimation

Extending the classical position bias model as shown in Eq. 1, when the user clicks on the hotel at position k_u, they have evaluated all the results on or above k_u:

$$P(E = 1 | k <= k_u) = 1 \tag{2}$$

On the other hand, the propensity of observing results below the lowest clicked hotel position k_u can be calculated as:

Discarded Search Logs   Used Search Logs

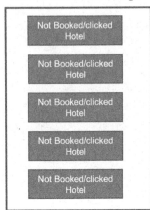 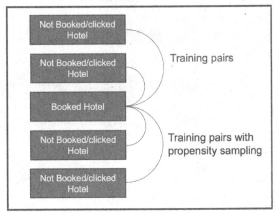

Fig. 2. Construction of training dataset from logged search results.

$$P(E = 1|k > k_u) = P(E = 1|k, k_u)$$
$$= \frac{P(E = 1|k)}{P(E = 1|k_u)} \qquad (3)$$

Apparently, the precise calculation of $P(E = 1|k > k_u)$ relies on an accurate estimation of $P(E = 1|k)$. As discussed in Sect. 2.2, estimating propensities with the help of result randomization degrades the user experience, while the existing evaluation methods from regular clicks suffer from the difficulty in separating hotel relevance from propensity. Here, we will use a simple relevance assignment strategy based on the historical number of bookings, which will be shown to be good enough for evaluating the average relevance of hotels at a certain position. According to the position bias model, we have:

$$P(E = 1|k) = \frac{E[P(C = 1|i, u, k)]}{E[P(R = 1|i, u, k)]} \qquad (4)$$

where we let $E[P(R = 1|i, u, k)] = $ mean of historical bookings at position k. We have found out that for online travel agencies (OTAs), the number of bookings (conversions) is a very strong signal of hotel relevance and is aligned with our final business goal. Figure 3 shows the measured click curve ($P(C = 1|k)$ vs position) and the calculated propensity curve ($P(E = 1|k)$ vs position) based on Eq. 4. The click curve confirms that users are highly biased towards clicking on higher ranked hotels, and since the click curve is steeper than the calculated propensity curve, it indicates that, in general, we are already promoting more relevant hotels to the top of the list.

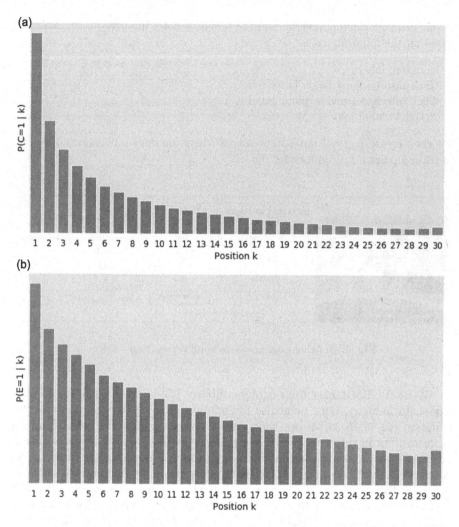

Fig. 3. a) Click curve, and b) propensity curve.

4   Experiments and Results

4.1   Model Implementation

The training dataset of our recommendation model includes search queries in the past 28 d, where at least one click/booking happens. We will be optimizing for bookings, similar to other OTAs [7,12,13], but will use clicks as supplemental data to facilitate the training process as we have far more clicks than bookings [12,22]. Specifically, two different types of clicks will be used: booking page clicks, and hotel review page clicks, as shown in Fig. 4. Moreover, optimizing for bookings to some extent addresses the concern of presentation bias. We use NDCG as our primary ranking metric, and the labels of hotel impressions are assigned based on the following rules:

- Booking: label = 5
- Click into booking page: label = 2
- Click into hotel review page: label = 1
- No click: label = 0

We then create pairs of hotel impressions whenever their labels do not match, to train a pairwise recommender model.

Fig. 4. Booking page clicks vs hotel review page clicks.

We use LGBMRanker from lightgbm library [23] to train a pairwise GBDT model. In industry, both pointwise formulation [9, 26–28, 41] and pairwise formulation [12, 13, 16, 26, 33] are widely used to solve real-world search ranking problems, but in this work we will use pairwise methods due to its three advantages over pointwise methods: (a) Focus on learning relevant things: for example, hotels in Boston have higher CTR than hotels in Maine. A pointwise model is supposed to predict such details correctly, which is unnecessary since we will never compare a hotel in Boston with a hotel in Maine, while pairwise learning will focus on solving problems that you will actually encounter [13]. (b) Quality-of-context bias: users make click decisions not only by the relevance of the clicked result, but also by the overall quality of the surrounding results in the list [19]. The pairwise formulation measures the relative relevance by constructing pairs. (c) Intention bias: for example, hotels on the second page generally have higher CTR than those on the first page because users entering second pages are more engaged. A pointwise model tends to incorrectly favor the best hotels on the second page.

To create personalization features, we trained hotel embeddings using word2vec [24, 25] with within-geo negative sampling, to account for congregated search (i.e. users frequently search only within a certain geographical region but not across regions), and these hotels embeddings were used to generate similarity features based on user behavior for real-time personalization similar to [12]. We modified the gensim library [32] to allow this within-geo negative sampling.

To reduce latency and better serve the online traffic, we use a two-stage ranking algorithm in our online ranking serving system, where an initial simple model retrieves a set of hotels (candidate generation) and a second complex model re-ranks them before presenting to users [11]. This approach allows fast real-time recommendations and has been widely used in Google [9], Facebook [15] and Pinterest [26,40]. In this work, the two models are trained with the same training dataset.

4.2   Experimental Setup

To evaluate the effectiveness of propensity sampling, we ran three online experiments in Tripadvisor Hotels Best Value Sort for 2 weeks, and evaluated the performance by the number of clicks (both booking page clicks and hotel review page clicks). For these experiments, the sampling rate of results on or above the lowest clicked hotel is kept as 1 (Eq. 2), while three different variants on how to sample results below the lowest clicked hotel will be tested. Specifically, we have chosen the 100% sampling strategy as the control, where all the hotel impressions of a query with at least one click/booking are kept in the training dataset. In Test 1, we use a sampling rate of 80% for the hotels below the lowest clicked position. In Test 2, we apply propensity sampling to hotel impressions based on our estimated propensity of observation.

- Control: 100% sampling, $P(E = 1|k > k_u) = 100\%$.
- Test 1: 80% sampling, $P(E = 1|k > k_u) = 80\%$.
- Test 2: propensity sampling, where $P(E = 1|k > k_u) = \frac{P(E=1|k)}{P(E=1|k_u)}$, and $P(E = 1|k)$ is estimated based on Eq. 4.

Since we use all the raw search logs from the past 28 d to construct the training pairs, the total number of pairs used to train the models in Test 1 and Test 2 is slightly lower than that in Control.

4.3   Results

The online A/B test result is shown in Table 1. Among the three experiments, the model with propensity sampling (Test 2) has the best performance in terms of clicks. Compared with the control model with a 100% sampling rate, it improves the clicks by 1.5%, which is statistically significant (p-value < 0.05), despite a lower number of training pairs used in model training. This model also outperforms the model with a constant sampling rate of 80% (Test 1), by 1.7% in clicks. The model with 80% sampling shows flat results compared with the control model. This result shows that our approach is effective at mitigating position bias, as it has generated more user clicks and engagements in the online test environment.

Table 1. Online test results of three experiments. Gain is relative to control.

Experiment	Clicks
Control: 100% sampling	0.0%
Test 1: 80% sampling	−0.2%
Test 2: propensity sampling	+1.5% (stats sig)

5   Conclusion

Although there is no widely accepted way of correcting position bias in training
LTR models, the importance of mitigating such bias should not be overlooked.
In this work, we put forward a simple and easily adoptable method that fully
leverages user actions with propensity sampling, and prove that it is effective
through an online experiment. Online test results show that this method leads
to significant performance improvements. Compared with large investments in
infrastructures to support more complex models [14], this method requires mini-
mal efforts without a higher level of model complexity, but is still able to improve
the recommender system significantly.

References

1. Agarwal, A., Wang, X., Li, C., Bendersky, M., Najork, M.: Addressing trust bias for
   unbiased learning-to-rank. In: The World Wide Web Conference, pp. 4–14 (2019)
2. Agarwal, A., Zaitsev, I., Joachims, T.: Consistent position bias estimation without
   online interventions for learning-to-rank. arXiv preprint arXiv:1806.03555 (2018)
3. Agarwal, A., Zaitsev, I., Wang, X., Li, C., Najork, M., Joachims, T.: Estimating
   position bias without intrusive interventions. In: Proceedings of the Twelfth ACM
   International Conference on Web Search and Data Mining, pp. 474–482 (2019)
4. Ai, Q., Bi, K., Luo, C., Guo, J., Croft, W.B.: Unbiased learning to rank with
   unbiased propensity estimation. In: The 41st International ACM SIGIR Conference
   on Research & Development in Information Retrieval, pp. 385–394 (2018)
5. Aslanyan, G., Porwal, U.: Direct estimation of position bias for unbiased learning-
   to-rank without intervention. arXiv preprint arXiv:1812.09338 (2018)
6. Aslanyan, G., Porwal, U.: Position bias estimation for unbiased learning-to-rank
   in ecommerce search. In: International Symposium on String Processing and Information Retrieval. pp. 47–64. Springer (2019)
7. Bernardi, L., Mavridis, T., Estevez, P.: 150 successful machine learning models:
   6 lessons learned at booking. com. In: Proceedings of the 25th ACM SIGKDD
   International Conference on Knowledge Discovery & Data Mining, pp. 1743–1751.
   ACM (2019)
8. Chen, J., Dong, H., Wang, X., Feng, F., Wang, M., He, X.: Bias and debias in recommender system: A survey and future directions. arXiv preprint arXiv:2010.03240
   (2020)
9. Covington, P., Adams, J., Sargin, E.: Deep neural networks for youtube recommendations. In: Proceedings of the 10th ACM Conference on Recommender Systems,
   pp. 191–198. ACM (2016)

10. Craswell, N., Zoeter, O., Taylor, M., Ramsey, B.: An experimental comparison of click position-bias models. In: Proceedings of the 2008 International Conference on Web Search and Data Mining, pp. 87–94. ACM (2008)
11. Dang, V., Bendersky, M., Croft, W.B.: Two-stage learning to rank for information retrieval. In: Serdyukov, P., Braslavski, P., Kuznetsov, S.O., Kamps, J., Rüger, S., Agichtein, E., Segalovich, I., Yilmaz, E. (eds.) ECIR 2013. LNCS, vol. 7814, pp. 423–434. Springer, Heidelberg (2013). https://doi.org/10.1007/978-3-642-36973-5_36
12. Grbovic, M., Cheng, H.: Real-time personalization using embeddings for search ranking at airbnb. In: Proceedings of the 24th ACM SIGKDD International Conference on Knowledge Discovery & Data Mining, pp. 311–320. ACM (2018)
13. Haldar, M., et al.: Applying deep learning to airbnb search. In: Proceedings of the 25th ACM SIGKDD International Conference on Knowledge Discovery & Data Mining, pp. 1927–1935. ACM (2019)
14. Hazelwood, K., et al.: Applied machine learning at facebook: a datacenter infrastructure perspective. In: 2018 IEEE International Symposium on High Performance Computer Architecture (HPCA), pp. 620–629. IEEE (2018)
15. He, X., et al.: Practical lessons from predicting clicks on ads at facebook. In: Proceedings of the Eighth International Workshop on Data Mining for Online Advertising, pp. 1–9. ACM (2014)
16. Hu, Z., Wang, Y., Peng, Q., Li, H.: Unbiased lambdamart: an unbiased pairwise learning-to-rank algorithm. In: The World Wide Web Conference, pp. 2830–2836 (2019)
17. Jin, J., et al.: A deep recurrent survival model for unbiased ranking. In: Proceedings of the 43rd International ACM SIGIR Conference on Research and Development in Information Retrieval, pp. 29–38 (2020)
18. Joachims, T.: Optimizing search engines using clickthrough data. In: Proceedings of the Eighth ACM SIGKDD International Conference on Knowledge Discovery and Data Mining, pp. 133–142. ACM (2002)
19. Joachims, T., Granka, L., Pan, B., Hembrooke, H., Radlinski, F., Gay, G.: Evaluating the accuracy of implicit feedback from clicks and query reformulations in web search. ACM Trans. Inf. Syst. (TOIS) 25(2), 7 (2007)
20. Joachims, T., Granka, L.A., Pan, B., Hembrooke, H., Gay, G.: Accurately interpreting clickthrough data as implicit feedback. In: Sigir, vol. 5, pp. 154–161 (2005)
21. Joachims, T., Swaminathan, A., Schnabel, T.: Unbiased learning-to-rank with biased feedback. In: Proceedings of the Tenth ACM International Conference on Web Search and Data Mining, pp. 781–789. ACM (2017)
22. Karmaker Santu, S.K., Sondhi, P., Zhai, C.: On application of learning to rank for e-commerce search. In: Proceedings of the 40th International ACM SIGIR Conference on Research and Development in Information Retrieval, pp. 475–484. ACM (2017)
23. Ke, G., et al.: Lightgbm: a highly efficient gradient boosting decision tree. In: Advances in Neural Information Processing Systems, pp. 3146–3154 (2017)
24. Li, Y., Anderson, J.: Introducing openstreetmap user embeddings: promising steps toward automated vandalism and community detection (2021)
25. Li, Y., Anderson, J., Niu, Y.: Vandalism detection in openstreetmap via user embeddings. In: Proceedings of the 30th ACM International Conference on Information & Knowledge Management, pp. 3232–3236 (2021)
26. Liu, D.C., et al.: Related pins at pinterest: the evolution of a real-world recommender system. In: Proceedings of the 26th International Conference on World

Wide Web Companion, pp. 583–592. International World Wide Web Conferences Steering Committee (2017)

27. Ma, X., et al.: Entire space multi-task model: an effective approach for estimating post-click conversion rate. In: The 41st International ACM SIGIR Conference on Research & Development in Information Retrieval, pp. 1137–1140. ACM (2018)

28. Naumov, M., et al.: Deep learning recommendation model for personalization and recommendation systems. arXiv preprint arXiv:1906.00091 (2019)

29. O'Brien, M., Keane, M.T.: Modeling result-list searching in the world wide web: the role of relevance topologies and trust bias. In: Proceedings of the 28th annual conference of the cognitive science society, vol. 28, pp. 1881–1886. Citeseer (2006)

30. Ovaisi, Z., Ahsan, R., Zhang, Y., Vasilaky, K., Zheleva, E.: Correcting for selection bias in learning-to-rank systems. In: Proceedings of The Web Conference 2020, pp. 1863–1873 (2020)

31. Radlinski, F., Joachims, T.: Minimally invasive randomization for collecting unbiased preferences from clickthrough. In: Logs, Proceedings of the 21st National Conference on Artificial Intelligence (AAAI). Citeseer (2006)

32. Řehůřek, R., Sojka, P.: Software framework for topic modelling with large corpora. In: Proceedings of the LREC 2010 Workshop on New Challenges for NLP Frameworks, pp. 45–50. ELRA, Valletta, Malta, May 2010. http://is.muni.cz/publication/884893/en

33. Ren, Y., Tang, H., Zhu, S.: Unbiased learning to rank with biased continuous feedback. In: Proceedings of the 31st ACM International Conference on Information & Knowledge Management, pp. 1716–1725 (2022)

34. Richardson, M., Dominowska, E., Ragno, R.: Predicting clicks: estimating the click-through rate for new ads. In: Proceedings of the 16th international conference on World Wide Web, pp. 521–530. ACM (2007)

35. Tagami, Y., Ono, S., Yamamoto, K., Tsukamoto, K., Tajima, A.: Ctr prediction for contextual advertising: Learning-to-rank approach. In: Proceedings of the Seventh International Workshop on Data Mining for Online Advertising, p. 4. ACM (2013)

36. Wang, X., Bendersky, M., Metzler, D., Najork, M.: Learning to rank with selection bias in personal search. In: Proceedings of the 39th International ACM SIGIR Conference on Research and Development in Information Retrieval, pp. 115–124 (2016)

37. Wang, X., Golbandi, N., Bendersky, M., Metzler, D., Najork, M.: Position bias estimation for unbiased learning to rank in personal search. In: Proceedings of the Eleventh ACM International Conference on Web Search and Data Mining, pp. 610–618. ACM (2018)

38. Yi, X., Hong, L., Zhong, E., Liu, N.N., Rajan, S.: Beyond clicks: dwell time for personalization. In: Proceedings of the 8th ACM Conference on Recommender Systems, pp. 113–120. ACM (2014)

39. Yue, Y., Patel, R., Roehrig, H.: Beyond position bias: examining result attractiveness as a source of presentation bias in clickthrough data. In: Proceedings of the 19th International Conference on World Wide Web, pp. 1011–1018. ACM (2010)

40. Zhai, A., et al.: Visual discovery at pinterest. In: Proceedings of the 26th International Conference on World Wide Web Companion, pp. 515–524. International World Wide Web Conferences Steering Committee (2017)

41. Zhou, G., et al.: Deep interest network for click-through rate prediction. In: Proceedings of the 24th ACM SIGKDD International Conference on Knowledge Discovery & Data Mining, pp. 1059–1068. ACM (2018)

42. Zhuang, H., et al.: Cross-positional attention for debiasing clicks. In: Proceedings of the Web Conference 2021, pp. 788–797 (2021)

Improving Recommender System Diversity with Variational Autoencoders

Sheetal Borar[3]([✉]) [iD], Hilde Weerts[1] [iD], Binyam Gebre[2] [iD],
and Mykola Pechenizkiy[1] [iD]

[1] Eindhoven University of Technology, 5612, AZ Eindhoven, The Netherlands
[2] Bol.com, 3528, BJ Utrecht, The Netherlands
[3] Amazon, London EC2A 2BA, UK
sborar12@gmail.com

Abstract. Focusing only on relevance when training recommender systems can lead to suboptimal recommendations. On eCommerce platforms, this not only leads to poor user experience for customers but also limits opportunities for vendors due to popularity bias. Consequently, there is an increasing interest in systems that produce recommendations that are not only relevant but also diverse. In this work, we have shown how diversity can be measured and improved in the context of a large eCommerce recommendation platform. We first evaluate how diversity should be measured feasibly in real-world recommender systems and introduce TILD: a novel diversity metric that measures representational diversity across user sessions. Second, we introduce VAE-based Generation of User Profiles (VAE-GUP), wherein we use the generative nature of VAEs to learn a user profile distribution and sample multiple user profiles. In a simple post-processing step, we combine the recommendations generated by these profiles to generate a final list of more diverse recommendations. Through empirical analysis of benchmark and real-world datasets, we show that VAE-GUP can improve several diversity metrics without significantly compromising relevance. This research has been done in collaboration with Bol.com, the largest e-commerce retailer in the Benelux region.

Keywords: Recommender systems · Popularity Bias · Diversity · Temporal Diversity · Aggregate Diversity · Intra-list Diversity · Temporal Inter-list Diversity · Relevance · Variational Autoencoders

1 Introduction

Recommender Systems (RSs) have emerged as a way to help users find relevant information as online item catalogs have multiplied in size. In the context of eCommerce platforms, users of RSs often find the recommendations to be too similar to their historical purchases, too homogeneous within each list, or too

S. Borar—Work was done prior to joining Amazon.

static over time, which can be observed from user complaints describing these systems as "too naive" or "not working" [15]. In addition to users, increased item diversity also benefits the platform and its vendors. Popularity bias in RSs causes popular items to be recommended frequently while the majority of other items are ignored. This leads to a long tail problem, where most items are not exposed to users [6]. Users are more likely to interact with items that are recommended to them creating a feedback loop [9], which results in a shift in consumption and homogenization of the user experience [6,18].

User profile generation is a crucial step in the recommendation process. A *user profile* is a numerical representation of the user where similar users are closer in the latent space in comparison to dissimilar users. Guo and Karl argue that current deep collaborative filtering (CF) approaches, which represent users as a single vector, fail to represent users' multiple interests, resulting in homogeneous recommendations [8]. Moreover, a real-world item catalog often contains many near-duplicates. As a result, an RS that only focuses on providing relevant recommendations would generate a list lacking diversity.

In this paper, we propose a method to increase the diversity of recommendations while maintaining a reasonable level of relevance. This will provide a better user experience for users and a fairer platform for vendors. Our contribution is twofold. First, we review the suitability of existing diversity metrics in the context of large-scale eCommerce platforms and introduce *temporal inter-list diversity* (TILD): a novel diversity metric for measuring temporal diversity that addresses the issue of near duplicates in item catalogs. Second, we propose a method to generate multiple user profiles called *VAE-based Generation of User Profiles* (VAE-GUP). Existing research shows that multiple profiles can be more effective at capturing users' varied interests compared to a single user profile [8], but no feasible methods have been proposed to generate these profiles. Our method uses the generative nature of Variational Autoencoders (VAEs) to generate multiple user profiles. In a simple post-processing step, we combine the recommendations generated by these profiles to generate a final list of more diverse recommendations. As the user profiles were sampled from the same distributions, we wanted to determine whether the lists generated in different sessions were representatively different or just near-duplicates. TILD was introduced in this paper to measure this aspect of VAE-GUP.

The remainder of this work is structured as follows: Sect. 2 evaluates existing diversity measures based on their feasibility for a real-world RS and proposes a new metric to evaluate diversity temporally. Section 3 describes existing methods for improving diversity in RSs. In Sect. 4, we explain and formalize VAE-GUP and in Sect. 5, we present the results of our experiment with both benchmark and real-world datasets. The paper is concluded with Sect. 6.

2 Diversity in RSs

In the context of large-scale eCommerce platforms, multiple stakeholders can benefit from more diverse recommendations, including users, vendors, and platform owners. As such, we set out to identify a set of diversity metrics that capture different stakeholder interests. Furthermore, given the increasing number of items on large-scale eCommerce platforms, another key consideration is scalability.

2.1   Existing Diversity Metrics

Most of the existing research on diversity metrics in RSs can be divided into individual and aggregate-level metrics of diversity. k is the size of the recommendation list, U is the total number of users, and I is the total number of items.

Individual diversity metrics aim to quantify how diverse the recommendations are for each user. Bradley and Smyth [4] introduce *intra-list diversity* (ILD), which is defined as the total distance (e.g., cosine or Manhattan distance) between each pair in a single recommended list, averaged across all users. Lathia et al. [15] introduce *temporal diversity* (TD), which computes the set-theoretic difference between recommendations for the same user at different time points, divided by the list size.

Aggregate diversity metrics seek to quantify the total number of items users are exposed to. Increasing aggregate diversity can help to tackle popularity bias, which could provide more business opportunities for vendors while making niche products more accessible to users. Adomavicius et al. [1] first introduce *aggregate diversity* (AD), which measures the total number of items recommended to all users. Guo et al. defined a concept of *joint accessibility* (JA), which measures the proportion of item sets that can be jointly recommended to a user [8]. This measure aims to capture whether users with niche interests will get recommendations that represent their interests. Compared to other diversity metrics, JA is considerably more costly to compute. The metric is not scalable to large datasets found in eCommerce systems. Table 6 in Appendix A provides a comparison of these measures, their formulas, and time complexities.

2.2   Temporal Inter-list Diversity (TILD)

Real-world RSs often contain many near-duplicates. A disadvantage of TD is that it does not take into account these near-duplicates. It only considers the number of distinct items that are different between sessions. It does not help us identify whether the items are diverse representationally or if they are just near duplicates. To measure temporal diversity representationally, we propose a new metric called *Temporal Inter-list Diversity* (TILD), which is the average pairwise distance between items of two different recommendation lists ($L1$: recommendation list at time $t = 0$ and $L2$: recommendation list at time $t=1$ of the same size) generated in separate sessions. In comparison to ILD, this distance measure is between two lists rather than the items of the same list and is normalized by the size of both lists. Eq. 1 describes the formula of TILD for one user, where *dist* could be any appropriate distance measure like the negative of Cosine or Euclidean distance. In this paper, we use Cosine distance in semantic space. We use a pre-trained model to generate the representation of the items based on their textual metadata. We use SBERT [19] for this purpose. This metric is normalized by the list size of the pairs and has a time complexity of $\mathcal{O}(k^2 \times |U|)$ over the entire user set.

$$TILD = \frac{1}{|L1| * |L2|} \sum_{i \in L1, j \in L2} dist(i, j) \tag{1}$$

3   Related Work

Existing approaches for improving diversity in RSs can be divided into post-processing and algorithmic techniques.

Post-processing techniques are employed after the candidate generation stage in RSs. Maximum Marginal Relevance (MMR) is the seminal work in this area [5]. This approach ranks items according to relevance and adds them to the list based on diversity with respect to the items already present in the recommendation list. Other techniques that aim to improve diversity by either re-ranking based on multiple objectives or candidate selection are based on a principle similar to MMR [3,4,23]. An advantage of post-processing approaches is that they are independent of the algorithm used to generate the recommendation list.

Algorithmic techniques adapt the algorithm used to generate the recommendations to improve diversity. For example, Hurley and Wasilewski proposed using regularization techniques in matrix factorization-based CF algorithms to optimize diversity in CF RSs [21]. Liu et al., propose a random-walk-based CF algorithm that enhances the opinions of small-degree users in a user-user similarity graph [17]. An advantage of algorithmic techniques is that diversification is inherent to the recommendation generation algorithm, increasing the solution space compared to post-processing algorithms. A disadvantage is that these techniques are typically designed for a specific architecture or model.

To our knowledge, existing approaches do not explicitly focus on improving diversity in recommender systems by making changes at the user profile generation stage(stage 1, Fig. 1. This paper focuses on this stage because if the user profile does not capture enough information about the users, it will be challenging for the system to generate a relevant yet diverse list at later stages [14].

4   VAE-GUP

In this section, we present the theory behind VAEs, the motivation for using VAEs to improve diversity in recommender systems, a step-by-step description of VAE-GUP: a method to improve diversity in RSs that leverages VAEs to generate multiple user profiles, and a formalization of the method.

4.1   Variational Autoencoders

VAEs are probabilistic generative models that aim to map an input vector x to a variational distribution with parameters mean μ and standard deviation σ.

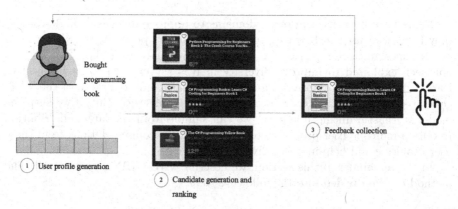

Fig. 1. Three stages of the recommendation process. 1. User profile generation using user features and past purchases, 2. Candidate item selection and ranking and 3. Feedback collection to further enrich the user profiles.

From this distribution, we can sample a latent vector z, rather than learning a mapping between x and z [12]. VAEs can be used to generate new data points by sampling the latent distribution. A generative model can be trained by maximizing Eq. 2, which is the likelihood of observing the input data through the model parameterized by θ.

$$\sum_{i=1}^{n} log\ P_{\theta}(x_i) \tag{2}$$

In most cases, $log\ P_{\theta}(x_i)$ is intractable, hence its lower bound is optimized [12] called *Variational lower bound (VLB)*. Expanding VLB will result in Eq. 3 [12]. VLB (VAE loss function) consists of two components - *Reconstruction loss* and *Kullback-Leibler (KL) divergence*. The first term in Eq. 3 is the reconstruction loss which is used to learn the model parameters to reconstruct the input. The second term aims to reduce the KL divergence between $Q_{\phi}(z|x)$ (latent distribution conditioned on the input) and $P(z)$, where $P(z)$ is a predefined tractable distribution like a Gaussian distribution. KL divergence serves as a regularizing factor that is designed to ensure that the latent distribution does not collapse to a point. The two components of the loss function must be balanced to reconstruct the input while generating a distribution to represent the input.

$$VLB = \mathbb{E}_{z \sim p(z|x)}\ log\ P_{\theta}(x,z) + \mathbb{E}_{z \sim p(z|x)}\ log\ \frac{P(z)}{Q_{\phi}(z|x)} \tag{3}$$

4.2   VAE-Based Generation of User Profiles

Recent work has proven theoretically that representing a user by multiple user profiles can represent their varied interests better than a single user profile [8]. Motivated by this finding, we propose to leverage VAEs to generate multiple user profiles that allow for a richer user representation.

VAEs have been used in other domains to improve diversity [10,20,22] and they have been used in RSs to give a state-of-the-art performance with respect to relevance measures [7,16], but the generative nature of these models has not been exploited to improve diversity in RSs as yet. VAEs can be used to learn a distribution to represent a user. Oftentimes, only the mean of the VAE-generated latent distribution is considered during inference. But, if we keep the model stochastic during inference, we can sample from the latent distribution to obtain multiple user profile vectors. Combining recommendations from these user profiles could help improve diversity in RSs.

In the remainder of this section, we describe VAE-GUP in more detail. The method can be divided into the following steps -

1. *Training*: train a VAE to generate a user profile distribution;
2. *Inference*: sample from the generated distribution to obtain multiple user profiles;
3. *Diverse item selection*: select recommendations generated by different user profiles based on diversity rank;
4. *Relevance Re-Ranking*: re-rank recommendations according to relevance.

Training. In the first step, we train a VAE that will be used to generate a user profile distribution. Formally, let I be an itemset associated with users $\forall u \in U$, which is divided into two itemsets I_1 and I_2 based on proportion p. A bag-of-words click matrices X_1 and $X_2 \in \mathbb{R}^{|U| \times |I|}$ are generated for a sample of users $u \in U$ using I_1 and I_2 respectively. I_1 will be used as the input and I_2 will be compared with the output of the VAE. X_1 is passed through the encoder network E to output two vectors μ and σ which parameterize the Gaussian user profile space. μ and σ are used to generate a user profile vector V_1. V_1 is passed through the decoder network D to generate the output $O \in \mathbb{R}^{|U| \times |I|}$. O, I_2, μ, and σ are used to calculate the loss value. The loss value is propagated backward using the reparametrization trick [12] to learn the optimal values for μ and σ and the network parameters. After E and D have converged, we can generate an optimal user profile distribution for all users.

Inference. During inference, we sample from the generated distribution to obtain multiple user profiles for each user. Each user profile produces a set of recommended items. Each user profile generated by the VAE should have slight differences such that the corresponding recommendation lists are not identical. Formally, we keep the network stochastic and sample n user profiles $P = \{P_1, P_2...P_n\}$ for each user. $\forall P_x \in P$ are passed through the decoder network D to generate n recommendation lists of size k, $R = \{R_1, R_2...R_n\}$.

Diverse Item Selection. We now combine the recommendations generated by different user profiles using a ranking based on diversity. This step ensures that we maximally exploit the recommendations generated through the different user profiles to improve diversity and can best be illustrated with an example. Imagine a user purchased a diaper. One user profile is most related to baby products and generates a list with items like milk powder and toys. In contrast, another user profile is most related to hygiene products like cleaning wipes. Combining these recommendations can ensure that the final recommendation list is more diverse compared to recommendations generated by a single, static user profile. We will give a diversity ranking to each item based on how different it is from all the other items on the list. We then select the items with the highest diversity rank. Formally, we generate a diversity ranking for all distinct items $i \in R$. We calculate the distance of each item from all the other items in the list and add it up. We then rank and select the top k items to generate $R_{diverse}$.

Relevance Re-Ranking. The combined list is ranked according to the relevance score. As users focus more on the items at the top, this step ensures the combined list will also have high relevance. That is, a relevance score is generated between I and the items in $R_{diverse}$ and $R_{diverse}$ is re-ranked by relevance to ensure that the final recommendation list is relevant as well as diverse.

We expect the recommendations generated by our method to be more diverse for a single list because we use multiple profiles which would better reflect the user's varied interests better and select items from these candidate lists based on diversity. The randomness in user profile generation ensures that recommendations are different over time. Finally, we expect the list to have higher aggregate diversity because our method should produce a personalized yet diverse list for each user.

5   Experiment to Evaluate the Method

In this experiment, we compare VAE-GUP to Vanilla autoencoder (AE) and β-VAE in terms of both relevance and diversity of the recommendations. We will use a benchmark dataset as well as a real-world dataset from Bol.com.

5.1   Experiment Details

Datasets

MovieLens-20M. MovieLens [9] is the most commonly used benchmark dataset in RSs. It contains 20 million records of user movie ratings collected from a movie recommendation service. The data has been filtered to remove movies rated less than five times and users who have rated less than five movies. The data was further divided into train, test, and validation sets (80-10-10). One-hot encoded vectors have been created for each user's item ratings to facilitate multinomial likelihood. We have also filtered out the ratings below 4/5 to reduce noise. The ranking was then binarized. This has resulted in a dataset with 138493 users and 26164 items, with a data sparsity of 0.541%.

Bol.com. We have taken a sample of a real-world dataset from Bol.com, which shows the categories (the most granular category level) users purchased items in a year. These were the users who were active on a given day. The same pre-processing steps, data split, and data pre-processing steps have been followed as the ML-20M dataset. This resulted in a dataset with 11547 categories, 6 million records, and 55 thousand users, with a data sparsity of 0.951%.

We use the MovieLens-20M dataset because the original authors of Multi-VAE [16], which VAE-GUP is based on, also used it for their experiments. This choice enabled us to start our experiments with confidence by first reproducing known results from the Multi-VAE paper. The motivation for VAE-GUP came from the need to improve diversity in Bol.com's recommender systems. Since the VAE-GUP proposal does not take advantage of any unique e-Commerce specific characteristics, the shift in domains should not change the principles behind VAE-GUP and the messages of the paper.

Setup. We used the β-VAE architecture as described [16]. In this study, we seek to find the sweet spot for each parameter that balances relevance and diversity. Table 1 reports the parameter values that have been chosen after tuning. The hyperparameters have been kept constant between the baselines and VAE-GUP to ensure a fair comparison. These hyperparameters were selected after evaluation over the following values -

1. Number of user-profiles: [1, 2, 3]
2. Latent vector size: [100, 200, 300]
3. Dropout Rate: [0.2, 0.5, 0.9]

The remaining hyperparameter values were the same as described in [16].

Table 1. Hyperparameter values

Hyperparameters	Values
Dropout	0.5
Batch Size	500
Number of user profiles	2
KL Divergence Weight	Monotonically increasing from 0 to 0.2
Latent Vector Size	200
Learning Rate	0.0001
Momentum	0.9

Baseline. We use a Vanilla-AE and a β-VAE of the same capacity as the baseline. Existing methods of improving diversity either focus on the candidate generation or the ranking stage or they do not explicitly focus on the user profile generation stage. Since we focus on the profile representation stage, we selected methods with existing representations as baselines. We chose to use a Vanilla-AE and $\beta-VAE$. A Vanilla-AE represents the user in the latent layer as a point estimate, while a β-VAE represents the user profile as a distribution, but only uses the mean of this distribution at inference time. Comparison with Vanilla-AE will help us understand if representing a user as a point estimate vs a distribution makes a difference. Comparison with β-VAE will help us understand the impact of keeping the model stochastic at inference time and combining several profiles sampled from the distribution to generate the recommendations.

Evaluation Methods. The relevance of recommendations was evaluated with *Normalized discounted cumulative gain* [11]. k is the size of the recommendation list and i is the item. DCG is used to calculate the weight for each item's relevance based on the position of the item in the recommendation list. NDCG is calculated by normalizing DCG by IDCG, which is the highest possible relevance that could be obtained with a particular recommendation list.

$$DCG@K = \sum_{i=1}^{k} \frac{rel_i}{log_2(i+1)} \tag{4}$$

The main strength of NDCG is that it utilizes also the order of recommended items and rewards relevant recommendations that occur early in the list. ILD, TILD, and AD were used to assess the recommendation lists on user and item-level diversity, as motivated in Sect. 2. For evaluating the method on NDCG, ILD, and AD, we generated a recommendation from the baseline methods and VAE-GUP and compared the metric value. Since TILD is measured across sessions, we generated two recommendations for each user at inference time (one for each session) from both the baselines and the VAE-GUP method and calculated the temporal diversity between the recommendations.

5.2   Results

Tables 2 and 3 report the results obtained from the experiment for MovieLens and Bol.com datasets for recommendation lists of sizes 5, 10, and 20. We have combined recommendations from the two user profiles sampled from the distribution generated by the VAE. We have only reported the % change for the Bol.com dataset to maintain confidentiality. The source code to reproduce the experimental results is available on GitHub[1]. Our method improved the diversity for the MovieLens datasets in all three dimensions over both the baselines. This came at a cost of [25.15% (Vanilla-AE), 13.13% (β-VAE)] decrease in relevance for a list of size 5. For the Bol.com dataset, our method showed improvement in all diversity measures over Vanilla-AE. It improved individual diversity (ILD, TILD) but suffered a small decrease in AD over β-VAE. This came at a cost of [5% (Vanilla-AE), 14.769% (β-VAE)] decrease in relevance for a list of size 5.

---

[1] https://github.com/sborar/vae_gup.

Table 2. The mean and standard deviation of the NDCG, ILD, TILD, and AD for the MovieLens data set for the baselines and proposed method. The standard deviation of NDCG, ILD, and TILD has been calculated at a user level. The standard deviation of AD has been calculated at a session level.

Metrics	Vanilla-AE	β-VAE	VAE-GUP
NDCG@5	0.456 ± 0.0032	0.392 ± 0.0030	0.3413 ± 0.0028
NDCG@10	0.4322 ± 0.0027	0.3826 ± 0.0026	0.3303 ± 0.0025
NDCG@20	0.3917 ± 0.0021	0.3896 ± 0.0024	0.3039 ± 0.0023
ILD@5	0.1622 ± 0.0006	0.1713 ± 0.0006	0.2134 ± 0.0008
ILD@10	0.1698 ± 0.0006	0.1767 ± 0.0005	0.2140 ± 0.0006
ILD@20	0.1789 ± 0.0004	0.1844 ± 0.0005	0.2180 ± 0.0006
TILD@5	0.1297 ± 0.0005	0.1279 ± 0.0005	0.1914 ± 0.0006
TILD@10	0.1529 ± 0.0005	0.153 ± 0.0005	0.2021 ± 0.0005
TILD@20	0.1701 ± 0.0004	0.1717 ± 0.0005	0.2114 ± 0.0005
AD@5	0.1076 ± 0.0000	0.1481 ± 0.0000	0.1599 ± 0.0004
AD@10	0.1367 ± 0.0000	0.18 ± 0.0000	0.1973 ± 0.0009
AD@20	0.1707 ± 0.0000	0.2199 ± 0.0000	0.2367 ± 0.0006

Table 3. The % difference between baselines and VAE-GUP for the Bol.com dataset

Metrics	Vanilla-AE	β-VAE
NDCG@5	−5.00%	−14.769%
NDCG@10	−2.79%	−12.456%
NDCG@20	−5.11%	−26.825%
ILD@5	9.41%	9.814%
ILD@10	9.07%	9.673%
ILD@20	9.22%	9.583%
TILD@5	18.99%	36.163%
TILD@10	13.33%	21.239%
TILD@20	11.17%	14.978%
AD@5	33.09%	−2.516%
AD@10	29.71%	−5.340%
AD@20	20.20%	−8.649%

Improvements over individual (ILD, TILD) and aggregate (AD) measures of diversity indicate that the recommendations are niche yet diverse for each user. While improvements over individual diversity at the cost of aggregate diversity suggest that recommendations are diverse but not necessarily niche. This can be explained with an example. If we suggest user 1 and user 2 - [popular phone, popular ice cream], this list might be individually diverse for most users, but it would result in a smaller AD since similar popular items are being suggested to each user. If we recommend user 1 - [phone, ice cream], and user 2 - [shoes, batteries], this list is not only diverse for each individual but also includes more niche products hence improving item coverage. VAE-GUP combines recommendations from different profiles by focusing on ILD, which causes the final list to favor individual user diversity over item diversity in some cases.

Table 4 reports VAE-GUP performance for [1,2,3] user profiles for a list of size 10 for the MovieLens dataset. We can see that NDCG reduces with an increase in the number of vectors and diversity increases. As we use more profile samples, we explore more items in the vicinity of the user preferences. These items could be relevant to the user, but might not be captured by NDCG as this metric does not take similar products into account when measuring relevance. We can also observe the rise in diversity plateaus with the increased number of vectors. This could be the result of repetitive recommendations provided by different vectors. It might be more feasible to choose fewer vectors to generate recommendations to ensure scalability and efficiency.

Table 4. Sensitivity of VAE-GUP towards number of user-profiles sampled: MovieLens dataset

Number of user-profiles	NDCG	ILD	TILD	AD
1	0.3826	0.1766	0.17001	0.1815
2	0.3303	0.214	0.20214	0.1984
3	0.3051	0.2302	0.21672	0.2036

5.3   Examples of Recommendations: Bol.com

A particular Bol.com user has purchased items from categories like 'pets', 'lamps', 'measuring equipment', 'health', and 'leisure hobbies'. Table 5 shows the categories that were recommended to this user by using a single user profile generated through a baseline (Vanilla-AE), and through the VAE-GUP method which combines results from two user profiles. We can observe that VAE-GUP captures the 'measuring equipment' category which the user has shown interest in, which was missed in the latter.

Table 5. Example of recommendations suggested to a single Bol.com user by Vanilla-AE and VAE-GUP

VAE-GUP Profile 1	VAE-GUP Profile 2	VAE-GUP combined	Vanilla-AE
Books	Books	Books	Books
Living	Cat toys	Living	Living
Electronics	Living	Electronics	Dogs
Literature novels	Dogs	Dogs	Feeding bowls
Dogs	Biology	Biology	Electronics
Blood sugar meters	Feeding bowls	Blood sugar meters	Feeding bowls
Kitchen Appliances	Cat gifts	Kitchen Appliances	Smart lighting
Personal Care	Drinking troughs	Drinking troughs	Medicine nursing
Projector Lamps	Animals	Animals	Toys
Health body	Smart lighting	Health Body	Cookbooks

6 Conclusion

In this work, we have set out to improve the diversity of recommendations in large-scale eCommerce systems. The main contribution of this work is VAE-GUP: a method that leverages the generative nature of VAEs to sample multiple user profiles and combines the recommendations to generate a diverse recommendation list and TILD: a metric to evaluate temporal diversity representationally. The VAE-GUP approach is conceptually simple and easy to implement. Our empirical analysis has shown that VAE-GUP substantially improves diversity across several dimensions while maintaining competitive relevance for a real-world dataset.

Even a slight increase in aggregate diversity can snowball, leading to richer user profiles and more opportunities for vendors and users looking for niche content [2]. As the decrease in relevance is small, exposure to more categories is expected to improve user experience as per existing studies [13] and mitigate feedback loops created by recommending only popular items. Future work is needed to validate the impact of implementing this change on user satisfaction, popularity bias, and vendor representation. In particular, we envision disaggregated analyses to assess how different user and vendor subgroups are affected by the system. We believe that increasing the diversity of recommendations will expose users to new interests and mitigate the dominance of a few products or vendors on e-commerce platforms. As increasing diversity is likely to lead to higher user satisfaction, this strengthens the position of the platform owner. At the same time, however, more diverse recommendations can benefit (small) vendors of more niche products. As such, we believe that our goal of increasing diversity in this context will be beneficial for all.

A   Appendix: Diversity Metric Comparison

Table 6 provides a comparison of all the diversity measures described in this paper.

k is the size of the recommendation list, U is the total number of users, and I is the total number of items. S is the set of items in the top K recommendations. $I_K(\{v_j\}_j^n = 1)$ is the space of all the subsets of I of size k.

Table 6. Comparison of different diversity measures

Metric	Explanation	Formula	Time Complexity
ILD	Dissimilarity between all item pairs in a recommendation list	$\frac{2}{|L|(|L|-1)} \sum_{i,j \in L} dist(i,j)$	$\mathcal{O}(k^2 \times |U|)$
Temporal Diversity	Proportion of different items recommended over time wrt to the list size	$\lvert \frac{L2/L1}{k} \rvert$	$\mathcal{O}(k \times |U|)$
Aggregate Diversity	Total items recommended to all users	$\lvert \bigcup_{u \in U} L(u) \rvert$	$\mathcal{O}(|I|)$
Joint Accessibility	For any item set of size k, it can be recommended to at least one user	$\forall S \in I_K(\{v_j\}_j^n = 1) = 1 \, if \, \exists u \in U,$ S is recommended	$\mathcal{O}(2^k \times |U|)$

References

1. Adomavicius, G., Kwon, Y.: Improving aggregate recommendation diversity using ranking-based techniques. IEEE Trans. Knowl. Data Eng. **24**(5), 896–911 (2012). https://doi.org/10.1109/TKDE.2011.15
2. Anderson, C.: The long tail (2004). https://www.wired.com/2004/10/tail/
3. Aytekin, T., Karakaya, M.Ö.: Clustering-based diversity improvement in top-n recommendation. J. Intell. Inf. Syst. **42**(1), 1–18 (2014)
4. Bradley, K., Smyth, B.: Improving recommendation diversity (2001)
5. Carbonell, J., Goldstein, J.: The use of MMR, diversity-based reranking for reordering documents and producing summaries. In: Proceedings of the 21st Annual International ACM SIGIR Conference on Research and Development in Information Retrieval, pp. 335–336. SIGIR 1998, Association for Computing Machinery, New York, NY, USA (1998). https://doi.org/10.1145/290941.291025. https://doi-org.libproxy.aalto.fi/10.1145/290941.291025
6. Chaney, A.J.B., Stewart, B.M., Engelhardt, B.E.: How algorithmic confounding in recommendation systems increases homogeneity and decreases utility. In: Proceedings of the 12th ACM Conference on Recommender Systems. ACM (2018). https://doi.org/10.1145/3240323.3240370

7. Dacrema, M.F., Cremonesi, P., Jannach, D.: Are we really making much progress? a worrying analysis of recent neural recommendation approaches. In: Proceedings of the 13th ACM Conference on Recommender Systems. ACM (2019). https://doi. org/10.1145/3298689.3347058
8. Guo, W., Krauth, K., Jordan, M.I., Garg, N.: The stereotyping problem in collaboratively filtered recommender systems (2021)
9. Harper, F.M., Konstan, J.A.: The MovieLens datasets: History and context. ACM Trans. Interact. Intell. Syst. **5**(4), 2827872 (2015). https://doi.org/10.1145/ 2827872
10. Jain, U., Zhang, Z., Schwing, A.G.: Creativity: generating diverse questions using variational autoencoders. In: Proceedings of the IEEE Conference on Computer Vision and Pattern Recognition (CVPR) (2017)
11. Järvelin, K., Kekäläinen, J.: Cumulated gain-based evaluation of IR techniques. ACM Trans. Inf. Syst.(TOIS) **20**(4), 422–446 (2002)
12. Kingma, D.P., Welling, M.: An introduction to variational autoencoders. Found. Trends® Mach. Learn. **12**(4), 307–392 (2019). https://doi.org/10.1561/ 2200000056
13. Knijnenburg, B.P., Willemsen, M.C., Gantner, Z., Soncu, H., Newell, C.: Explaining the user experience of recommender systems. User Model. User-Adap. Inter. **22**(4), 441–504 (2012)
14. Kunaver, M., Požrl, T.: Diversity in recommender systems-a survey. Knowl.-Based Syst. **123**, 154–162 (2017)
15. Lathia, N., Hailes, S., Capra, L., Amatriain, X.: Temporal diversity in recommender systems. In: Proceedings of the 33rd International ACM SIGIR Conference on Research and Development in Information Retrieval, pp. 210–217. SIGIR 2010, Association for Computing Machinery, New York, NY, USA (2010). https://doi. org/10.1145/1835449.1835486
16. Liang, D., Krishnan, R.G., Hoffman, M.D., Jebara, T.: Variational autoencoders for collaborative filtering (2018)
17. Liu, J.G., Shi, K., Guo, Q.: Solving the accuracy-diversity dilemma via directed random walks. Phys. Rev. E **85**(1), 016118 (2012). https://doi.org/10.1103/ physreve.85.016118
18. Mansoury, M., Abdollahpouri, H., Pechenizkiy, M., Mobasher, B., Burke, R.: Feedback loop and bias amplification in recommender systems. In: Proceedings of the 29th ACM International Conference on Information & Knowledge Management, pp. 2145–2148. CIKM 2020, Association for Computing Machinery, New York, NY, USA (2020). https://doi.org/10.1145/3340531.3412152. https://doi-org.libproxy. aalto.fi/10.1145/3340531.3412152
19. Reimers, N., Gurevych, I.: Sentence-BERT: sentence embeddings using Siamese BERT-networks. In: Proceedings of the 2019 Conference on Empirical Methods in Natural Language Processing. Association for Computational Linguistics (2019). http://arxiv.org/abs/1908.10084
20. Wang, L., Schwing, A., Lazebnik, S.: Diverse and accurate image description using a variational auto-encoder with an additive gaussian encoding space. In: Guyon, I., Luxburg, U.V., Bengio, S., Wallach, H., Fergus, R., Vishwanathan, S., Garnett, R. (eds.) Advances in Neural Information Processing Systems, vol. 30. Curran Associates, Inc. (2017). https://proceedings.neurips.cc/paper/2017/file/ 4b21cf96d4cf612f239a6c322b10c8fe-Paper.pdf
21. Wasilewski, J., Hurley, N.: Incorporating diversity in a learning to rank recommender system. In: the Twenty-ninth International Flairs Conference (2016)

22. Zhang, Y., Wang, Y., Zhang, L., Zhang, Z., Gai, K.: Improve diverse text generation by self labeling conditional variational auto encoder. In: ICASSP 2019–2019 IEEE International Conference on Acoustics, Speech and Signal Processing (ICASSP), pp. 2767–2771 (2019). https://doi.org/10.1109/ICASSP.2019.8683090
23. Ziegler, C.N., McNee, S.M., Konstan, J.A., Lausen, G.: Improving recommendation lists through topic diversification. In: Proceedings of the 14th International Conference on World Wide Web, pp. 22–32. WWW 2005, Association for Computing Machinery, New York, NY, USA (2005). https://doi.org/10.1145/1060745.1060754

Addressing Biases in the Texts Using an End-to-End Pipeline Approach

Shaina Raza[1]([envelope]), Syed Raza Bashir[2], Sneha[2], and Urooj Qamar[3]

[1] University of Toronto, Toronto, ON, Canada
shaina.raza@utoronto.ca
[2] Toronto Metropolitan University, Toronto, ON, Canada
{syedraza.bashir,fnu.sneha}@torontomu.ca
[3] Institute of Business and Information Technology, University of the Punjab, Lahore, Pakistan
uroojqamar@ibitpu.edu.pk

Abstract. The concept of fairness is gaining popularity in academia and industry. Social media is especially vulnerable to media biases and toxic language and comments. We propose a fair ML pipeline that takes a text as input and determines whether it contains biases and toxic content. Then, based on pre-trained word embeddings, it suggests a set of new words by substituting the biased words, the idea is to lessen the effects of those biases by replacing them with alternative words. We compare our approach to existing fairness models to determine its effectiveness. The results show that our proposed pipeline can detect, identify, and mitigate biases in social media data.

Keywords: Bias · Fairness · Transformer-model · Pipeline · Machine learning

1 Introduction

Social media platforms allow users to interact with one another in a variety of ways, such as messaging, photo and video sharing apps and even allow users to leave comments and communicate with one another. This functionality is vulnerable to several internet crimes, including personal insults and threats, propaganda, fraud, and the advertisement of illegal goods and services. It is critical to identify and eliminate these toxic comments from social media that reflect biases.

The Conversation AI team, a joint venture between Jigsaw and Google develops technology to protect human voices during a conversation [1]. They are particularly interested in developing machine learning (ML) models that can detect toxicity in online conversations, with toxicity defined as anything biased, rude, disrespectful, offensive, or otherwise likely to cause someone to leave a discussion. This initiative has generated a substantial number of published words and competitions [2, 3].

In this paper, we propose a novel ML pipeline that ingests data and identifies toxic words early in the pre-processing stage; the identified words are then replaced with substitute words that retain the lexical meaning of the word but reduce or eliminate its effect. The main contribution of this work is to identify and mitigate biases during

© The Author(s), under exclusive license to Springer Nature Switzerland AG 2023
L. Boratto et al. (Eds.): BIAS 2023, CCIS 1840, pp. 100–107, 2023.
https://doi.org/10.1007/978-3-031-37249-0_8

the pre-processing stage and avoid these biases replicate in the ML predictions. In this work, the term bias refers to any behavior, attitude, or expression that negatively affects a specific identity group, including actions that are hurtful, disrespectful, or disruptive. This definition is consistent with the bias definitions found in relevant literature [4–7]. The specific contribution of this work is as:

- We propose a fair ML pipeline that takes any data and detects if the biases exist, if existing then it mitigate those biases.
- We annotate the dataset with bias-bearing words, which are generally biased words used in toxic contexts to refer to specific identities (race, ethnicity, religion, gender), and are taken from various literature sources [8, 9], and [10].
- We test each pipeline component individually to determine the method effectiveness, and we also quantify fairness (i.e., non-biased words in this context, for each sub-group based on identities- race, gender etc.).

2 Related Work

Fairness [11] is a multi-faceted concept that vary by culture and context. Bias mitigation or fairness methods are categorized into three broad types: (1) pre-processing; (2) in-processing; and (3) post-processing algorithms. The pre-processing algorithms [12] attempt to learn a new representation of data by removing the biases prior to algorithm training. In-processing algorithms influences the loss function during the model training to mitigate biases [13]. Post-processing algorithms [14] manipulate output predictions after training to reduce bias.

Several models have been proposed to address the issue of bias in ML algorithms and data. For example Fairness GAN [15] is a Generative Adversarial Network that learns to generate synthetic data samples to ensure demographic parity. Aequitas [16] is a toolkit for assessing and mitigating bias in predictive models. Themis-ML [17] is a library for creating fair ML models that utilizes algorithms for fairness-aware classification, regression, and clustering. Fairlearn [18] is another library for ML fairness built on top of the popular scikit-learn library. It provides metrics and algorithms for fairness evaluation and mitigation. Google's What-If Tool [19] is a visual interface for exploring ML models. It allows users to see the impact of changes to inputs and models on predictions and fairness metrics. AI Fairness 360 [20] is an open-source software toolkit that contains a comprehensive set of metrics, algorithms, and tutorials for detecting and mitigating bias in ML models. Other models such as Counterfactual Fairness [21], and Disentangled Representation Learning [22], also tackle the problem of bias mitigation in ML. It is important to note that while these models have shown promise in reducing bias, more research is needed to ensure the generalizability and effectiveness of these techniques. Each of the previous works is valuable and incremental, focusing on task fairness (pre/in/post-processing). Unlike previous works, we detect and mitigate many biases from text, and we build a pipeline to achieve fairness.

3 Proposed Methodology

We develop a fair ML pipeline (Fig. 1) that accepts raw text, detects if the text is biased or not (detection task), then identifies the bias-bearing words in the text (recognition task), and finally substitutes those words with alternative words (mitigation task). We explain each phase next.

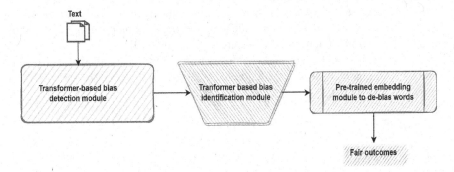

Fig. 1. Fair ML pipeline

Bias Detection: The problem of bias detection involves identifying whether a given document, such as a news article or social media post, contains any biased language or perspectives. To address this problem, we have treated it as a multi-label classification task. Specifically, we have used a Transformer-based model called ELECTRA [23] and fine-tune the model for bias detection. We have used the labelled data provided by the Jigsaw Toxic Comment Classification [1] competition. This competition involved identifying whether comments on online forums were toxic or not. The dataset is also used in the competition to identify different types of language biases [1, 2]. By fine-tuning the ELECTRA model on this labeled data, we are able to adapt it to the specific task of bias detection. The output of the detection model is a sentence or text that has been labeled with one or more bias labels. These labels can indicate various types of biases, such as political bias, gender bias, or racial bias.

Bias Identification: The second step in the pipeline involves a module designed to identify biases within the dataset, which we refer to as the bias identification module. To create this module, we compiled a comprehensive list of biases that includes gender, race, religion, mental health, and disability. We also incorporated biases from sources such as [8, 24]; [9]; and [10] to ensure that our list is comprehensive and up-to-date. Using this list of biases, we tag each comment in the dataset with relevant biases. Once the comments are tagged, we fine-tune the BERT model for named entity recognition (NER) to identify the biased words within the text. This fine-tuned model is then used to identify instances of bias in the comments, allowing us to analyze the extent and nature of biases present in the dataset.

In the bias identification task, certain categories of bias may be more easily or hardly detected depending on the nature of the biases and the dataset being analyzed. For example, some biases may be more explicit, while others may be more subtle or implicit. Similarly, some biases may be more prevalent in certain types of texts or domains, such as gender bias in job postings or racial bias in news articles. Based on our initial assessment of the data, we find that we are able to cover a range of topics, including online toxicity, hate speech, and misinformation.

Bias Mitigation: After identifying the biased words in the text, our next step is to mitigate these biases by recommending alternative words that can be used in place of the biased words. We typically recommend between 5 to 10 substitute words per biased word, based on their similarity and appropriateness in the context of the text.

To generate these substitute words, we utilize publicly available pre-trained word embeddings, specifically Word2Vec [25], which operates in a 300-dimensional space. BERT can also be used to understand the contextual meaning of words and phrases in text data, and to fill in for the words as the substitute task. However, BERT can be computationally expensive and may require extensive training data to perform well. So we choose to work the Word2Vec in this paper.

Our method for identifying appropriate substitute words is based on semantic similarity and word analogy benchmarks [26]. By using this method, we aim to preserve the semantic information present in word embeddings while removing any biases that may be present in the text. The idea behind using Word2Vec here is to offer suitable substitutes that can help ensure a more equitable and inclusive representation of the target groups through words/phrases.

4 Experimental Setup

In this work, we use Google's Jigsaw Multilingual Toxic Comment Classification [1] dataset. It includes 223,549 annotated user comments collected from Wikipedia talk pages. These comments were annotated by human raters with six labels 'toxic', 'severe toxic, 'insult', 'threat', 'obscene', and 'identity hate'.

We use the F1-score (F1) for the accuracy, and a bias metric ROC-AUC (b-AUC) [2] to evaluate fairness. This bias metric combines several sub-metrics to balance overall performance. We also use the disparate impact ratio [27] to quantify fairness.

For our experiments, we utilized a standard set of hyperparameters to train our models, including a batch size of 16, a sequence length of 512, and 6 labels for the classification task. We trained the models for 10 epochs and optmize the learning rate in the range of 0.0001–0.001, the dropout rate in the range of 0.1–0.5, and the weight decay in the range of 0.0001–0.001. Our experiments were conducted on an NVIDIA P100 GPU with 32 GB RAM, and we implemented our models using TensorFlow. We fine-tuned our models using pre-trained weights from Huggingface.co. These settings ensured that our models were optimized for performance and accuracy.

5 Results

Evaluation of Bias Detection Task: We evaluate our multi-label classifier with baseline methods: Logistic Regression with TFIDF (LG-TFIDF), LG with ELMO [28], BERT-base and DistillBERT.

Table 1. Performance of bias detection task. Bold means best performance.

Model	b-AUC	F1
LG-TFIDF	0.547	0.585
LG- ELMO	0.684	0.625
BERT-base	0.692	0.687
DistilBERT	0.742	0.753
Our model	**0.837**	**0.812**

We observe in Table 1 that LG-TFIDF model has the lowest performance, achieving a b-AUC score of 0.547 and an F1-score of 0.585. The LG-ELMO model has an improved b-AUC score of 0.684 and F1 score of 0.625. The BERT-base model achieves a higher b-AUC score of 0.692, but its F1 score is comparatively lower at 0.687. Distilbert model achieves the b-AUC score of 0.742 and the F1 score of 0.753. Our model outperforms all other models, achieving the highest b-AUC score of 0.837 and the highest F1 score of 0.812. The significant improvement in the performance of our model suggests that it is effective in detecting bias in text data.

Effectiveness of Bias Identification Task: We compare different configurations of NER: Spacy core web small (core-sm), core web medium (core-md), and core web large (core-lg) methods (that are based on RoBERTa [29]) against our NER.

Table 2. Performance of bias recognition task

Model	AUC	F1
Core-sm	0.427	0.432
Core-md	0.532	0.524
Core-lg	0.643	0.637
Our model	**0.832**	**0.828**

Based on the performance metrics reported in Table 2, it is clear that our model outperformed the three baseline models (Core-sm, Core-md, Core-lg) by a significant margin in both AUC and F1 score. Our model achieved an AUC of 0.832 and F1 score of 0.828, while the best-performing baseline (Core-lg) achieved an AUC of 0.643 and F1 score of 0.637. This indicates that our model is fine-tuned properly on the biased labels and is more effective in recognizing bias in the dataset than the baseline models. It is also worth noting that the performance of the baseline models improved as the model size increased, with Core-lg performing better than Core-md and Core-sm. This also suggests that the size of the model can have a significant impact on its performance.

Overall Performance Comparison: To evaluate the pipeline as a whole, we use the adversarial debiasing (AD) [13] and meta-fair (MF) classifier [30] methods as the baselines. AD is a fairness method that addresses fairness during the data pre-processing time and MF is an in-processing method that addressed biases during the optimization phase.

In this experiment, we provide the labeled data to each method. First, we use our detection module to find if a text is biased or not, and then use each method's debiasing technique to introduce fairness in the data. The new data that is produced in the transformed data. These methods calculate fairness based on the ratio of fair outcomes (non-biased words) for each sub-group (e.g., gender, and identities). For example, these methods see how many biased or unbiased words are associated with each identity group, and then remove the biases for the subgroup that is more prone to negative outcomes.

We consider the sub-groups based on gender and race as the use cases. For gender, we consider the privileged class to be "male," while the unprivileged class is "female". For race, we consider "Asians" and "American-Africans" to be unprivileged, and "white" to be privileged. These groups are chosen based on an initial analysis of the data. We use the disparate impact ratio evaluation metric to quantify fairness. A good range of DI ratio is between 0.8 and 1.25 [27] with scores lower than 0.8 showing favorable outcomes for privileged sub-group and values above 1.25 favoring the unprivileged class. The results are shown in Fig. 2.

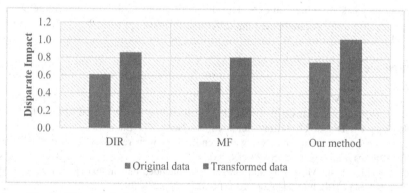

Fig. 2. Disparate impact scores to quantify fairness using different methods.

The results in Fig. 2 show that the DI score in the original data is lower than 0.8, which means biased outcomes toward unprivileged identities. Before mitigation, the DI score is the same for all methods, since it is calculated based on original data. The DI score after fairness methods is above 0.8 for all methods. Our approach gives us a DI score close to 1, which shows that we achieve a balance between unprivileged and privileged groups. Other methods also get fairer on transformed data, but they seem to skewed toward privileged groups (score close to 0.8).

6 Discussion

The main implications of the proposed model are in applications where bias in textual data can have significant real-world impacts, such as in hiring and admissions decisions, financial lending, and predictive policing. Prior work [13, 15–21, 31, 32] in this area has also explored various techniques for detecting and mitigating text biases. However, the proposed method has the advantage of being a scalable and easy-to-implement solution that does not require additional annotation or training data. There are some limitations of this study, which are also suggestions for future work. First, the current work assumes that the biased words can be easily identified and replaced with alternative words, which may not always be the case. We need to consider the epistemology and tone in the biased language as well. The method also relies on pre-trained embeddings, which may contain biases and affect the quality of the mitigation. Further, the effectiveness of the method may vary across different domains and languages, which needs to be further investigated.

7 Conclusion

The proposed fair ML pipeline for detecting and mitigating text biases is an important step towards developing more equitable and just AI models. However, there is still much to learn about applying and interpreting fairness in our study. We plan to further evaluate the pipeline using other evaluation metrics and extend it to other domains such as health and life sciences. The bias mitigation task will also be evaluated to enhance the effectiveness of the pipeline. Additionally, we will explore other datasets to see how the pipeline works in other contexts. Through continuous evaluation and refinement, we aim to develop more sophisticated and effective fairness approach.

References

1. AI, J.: Jigsaw Multilingual Toxic Comment Classification (2022). https://www.kaggle.com/c/jigsaw-multilingual-toxic-comment-classification/overview. Accessed 03 Feb 2022
2. Borkan, D., Dixon, L., Jeffrey Sorensen, J., Thain, N., Lucy Vasserman, J., Sorensen, J.: Nuanced metrics for measuring unintended bias with real data for text classification (2019)https://doi.org/10.1145/3308560.3317593
3. Dixon, J.L., et al.: Measuring and mitigating unintended bias in text classification. Ethics, Soc. 67–73 (2018). https://doi.org/10.1145/3278721.3278729
4. Nielsen, A.: Practical Fairness. O'Reilly Media (2020)
5. Google developers: machine learning glossary|Google developers (2018). https://developers.google.com/machine-learning/glossary#m%0A https://developers.google.com/machine-learning/glossary/#t
6. Wang, Y., Ma, W., Zhang, M., Liu, Y., Ma, S.: A survey on the fairness of recommender systems. ACM Trans. Inf. Syst. (2022)https://doi.org/10.1145/3547333
7. Mastrine, J.: Types of Media Bias and How to Spot It AllSides (2018). https://www.allsides.com/media-bias/how-to-spot-types-of-media-bias
8. Matfield, K.: Gender decoder: find subtle bias in job ads (2016). http://gender-decoder.katmatfield.com
9. Service-Growth: Examples of gender-sensitive language (2003)

10. Barbour, H.: 25 Examples of Biased Language|Ongig Blog (2022). https://blog.ongig.com/diversity-and-inclusion/biased-language-examples. Accessed 03 Feb 2022

11. Narayanan, A.: Fairness Definitions and Their Politics. In: Tutorial Presented at the Conference on Fairness, Accountability, and Transparency (2018)

12. Kamiran, F., Calders, T.: Data preprocessing techniques for classification without discrimination (2012)https://doi.org/10.1007/s10115-011-0463-8

13. Zhang, B.H., Lemoine, B., Mitchell, M.: Mitigating unwanted biases with adversarial learning. In: Proceedings of the 2018 AAAI/ACM Conference on AI, Ethics, and Society, pp. 335–340 (2018)

14. Pleiss, G., Raghavan, M., Wu, F., Kleinberg, J., Weinberger, K.Q.: On fairness and calibration. arXiv Prepr. arXiv:1709.02012 (2017)

15. Sattigeri, P., Hoffman, S.C., Chenthamarakshan, V., Varshney, K.R.: Fairness GAN: generating datasets with fairness properties using a generative adversarial network. IBM J. Res. Dev. **63**, 1–3 (2019)

16. Saleiro, P., et al.: Aequitas: A bias and fairness audit toolkit. arXiv Prepr. arXiv:1811.05577 (2018)

17. Bantilan, N.: Themis-ml: a fairness-aware machine learning interface for end-to-end discrimination discovery and mitigation. J. Technol. Hum. Serv. **36**, 15–30 (2018)

18. Bird, S., et al.: A toolkit for assessing and improving fairness in AI

19. Using the what-if tool AI platform prediction Google Cloud

20. Bellamy, R.K.E., et al.: AI fairness 360: an extensible toolkit for detecting and mitigating algorithmic bias. IBM J. Res. Dev. 63 (2019). https://doi.org/10.1147/JRD.2019.2942287

21. Kusner, M.J., Loftus, J., Russell, C., Silva, R.: Counterfactual fairness. In: Advances Neural Information Processing System 30 (2017)

22. Locatello, F., Abbati, G., Rainforth, T., Bauer, S., Schölkopf, B., Bachem, O.: On the fairness of disentangled representations. In: Advances Neural Information Processing System 32 (2019)

23. Clark, K., Luong, M.-T., Le, Q.V, Manning, C.D.: Electra: pre-training text encoders as discriminators rather than generators. arXiv Prepr. arXiv:2003.10555 (2020)

24. Gaucher, D., Friesen, J., Kay, A.C.: Evidence that gendered wording in job advertisements exists and sustains gender inequality. J. Pers. Soc. Psychol. **101**, 109–128 (2011). https://doi.org/10.1037/a0022530

25. Goldberg, Y., Levy, O.: word2vec explained: deriving Mikolov et al.'s negative-sampling word-embedding method. arXiv Prepr. arXiv:1402.3722 (2014)

26. Kaneko, M., Bollegala, D.: Dictionary-based debiasing of pre-trained word embeddings, pp. 212–223 (2021)

27. MacCarthy, M.: Standards of fairness for disparate impact assessment of big data algorithms. Cumb. L. Rev. **48**, 67 (2017)

28. AllenNLP: AllenNLP - ELMo—Allen Institute for AI (2022). https://allenai.org/allennlp/software/elmo

29. Liu, Y., et al.: Roberta: a robustly optimized bert pretraining approach. arXiv Prepr. arXiv:1907.11692 (2019)

30. Celis, L.E., Huang, L., Keswani, V., Vishnoi, N.K.: Classification with fairness constraints: a meta-algorithm with provable guarantees. In: Proceedings of the Conference on Fairness, Accountability, and Transparency, pp. 319–328 (2019)

31. Welcome to the Adversarial Robustness Toolbox—Adversarial Robustness Toolbox 1.10.3 documentation. https://adversarial-robustness-toolbox.readthedocs.io/en/latest/

32. Raza, S., Ding, C.: A regularized model to trade-off between accuracy and diversity in a news recommender system. In: 2020 IEEE International Conference on Big Data (Big Data), pp. 551–560 (2020)

Bootless Application of Greedy Re-ranking Algorithms in Fair Neural Team Formation

Hamed Loghmani and Hossein Fani(✉)

University of Windsor, Windsor, Canada
{ghasrlo,hfani}@uwindsor.ca

Abstract. Team formation aims to automate forming teams of experts who can successfully solve difficult tasks, which have firsthand effects on creating organizational performance. While existing neural team formation methods are able to efficiently analyze massive collections of experts to form effective collaborative teams, they largely ignore the fairness in recommended teams of experts. Fairness breeds innovation and increases teams' success by enabling a stronger sense of community, reducing conflict, and stimulating more creative thinking. In this paper, we study the application of state-of-the-art deterministic greedy re-ranking algorithms to mitigate the potential popularity bias in the neural team formation models based on *demographic parity*. Our experiments show that, first, neural team formation models are biased toward popular experts. Second, although deterministic re-ranking algorithms mitigate popularity bias substantially, they severely hurt the efficacy of teams. The code to reproduce the experiments reported in this paper is available at https://github.com/fani-lab/Adila/tree/bias23 (عادلة, a feminine Arabic given name meaning just and fair.)

1 Introduction

Algorithmic search for collaborative teams, also known as team formation, aims to automate forming teams of experts whose combined skills, applied in coordinated ways, can successfully solve complex tasks such as producing the next blockbuster *'thriller'* with a touch of *'sci-fi'* in the movie industry. Team formation can be seen as social information retrieval (Social IR) where the right group of talented people are searched and hired to solve the task at hand [1,2]. Successful teams have firsthand effects on creating organizational performance in the industry [3–5], academia [6–8], law [9,10], and the healthcare sector [11,12]. Forming a successful team whose members can effectively collaborate and deliver the outcomes within the constraints such as planned budget and timeline is challenging due to the immense number of candidates with various backgrounds, personality traits, and skills, as well as unknown synergistic balance among them; not *all* teams with the best experts are necessarily successful [13].

© The Author(s), under exclusive license to Springer Nature Switzerland AG 2023
L. Boratto et al. (Eds.): BIAS 2023, CCIS 1840, pp. 108–118, 2023.
https://doi.org/10.1007/978-3-031-37249-0_9

Historically, teams have been formed by relying on human experience and instinct, resulting in suboptimal team composition due to (1) an overwhelming number of candidates, and (2) hidden societal biases, among other reasons. To address the former, the earliest algorithmic methods of team formation were conceived in the *i*) Operations Research (OR) [14], where multiple objective functions must be optimized in a large search space of *all* possible combinations of skillful experts, given constraints for human and non-human factors as well as scheduling preferences. Such work, however, was premised on the mutually independent selection of experts and overlooked the organizational and collaborative ties among experts. Next, *ii*) social network analysis has been employed to fill the gap by the network representation of the experts with links that shows collaborations in the past [15–17]. They search for the optimum teams over *all* possible subnetworks, which is daunting. Recently, *iii*) a paradigm shift to machine learning has been observed, opening doors to the analysis of massive collections of experts coming from different fields. Machine learning approaches efficiently learn relationships between experts and their skills in the context of successful (positive samples) and unsuccessful teams (negative samples) from all past instances to excel at recommending teams of experts [18–20]. We can observe the commercial application of machine learning-based algorithmic search for an optimum team in online platforms like LinkedIn[1] to help the industry browse the enormous space of experts and form *almost surely* successful teams.

However, the primary focus of existing machine learning-based methods in team formation is the maximization of the success rate (utility) by tailoring the recommended experts for a team to the required skills only, largely ignoring the *fairness* in recommended experts. Indeed, it has been well-explored that machine learning methods that produce recommendations suffer from unfair biases. They result in discrimination and reduced visibility for an already disadvantaged group [21,22], disproportionate selection of popular candidates [23–25], and over/under-representation and racial/gender disparities [26] since they are trained on real-world datasets that already inherit hidden societal biases. On the other hand, social science research provides compelling evidence about the synergistic effects of diversity on team performance [27–29]; diversity breeds innovation and increases teams' success by enabling a stronger sense of community and support, reducing conflict, and stimulating more creative thinking.

Surprisingly, there is little to no fairness-aware algorithmic method that mitigates societal biases in team formation algorithms except that of the recent work by Barnabò et al. [30] that proves fair team formation is NP-complete; therefore, computationally prohibitive for practical use. Recent state-of-the-art neural team formation models have *weakly* attributed their performance gain to mitigating popularity bias inherent in the underlying real-world training data [19,20]. Rad et al. [20] employed uncertainty in learnable parameters by variational Bayesian neural model, and Dashti et al. [19] applied *virtually* negative samples from popular experts during the neural model learning procedure. However, they overlook substantiating the attribution by evidence using fairness metrics.

---

[1] business.linkedin.com/talent-solutions.

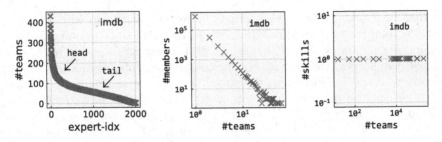

Fig. 1. Left: Long-tail distribution of casts and crews (experts) in movies (teams). Middle: Long-tail distribution in `log` scale. The figure reads y number of members have x number of teams. Right: uniform distribution of movies over genres (skills).

A purely diversity-centric design for team formation algorithms that solely overfit to satisfy diversity, neglecting the team's success, is also unfair to the organizations, e.g., a team of *non*popular individuals who cannot accomplish the tasks. In this paper, we propose to model team formation as a two-sided marketplace between two stakeholders: *i) experts* who hold skills, e.g., artists, and *ii) organizations* who recruit experts for their teams, e.g., entertainment industries. We investigate the trade-off between success rate (utility) and fairness in the recommended teams by neural team formation methods in terms of popularity bias, given the required skills. The choice of popularity bias in this study is motivated due to: (1) training sets in team formation suffer from popularity bias; that is, the majority of experts have scarcely participated in the (successful) teams (nonpopular experts), whereas few experts (popular ones) are in many teams [19,20]. Therefore, popular experts receive higher scores and are more frequently recommended by the machine learning model, leading to systematic discrimination against already disadvantaged nonpopular experts. Statistically, popularity bias can be observed as long tail distribution (power law). For instance, in `imdb`[2] dataset of movies, given a movie as a team of casts and crews such as actors and directors [16,31], from Fig. 1(left), we observe a long tail of many nonpopular experts, while few popular experts in the head that dominate. Figure 1(middle) shows the same observation in `log` scale based on y number of experts participating in x number of teams. (2) Moreover, experts' labels of being popular or otherwise can be calculated from datasets based on their position in the statistical distribution; that is, those in the *'tail'* are assumed to be nonpopular experts, while those in the *'head'* are the popular ones.

In this paper, we employ the framework by Geyik et al. [32] for quantifying and mitigating popularity bias in state-of-the-art neural team formation methods [19] in terms of normalized discounted cumulative KL-divergence (`ndkl`) for re-ranking experts in the recommended teams to achieve fairness based on the *demographic parity* (statistical parity) [33] depending on the distribution of teams over popular and nonpopular experts in the training datasets. Meanwhile, we measure the impact of the popularity bias mitigation on the success

---

[2] imdb.com/interfaces/.

rate (utility) of the recommended teams using information retrieval metrics, namely mean average precision (map) and normalized discounted cumulative gain (ndcg). Our early results on imdb using three re-ranking algorithms by Geyik et al. [32] demonstrate that (1) state-of-the-art Bayesian neural models fall short in producing fair teams of experts in terms of popularity, and (2) state-of-the-art deterministic re-ranking algorithms improve the fairness of neural team formation models but at the cost of a substantial decrease in accuracy of predicted teams in terms of success rate. Our findings encourage further development of fairness-aware re-ranking methods for the task of team formation.

2   Research Methodology

Ranking is the primary output interface of the neural team formation model for producing expert recommendations where all available experts are recommended for a given required subset of skills but with different scores, usually a probability value after a softmax layer, and the final recommended experts are selected among the top-k highest scores. This enables further post-processing refinements like re-ranking the list of recommended items to improve fairness in the recommended list. Therefore, our research includes two pipelined steps: *i*) training state-of-the-art neural team formation model to produce experts recommendations for given subsets of skills while measuring the accuracy and diversity of top-k experts as the optimum team, and *ii*) applying state-of-the-art re-ranking algorithms to reorder the top-k experts and to improve fairness while maintaining accuracy. For example, when two or more experts have been assigned the same probability score in the final ranked list by a model, a re-ranking algorithm can prioritize nonpopular experts over popular ones and reassign new higher scores.

We follow the *demographic parity* [33] notion of fairness; that is, for being a member of a team (a preferred label that benefits an expert), a neural team formation model should predict an expert's membership with equal odds based on the underlying training dataset for all popular and nonpopular experts. In other words, demographic parity measures whether the experts who should qualify for a team are equally *likely* regardless of their popularity status. For instance, given the percentage of popular experts to nonpopular ones is 10% to 90%, the neural model satisfies demographic parity for forming a team of k experts should the team include $k \times 10\%$ popular and $k \times 90\%$ nonpopular experts. It is noteworthy that a random baseline that assigns experts to teams from a uniform distribution of experts regardless of popularity labels is an *ideally* fair model yet at the cost of very low success rates for the predicted teams.

Intuitively, a few popular experts who participated in many training instances of teams reinforce a neural model to forget about the majority nonpopular experts for their scarce number of teams, leading to popularity bias. As a result, a new predicted team would only include experts from the minority popular experts ($k \times 100\%$), which is disproportionate compared to their population size (10%). In this paper, we aim to dampen the popularity bias by adjusting the distributions of popular and nonpopluar experts in the top-k recommended experts for a team according to their ratio in the training dataset via deterministic algorithms and study the impacts on the team's quality in terms of success rate; that is measuring the accuracy of top-k experts for teams whose all $k \times 100\%$ members are popular experts compared to teams with $k \times 10\%$ popular and $k \times 90\%$ nonpopular experts.

3 Experiments

In this section, we lay out the details of our experiments and findings toward answering the following research questions:

RQ1: Do state-of-the-art neural team formation models produce fair teams of experts in terms of popularity bias? To this end, we benchmark state-of-the-art Bayesian neural model with negative sampling heuristics [19] and measure the fairness scores of predicted teams.

RQ2: Do state-of-the-art deterministic greedy re-ranking algorithms improve the fairness of neural team formation models while maintaining their accuracy? To this end, we apply three deterministic greedy re-ranking algorithms on the neural model predictions and measure the diversity and utility scores afterwards.

3.1 Setup

Dataset. Our testbed includes `imdb` [16,31] dataset where each instance is a movie consisting of its cast and crew such as actors and director, as well as the movie's genres. We consider each movie as a team whose members are the cast and crew, and the movie's genres are the skills. The choice of `imdb` in team formation literature is not to be confused with its use cases in recommender systems or review analysis research; herein, the goal is to form a team of casts and crews for a movie production as opposed to a movie recommendation. As shown in Fig. 1, we can observe a long tail in the distributions of teams over experts; many casts and crews have participated in very few movies. However, the distribution with respect to the set of skills follows a more fair distribution. Specifically, `imdb` has a limited variety of skills (genres) which are, by and large, employed by many movies. We filter out singleton and sparse movies with less than 3 members as well as casts and crews who relatively participated in very few movies, as suggested by [20,34]. The latter also reduced the computational complexity of the neural models in their last layer where the size equals the number of experts. We ensured that the preprocessing step made no major change to the statistical distributions of the dataset. Table 1 reports additional point-wise statistics on the dataset before and after preprocessing.

Popularity Labels. We label an expert as popular if she participated in more than the average number of teams per expert over the whole dataset, and nonpopular otherwise. As seen in Table 1, this number is 62.45 and the popularity ratio (popular/nonpopular) is 0.426/0.574.

Table 1. Statistics of the raw and preprocessed `imdb` dataset.

	imdb	
	raw	preprocessed
#movies	507,034	32,059
#unique casts and crews	876,981	2,011
#unique genres	28	23
average #casts and crews per team	1.88	3.98
average #genres per team	1.54	1.76
average #movie per cast and crew	1.09	62.45
average #genre per cast and crew	1.59	10.85
#team w/ single cast and crew	322,918	0
#team w/ single genre	315,503	15,180

Baselines. Our neural team formation baselines include variational Bayesian neural network [20] with unigram negative sampling strategy in minibatches [19] (`bnn`) and Kullback-Leibler optimization. The model includes a single hidden layer of size d=100, `leaky relu` and `sigmoid` are the activation functions for the hidden and the output layers, respectively, and `Adam` is the optimizer. The input and output layers are sparse occurrence vector representations (one-hot encoded) of skills and experts of size $|\mathcal{S}|$ and $|\mathcal{E}|$, respectively. Moreover, we also used pre-trained dense vector representations for the input skill subsets (`-emb`). Adapted from paragraph vectors of Le and Mikolov [35], we consider each team as a document and the skills as the document's words. We used the distributed memory model to generate the real-valued embeddings of the subset of skills with a dimension of d=100. We evaluate baselines with and without the application of re-ranking methods (`before`, `after`). To have a minimum level of comparison, we also add a model that randomly assigns experts to a team (`random`). The re-ranking methods include the *i*) score maximizing greedy mitigation algorithm (`greedy`), *ii*) greedy conservative mitigation algorithm (`conservative`), and *iii*) the relaxed variant of greedy conservative algorithm (`relaxed`) [32].

Evaluation Strategy and Metrics. To demonstrate prediction effectiveness, we randomly select 15% of teams for the test set and perform 5-fold cross-validation on the remaining teams for model training and validation that results in one trained model per each fold. Let (s, e) a team of experts e for the required skills s from the test set, we compare the top-k ranked list of experts e', predicted by the model of each fold for the input skills s, with the observed subset of experts e and report the average performance of models on all folds in terms of utility metrics (the higher, the better) including mean average precision (`map`) and normalized discounted cumulative gain (`ndcg`) at top-{2,5,10}. Formally,

$$\text{ap}(k) : \frac{\sum_{i=1}^{k} \text{p}(i) \times \delta_e(i)}{|e \cap e'|} \tag{1}$$

where $\text{p}(k) = \frac{|e \cap e'|}{k}$ is the precision, i.e., how many of the k predicted experts e' are correctly identified from the test instance of the team e and $\delta_e(i)$ returns 1 if the i-th predicted expert is in e. Finally, we report the mean of average precisions (map) on all test instances of teams. For normalized discounted cumulative gain (ndcg),

$$\text{dcg}(k) = \sum_{i=1}^{k} \frac{\text{rel}(i)}{\log(i+1)} \tag{2}$$

where $\text{rel}(i)$ captures the degree of relevance for the predicted expert at position i. In our problem setting, however, all members of a test team are considered of the same importance. Therefore, $rel(i) = 1$ if $i \in e$ and 0 otherwise, and Eq. (2) becomes:

$$\text{dcg}(k) = \sum_{i=1}^{k} \frac{\delta_e(i)}{\log(i+1)} \tag{3}$$

This metric can be *normalized* relative to the ideal case when the top-k predicted experts include members of the test team e at the lowest possible ranks, i.e.,

$$\text{ndcg}(k) = \frac{\sum_{i=1}^{k} \frac{\delta_e(i)}{\log(i+1)}}{\sum_{i=1}^{|e|} \frac{1}{\log(i+1)}} \tag{4}$$

To evaluate fairness, we used ndkl with no cutoff [32] (the lower, the better) with being 0 in the ideal fair cases. Formally, let $d_{e'}$ the distribution of popular and nonpopular experts in the predicted top-k experts e' (the proportions of popular and nonpopular experts) and d_e the ideal fair distribution for a test instance of a team (s, e), the Kullback-Leibler (kl) divergence of $d_{e'}$ from d_e is:

$$\text{kl}(d_{e'}(k)\|d_e(k)) = \sum_{i=1}^{k} d_{e'}(i) \log \frac{d_{e'}(i)}{d_e(i)} \tag{5}$$

This metric has a minimum value of 0 when both distributions are identical up to position i. A higher value indicates a greater divergence between the two distributions, and the metric is always non-negative. We report the *normalized discounted cumulative* KL-divergence (ndkl) [32]:

$$\text{ndkl}(d_{e'}) = \frac{\sum_{k=1}^{|e|} \frac{1}{\log(k+1)} \text{kl}(d_{e'}(k)\|d_e(k))}{\sum_{i=1}^{|e|} \frac{1}{\log(i+1)}} \tag{6}$$

3.2   Results

In response to **RQ1**, i.e., whether state-of-the-art neural team formation models produce fair teams of experts, from Table 2, we observe that state-of-the-art Bayesian neural models with negative sampling (bnn and bnn_emb) suffer from popularity bias having regard to their high ndkl compared to random baseline

Table 2. Average performance of 5-fold on test set in terms of fairness (ndkl; the lower, the better) and utility metrics (map and ndcg, the higher, the better)

	bnn [19, 20]						
		greedy		conservative		relaxed	
	before	after	Δ	after	Δ	after	Δ
ndcg2↑	0.695%	0.126%	-0.569%	0.091%	-0.604%	0.146%	-0.550%
ndcg5↑	0.767%	0.141%	-0.626%	0.130%	-0.637%	0.130%	-0.637%
ndcg10↑	1.058%	0.247%	-0.811%	0.232%	-0.826%	0.246%	-0.812%
map2↑	0.248%	0.060%	-0.188%	0.041%	-0.207%	0.063%	-0.185%
map5↑	0.381%	0.083%	-0.298%	0.068%	-0.313%	0.079%	-0.302%
map10↑	0.467%	0.115%	-0.352%	0.101%	-0.366%	0.115%	-0.352%
ndlkl↓	0.2317	0.0276	-0.2041	0.0276	-0.2041	0.0273	-0.2043

	bnn_emb [19, 20]						
		greedy		conservative		relaxed	
	before	after	Δ	after	Δ	after	Δ
ndcg2↑	0.921%	0.087%	-0.834%	0.121%	-0.799%	0.087%	-0.834%
ndcg5↑	0.927%	0.117%	-0.810%	0.150%	-0.777%	0.117%	-0.810%
ndcg10↑	1.266%	0.223%	-1.043%	0.241%	-1.025%	0.223%	-1.043%
map2↑	0.327%	0.034%	-0.293%	0.057%	-0.270%	0.034%	-0.293%
map5↑	0.469%	0.059%	-0.410%	0.084%	-0.386%	0.059%	-0.410%
map10↑	0.573%	0.093%	-0.480%	0.111%	-0.461%	0.093%	-0.480%
ndkl↓	0.2779	0.0244	-0.2535	0.0244	-0.2535	0.0241	-0.2539

	random						
		greedy		conservative		relaxed	
	before	after	Δ	after	Δ	after	Δ
ndcg2↑	0.1711%	0.136%	-0.035%	0.205%	0.034%	0.205%	0.034%
ndcg5↑	0.1809%	0.170%	-0.011%	0.190%	0.009%	0.190%	0.009%
ndcg10↑	0.3086%	0.258%	-0.051%	0.283%	-0.026%	0.283%	-0.026%
map2↑	0.0617%	0.059%	-0.003%	0.089%	0.028%	0.089%	0.028%
map5↑	0.0889%	0.095%	0.006%	0.110%	0.021%	0.110%	0.021%
map10↑	0.1244%	0.121%	-0.003%	0.140%	0.016%	0.140%	0.016%
ndkl↓	0.0072	0.0369	0.0296	0.0366	0.0293	0.0366	0.0294

before applying deterministic re-ranking algorithms, thus answering **RQ2** negatively. Indeed, the random baseline which blindly assigns experts to teams is following the experts' popularity label distribution in the training dataset, and hence, yields the best fair model based on *demographic parity* (statistical parity). However, random baseline has the lowest utility metric values while bnn and bnn_emb achieve the highest.

In response to **RQ2**, i.e., whether state-of-the-art deterministic re-ranking algorithms improve the fairness of neural team formation models while maintaining their accuracy, from Table 2, although applying all re-ranking algorithms resulted in lower `ndkl` values by increasing the diversity of experts in the recommended teams, they substantially reduced the teams' accuracy at the same time for all neural models in terms of all utility metrics, proving the ineffectiveness of deterministic greedy re-ranking algorithms for the task of team formation. Among the re-ranking algorithms, `relaxed` is the best since it decreases the `ndkl` of neural models the most while the drop in the utility metrics is the lowest compared to the other two algorithms.

4   Concluding Remarks

We focused on the problem of fair team formation. We showed that state-of-the-art neural models, which can efficiently learn relationships between experts and their skills in the context of successful and unsuccessful teams from all past instances, suffer from popularity bias. To mitigate the popularity bias while maintaining the success rates of recommended teams, we applied three state-of-the-art deterministic re-ranking algorithms to reorder the final ranked list of experts against the popular experts in favour of nonpopular ones. We found that while deterministic re-ranking algorithms improve the fairness of neural team formation models, they fall short of maintaining accuracy. Our future research directions include i) investigating other fairness factors like demographic attributes, including age, race, and gender; and ii) developing machine learning-based models using learning-to-rank techniques to mitigate popularity bias as opposed to deterministic greedy algorithms.

References

1. Horowitz, D., Kamvar, S.D.: The anatomy of a large-scale social search engine. In: WWW, pp. 431–440. Association for Computing Machinery, New York (2010)
2. Horowitz, D., Kamvar, S.D.: Searching the village: models and methods for social search. Commun. ACM **55**(4), 111–118 (2012)
3. Bursic, K.M.: Strategies and benefits of the successful use of teams in manufacturing organizations. IEEE Trans. Eng. Manage. **39**(3), 277–289 (1992)
4. Askari, G., Asghri, N., Gordji, M.E., Asgari, H., Filipe, J.A., Azar, A.: The impact of teamwork on an organization' performance: a cooperative game' approach. Mathematics **8**(10), 1–15 (2020)
5. Almagul, K., Nurul M.Z.: The effect of teamwork on employee productivity(2021)
6. Julie, Y.-W., Barbara, G., Charles, W.A., Amy, P.T.: The dynamics of multidisciplinary research teams in academia. Rev. High. Educ. **22**(4), 425–440 (1999)
7. Erin, L.: From sole investigator to team scientist: trends in the practice and study of research collaboration. Annu. Rev. Soc. **42**(1), 81–100 (2016)
8. Hall, K.L., et al.: The science of team science: a review of the empirical evidence and research gaps on collaboration in science. Am. Psychol. **73**, 532–548 (2018)
9. Sherer, P.D.: Leveraging human assets in law firms: human capital structures and organizational capabilities. ILR Rev. **48**(4), 671–691 (1995)

10. Hu, J., Liden, R.C.: Making a difference in the teamwork: linking team prosocial motivation to team processes and effectiveness. Acad. Manag. J. **58**, 1102–1127 (2014)

11. Craig, M., McKeown, D.: How to build effective teams in healthcare. Nurs. Times **111**(14), 16–18 (2015)

12. Rosen, M.A., et al.: Teamwork in healthcare: key discoveries enabling safer, high-quality care. Am. Psychol. **73**(4), 433–450 (2018)

13. Swaab, R., Schaerer, M., Anicich, E.M., Ronay, R., Galinsky, A.D.: The too-much-talent effect: team interdependence determines when more talent is too much or not enough. Psychol. Sci. **25**(8), 1581–1591 (2014)

14. Rahmanniyay, F., Yu, A.J., Seif, J.: A multi-objective multi-stage stochastic model for project team formation under uncertainty in time requirements. Comput. Ind. Eng. **132**, 153–165 (2019)

15. Lappas, T., Liu, K., Terzi, E.: Finding a team of experts in social networks. In: SIGKDD 2009, pp. 467–476 ACM (2009)

16. Kargar, M., An, A.: Discovering top-k teams of experts with/without a leader in social networks. In: Proceedings of the 20th ACM International Conference on Information and Knowledge Management, pp. 985–994 (2011)

17. Kargar, M., An, A.: Efficient top-k keyword search in graphs with polynomial delay. In: 2012 IEEE 28th International Conference on Data Engineering, pp. 1269–1272 (2012)

18. Rad, R.H., Mitha, A., Fani, H., Kargar, M., Szlichta, J., Bagheri, E.: PyTFL: a python-based neural team formation toolkit. In: CIKM, pp. 4716–4720 ACM (2021)

19. Dashti, A., Samet, S., Fani, H.: Effective neural team formation via negative samples. In: CIKM, pp. 3908–3912 ACM (2022)

20. Rad, R.H., Fani, H., Kargar, M., Szlichta, J., Bagheri, E.: Learning to form skill-based teams of experts. In: CIKM 2020, pp. 2049–2052. ACM (2020)

21. Dwork, C., Hardt, M., Pitassi, T., Reingold, O., Zemel, R.S.: Fairness through awareness. In: Innovations in Theoretical Computer Science 2012, Cambridge, MA, USA, January 8–10, 2012, pp. 214–226. ACM (2012)

22. Hajian, S., Bonchi, F., Castillo, C.: Algorithmic Bias: from discrimination discovery to fairness-aware data mining. In: Proceedings of the 22nd ACM SIGKDD International Conference on Knowledge Discovery and Data Mining, San Francisco, CA, USA, August 13–17, 2016, pp. 2125–2126. ACM (2016)

23. Yalcin, E., Bilge, A.: Investigating and counteracting popularity bias in group recommendations. Inf. Process. Manag. **58**(5), 102608 (2021)

24. Zhu, Z., He, Y., Zhao, X., Caverlee, J.: Popularity bias in dynamic recommendation. In: KDD, pp. 2439–2449. ACM (2021)

25. Sun, J., et al.: A framework for recommending accurate and diverse items using Bayesian graph convolutional neural networks. In: KDD, pp. 2030–2039. ACM (2020)

26. Kay, M., Matuszek, C., Munson, S.A.: Unequal representation and gender stereotypes in image search results for occupations. In: Proceedings of the 33rd Annual ACM Conference on Human Factors in Computing Systems, CHI 2015, Seoul, Republic of Korea, April 18–23, 2015, pp. 3819–3828. ACM (2015)

27. Tannenbaum, C., Ellis, R.P., Eyssel, F., Zou, J., Schiebinger, L.: Sex and gender analysis improves science and engineering. Nature **575**(7781), 137–146 (2019)

28. Lauring, J., Villesèche, F.: The performance of gender diverse teams: what is the relation between diversity attitudes and degree of diversity? Eur. Manag. Rev. **16**(2), 243–254 (2019)

29. Hofstra, B., Kulkarni, V.V., Galvez, S.M.N., He, B., Jurafsky, D., McFarland, D.A.: The diversity-innovation paradox in science. Proc. Nat. Acad. Sci. **117**(17), 9284–9291 (2020)
30. Barnabò, G., Fazzone, A., Leonardi, S., Schwiegelshohn, C.: Algorithms for fair team formation in online labour marketplaces. In: WWW, pp. 484–490 (2019)
31. Kargar, M., Golab, L., Srivastava, D., Szlichta, J., Zihayat, M.: Effective keyword search over weighted graphs. IEEE Trans. Knowl. Data Eng. **34**(2), 601–616 (2022)
32. Geyik, S.C., Ambler, S., Kenthapadi, K.: Fairness-aware ranking in search recommendation systems with application to linkedin talent search. In: KDD, pp. 2221–2231. ACM (2019)
33. Dwork, C., Hardt, M., Pitassi, T., Reingold, O., Zemel, R.: Fairness through awareness. In: Proceedings of the 3rd Innovations in Theoretical Computer Science Conference (ITCS 2012), pp. 214–226. Association for Computing Machinery, New York (2012). https://doi.org/10.1145/2090236.2090255
34. Dashti, A., Samet, S., Fani. H.: Effective neural team formation via negative samples. In: CIKM, pp. 3908–3912. Association for Computing Machinery, New York (2022)
35. Le, Q., Mikolov, T.: Distributed representations of sentences and documents. In: ICML, ICML 2014, pp. II-1188–II-1196. JMLR.org (2014)

How Do You Feel? Information Retrieval in Psychotherapy and Fair Ranking Assessment

Vivek Kumar[1] , Giacomo Medda[1](✉) , Diego Reforgiato Recupero[1] ,
Daniele Riboni[1] , Rim Helaoui[2] , and Gianni Fenu[1]

[1] University of Cagliari, Via Ospedale 72, 09124 Cagliari, Italy
{vivek.kumar,giacomo.medda,diego.reforgiato,riboni,fenu}@unica.it
[2] Philips Research, High-Tech Campus, Eindhoven, Netherlands
rim.helaoui@philips.com

Abstract. The recent pandemic Coronavirus Disease 2019 (COVID-19) led to an unexpectedly imposed social isolation, causing an enormous disruption of daily routines for the global community and posing a potential risk to the mental well-being of individuals. However, resources for supporting people with mental health issues remain extremely limited, raising the matter of providing trustworthy and relevant psychotherapeutic content publicly available. To bridge this gap, this paper investigates the application of information retrieval in the mental health domain to automatically filter therapeutical content by estimated quality. We have used AnnoMI, an expert annotated counseling dataset composed of high- and low-quality Motivational Interviewing therapy sessions. First, we applied state-of-the-art information retrieval models to evaluate their applicability in the psychological domain for ranking therapy sessions by estimated quality. Then, given the sensitive psychological information associated with each therapy session, we analyzed the potential risk of unfair outcomes across therapy topics, i.e., mental issues, under a common fairness definition. Our experimental results show that the employed ranking models are reliable for systematically ranking high-quality content above low-quality one, while unfair outcomes across topics are model-dependent and associated low-quality content distribution. Our findings provide preliminary insights for applying information retrieval in the psychological domain, laying the foundations for incorporating publicly available high-quality resources to support mental health. Source code available at https://github.com/jackmedda/BIAS-FairAnnoMI.

Keywords: Psychology · Motivational Interviewing · Therapeutical Session · Information Retrieval · Ranking Task

1 Introduction

The recent pandemic has forced people to confine themselves to four walls and has limited human interactions. This living condition does not align with the

---

V. Kumar and G. Medda—These authors contributed equally to this work.

© The Author(s), under exclusive license to Springer Nature Switzerland AG 2023
L. Boratto et al. (Eds.): BIAS 2023, CCIS 1840, pp. 119–133, 2023.
https://doi.org/10.1007/978-3-031-37249-0_10

definition of leading an everyday human life. Psychological issues such as anxiety and depression have surfaced due to this prolonged situation [3]. The pandemic also emphasized the importance of psychologists and remote therapy access. These services are cost-intensive, and people are forced to make sacrifices or wait for bonus payments issued by the governments. Furthermore, common people do not have familiarity and awareness of mental health issues, which puts them at risk of incurring misinformative content publicly available online [27,28].

This scenario has captured the interest of the research community towards the application of Natural Language Processing (NLP) in mental health [1,20,30] and healthcare [10,17,19,21,38] to provide reliable resources for the common good. However, some of these works studied systems that still impose people to interact actively, e.g. with a chatbot. Though patients have positive perceptions about such tools [1], the knowledge and support provided by chatbots are limited by the conversation carried on by the users. Hence, patients are unable to browse and analyze personalized resources to support their own mental health.

Conversely, the motivation of this study is to facilitate individuals in autonomously evaluating therapeutical content personalized for their psychological issues. This objective is inspired by a publication over 20 years old [28] that emphasized the potential benefits that information retrieval (IR) methods could offer to both patients and therapists. IR can help in addressing mental health issues by efficiently providing relevant and reliable information, personalizing treatment options based on specific needs and preferences, and monitoring mental health trends in the population.

In this paper, we aim to examine the application of IR tools to rank relevant therapy counseling sessions according to the psychological disease a patient aims to solve. Therefore, in such a system, users expect to find counseling sessions of high quality ranked in higher positions because they could significantly reflect their personal mental health issues and offer emotional support. Nonetheless, applying automatic decision-making systems to data that includes such sensitive attributes raises the need to account for unfairness issues, being fairness one of the key requirements artificial intelligence (AI) systems should meet according to the European Commission [7]. AI responsibility towards the entity receiving the ranked content is especially studied in the IR subfield of recommendation systems. Researchers have faced beyond-accuracy issues, such as explainability [2] and fairness [4,5,24], to make these systems more trustworthy. Along the same lines, ranking methods for therapeutical content should be examined to assess that the IR task is performed fairly across psychological diseases.

To this end, we first highlighted the scarcity of therapeutical counseling data, the application of IR techniques in healthcare, and fairness assessments performed in the same field (Sect. 2). We presented the data and fairness definition used to evaluate the formulated problem (Sect. 3). We described the procedure to reduce the number of psychological topics, prepare the data, model the ranking task (Sect. 4). We performed a set of experiments to evaluate the applicability of IR to therapeutical data and assessed the rankings fairness across topics

(Sect. 5). Finally, we discussed the open issues, limitations, and future research of ranking in the psychological domain (Sect. 6).

2   Related Works

This section raises the issue of scarce data in the psychology domain, as well as gives an overview of the literature on healthcare that applies IR techniques and evaluates the unfairness of AI model outcomes.

2.1   Data Scarcity in Psychological Domain

Ironically, despite the massive amount of data that humanity produces, there is a scarcity of publicly accessible data in healthcare and its sub-domains, e.g., mental health. Due to such issue, psychology research is limited and machine learning models cannot be sufficiently trained to achieve the performance level required to solve the provided task.

To bridge this gap, researchers have recently worked towards releasing freely accessible datasets in the psychological domain. The work in [32] proposed a new benchmark for empathetic dialogue generation and released *EMPATHETICDI-ALOGUES*, a dataset containing 224,850 conversations grounded in emotional situations and gathered from 810 different participants. [37] released AnnoMI, a dataset of conversational therapy sessions annotated by experts, composed of 110 high-quality and 23 low-quality Motivational Interviewing (MI) dialogues. The work in [6] presented a dataset containing 1860 short texts together with ratings for two kinds of empathetic states, personal distress and empathetic concern.

2.2   Information Retrieval and Fairness in Healthcare

Publications regarding IR in healthcare range across several goals, e.g. real-time monitoring and management of diabetes [29], and improvement of biomedical content retrieval [23]. Psychological diseases do not seem to be analyzed in detail, but IR models applied to ranking tasks with large datasets, e.g. PubMed [23], could also handle data related to mental health issues.

Literature on fairness in mental health is scarce because psychological diseases are mentioned as part of the wider and general healthcare field. This is probably because the community started to recognize healthcare disparities in the early 2000s [8]. Driven by the fairness key requirements set up by the European Commission [7], recent works in healthcare [9,11,22,25] addressed unfairness issues of AI outcomes, e.g. in neural medicine and kidney function estimation. In the mental health domain, [33,35] examined unfair gaps in access and questionable diagnostic practices against racial and ethnic groups, e.g. African Americans receiving a medical prescription less likely than Whites.

Hence, this paper adds a significant contribution to both domains, dealing with scarce therapeutical data for IR tasks, performing a fairness assessment of the entities being queried, i.e. the psychological topics, and employing a tool to support mental health issues, only envisioned more than 20 years ago.

3   Problem Formulation, Dataset and Fairness Definition

In this section, we describe the problem formulation for the ranking task, the dataset and the fairness notion used to perform the experiments.

3.1   Problem Formulation

We model an IR task where documents are represented as therapy sessions and queries as psychological topics. Let S be the set of queries, i.e., topics, T the set of documents, i.e. therapy sessions, $Y = \{0, 1\}$ the set of relevance labels, which represent the extent to which a document is relevant for a specific query, where higher values denote higher relevance. In particular, given $s_i \in S$, a subset of documents $T_i = \{t_{i,1}, t_{i,2}, ..., t_{i,n}\}$, sorted in descending order by relevance, is retrieved to satisfy s_i. The relevance of each document in T_i is denoted by $y_i = \{y_{i,1}, y_{i,2}, ..., y_{i,n}\}$, such that $y_{i,j}$ is the relevance degree of $t_{i,j}$ for s_i.

A ranking model $\mathcal{F} : S \times T \rightarrow \hat{Y}$ takes queries and documents as input and predicts the relevance score $\hat{y}$ for each query-document pair. Therefore, training a ranking model becomes an optimization problem. Given relevance-graded query-document pairs, this means finding the model hyper-parameters θ that minimize the following objective function:

$$\underset{\theta}{\operatorname{argmax}} \mathcal{L}(\mathcal{F}, s_i, t_{i,j}, y_{i,j}) \tag{1}$$

3.2   Dataset

For our work, we have used AnnoMI[1] [37], a high-quality dataset of expert-annotated MI transcripts of 133 therapy sessions distributed over 44 topics, e.g. smoking cessation, anxiety management, and 9695 utterances. Dialogues comprise several utterances of the therapists and the patients, labeled according to the therapist's approach, e.g. question, reflection, and the patient's reaction, e.g. neutral, change. AnnoMI is the first dataset of its kind to be publicly accessible in the psychology domain, which is suitable for several tasks, such as the classification of the therapy quality or the patient's reaction.

Our work focuses on providing therapeutical content in response to a particular psychological disease, then we have only considered the therapist dialogue sessions and, thus, the AnnoMI therapist's utterances. However, due to the low number of therapy sessions per topic, we reduced the ranking task to use only the therapist's utterances text in each session, instead of the whole session. Nonetheless, the quality of each therapist's utterance text is considered to be the same as the therapy session it belongs to, given that the quality assigned to each session is dependent on the utterances it is made up of.

---

[1] Data available at https://github.com/vsrana-ai/AnnoMI.

3.3   Fairness Definition

A relevant amount of the IR literature analyzes fairness regarding the entities being ranked [12,13,31]. Here we focus on the impact of ranking utility disparity on psychological topics, which are considered proxies of psychological diseases. The therapeutical content being retrieved should help and support any query with the same level of therapy quality, regardless of the psychological disease being searched. To this purpose, we operationalized the fairness definition of *Demographic/Statistical Parity*. This definition is satisfied if the likelihood of relevant content is the same for any psychological disease. Following other works focusing on the entity receiving the ranked lists in IR [4,36], unfairness is assessed as the disparity of ranking utility across consumers. Let the Normalized Discounted Cumulative Gain (NDCG@k) be the ranking utility metric, the disparity across topics D_S is measured as the average pairwise absolute difference between NDCG@k values and defined as follows:

$$D_S = \frac{1}{\binom{|S|}{2}} \sum_{1 \leq i < j \leq |S|} \|NDCG_i@k - NDCG_j@k\|_2^2 \tag{2}$$

4   Methodology

In this section, we present the methodology followed to apply IR techniques on AnnoMI under the problem statement in Sect. 3.1. In particular, we describe the strategy of re-labeling the topics, the procedure to prepare the data, the ranking task, and the selected models.

4.1   Topics Re-labeling

The AnnoMI topics distribution is composed of a single or more than one treatment/goal/morbidity, which makes the distinction between the topics difficult for machine learning approaches. As a result of an exploratory analysis supported by a psychology researcher, we aggregated the topics based on (i) similarities between the psychological diseases being treated and (ii) families of topics that could be envisioned in a more general group.

(i) several topics regard an equal or similar problem, but, in some cases, they are associated with other aspects mainly related to the central topic, e.g. the topics *weight loss; diet* and *weight loss* were merged into the single topic *diet and weight loss management*

(ii) some new groups can be defined to include several topics to represent a broader psychological problem that connects all the considered topics, e.g. the new topic *motivated towards adopting better life style* envisions the same issue depicted by *increasing self-confidence* and *reducing violence*

The two AnnoMI topics *birth control* and *opening up* were instead discarded because they did not fit the new topics labeling. 51 utterances were then removed from the dataset, which does not affect the integrity of the whole corpus.

4.2   Data Preparation

As mentioned in Sect. 3.2, due to the low number of therapy sessions per topic, we treat the transcription text of therapists' individual utterances as documents. To make each utterance text reflect as much as possible the quality of the respective therapy session, we filtered out the utterance with less than 5 tokens, leading to a total of 3984 utterances. The value was selected empirically to remove most of the classic expressions not related to the respective topic or therapy quality, e.g. "Okay, all right.", "Yes, I think so.".

Given the thorny type of sensitive data, it is fundamental to assess the outcomes fairness of the rankers used in our experiments. Based on the definition in Sect. 3.3, the dataset is split into training and testing sets following the ratio 80:20, respectively, such that the distribution of each psychological disease follows the same ratio across the sets. Furthermore, the topics not representing both the low and high MI dialogues quality were dropped, otherwise, the ranking utility for such topics would be minimum or maximum respectively and disparities could be misinterpreted as an unfairness issue.

Table 1. Distribution of topics over each *MI quality* class.

Topic (Psychological Disease)	MI quality	
	Low (0)	High (1)
adhering to medical procedure (AMP)	2.36%	7.83%
asthma management (AM)	0.66%	3.12%
compliance with rules (CR)	0.43%	9.50%
diabetes management (DM)	0.18%	11.45%
managing life (MF)	0.86%	12.18%
reducing alcohol consumption (RAC)	7.14%	24.95%
reducing alcohol consumption—smoking cessation (RAC—SC)	0.51%	0.66%
smoking cessation (SC)	3.70%	14.49%

Table 1 lists the remaining topics after the just described filtering procedure and their distribution over the high (1) and low (0) *MI quality* classes characterizing the 3984 utterances. There is a clear over-representation of the high *MI quality*, but envisioning the next experiments under the viewpoint of a therapeutical retrieval system, ranking high-quality content in higher positions would be beneficial to support patients. The utterances with the aggregated topic *RAC—SC* were not divided and assigned to the individual ones because of the subjective nature of the counseling sessions, which are tailored to support the patients with their specific disease, even if the combination of multiple ones.

4.3   Ranking Task and Models

A simple IR system takes a query as input and retrieves a list of documents ranked by the predicted relevance. The query is usually in the form of a simple sentence, e.g., "what is a corporation?", consisting also of words that could add no information to the documents expected to be retrieved. In this work, we instead use as a query the name of the psychological disease being treated in a therapeutical counseling session, e.g., "diabetes management." The ranking task modeled in this work takes as input these keywords-like topics and retrieves therapist's utterances text, ranked by the predicted quality, with the goal of providing therapeutical material to support patients with the queried disease.

The focus of this paper is to analyze the applicability of IR tasks in the psychological domain. Therefore, we use a high diversity of neural rankers, selected to cover different levels of network complexity. Arc-I [16], Arc-II [16], DRMMTKS [40], DUET [26], Dense Baseline [14], HBMP [34], KNRM [39], Naive [14] are some of the models provided in the MatchZoo Python library[2]. TFR BERT [15] is a ranker based on the popular BERT proposed by TensorFlow and represents the most complex network in this study. All the models were optimized with a Softmax cross entropy loss and the selected hyper-parameters can be found in the linked source code. We selected the best predictions generated by each model based on the NDCG@5 on the training set.

5   Experiments and Fairness Assessment

In this section, we perform a suite of experiments to evaluate the ranking models under AnnoMI in terms of utility and fairness. The analysis, evaluation, discussion of each experiment results are guided by the following research questions:

- **RQ1:** to what extent can the ranking utility be considered reliable for IR tasks in therapeutical settings?
- **RQ2:** how does the ranking utility variation across different psychological topics impact the fairness of ranking algorithms?
- **RQ3:** do the rankers systematically exhibit bias towards specific psychological diseases that result in negative impacts on the ranking utility?

5.1   RQ1: Ranking in Psychological Domain

Research in IR applied in the psychological domain, more specifically in therapeutical counseling, is hard to be found in healthcare literature. As far as our knowledge, this is the first paper addressing the problem of ranking therapeutical documents to support users with psychological diseases. To this end, we first investigated whether the rankings produced by IR techniques guarantee a good level of utility on therapeutical counseling data.

---

[2] https://github.com/NTMC-Community/MatchZoo.

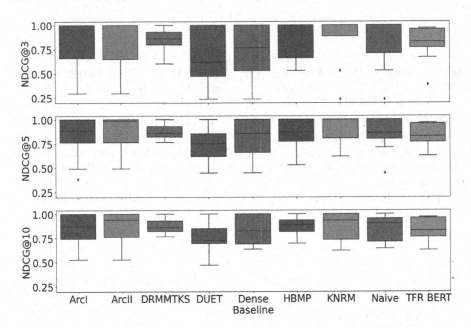

Fig. 1. Distribution of NDCG@k, $k \in \{3, 5, 10\}$ across topics for each ranker. Higher NDCG denotes higher utility.

Analyzing the ranking utility over different relevance levels could provide insights into the decision-making process of each ranker. A model reporting utility values quite different across relevance levels could be affected by the similarity between the utterance text and the queried topic, instead of finding a pattern that connects high-quality utterances to the relative psychological disease. Under this viewpoint, Fig. 1 depicts the distribution of NDCG@k, $k \in \{3, 5, 10\}$ over topics, i.e. queries, measured on the rankings generated by the trained models. The performance of most of the models is positively affected as the relevance level increases, with higher medians and narrower ranges. Conversely, two of the most performing rankers, *DRMMTKS* and *TFR BERT*, are robust against the k used to measure the NDCG, except for one outlier when the top 3 results are considered. The rankings generation by these two models seems then more reliable because their predictions better map the relation between the queried diseases and the *MI quality* of therapeutical content.

Other than that, even if the complexity of the underlying structure is significantly different across models, there is no evidence of a relationship between higher model complexity and higher NDCG average. For instance, *TFR-BERT*, one of the most complex rankers, reports a slightly lower performance than the simpler *Naive*. Nonetheless, the NDCG@10 distribution across topics for all models spans ranges higher than 0.5, and, considering the over-representation of the high *MI quality* class, it is reasonable to obtain such measures.

We can then positively answer our first research question, with all the models reporting rankings of high utility on therapeutical counseling data.

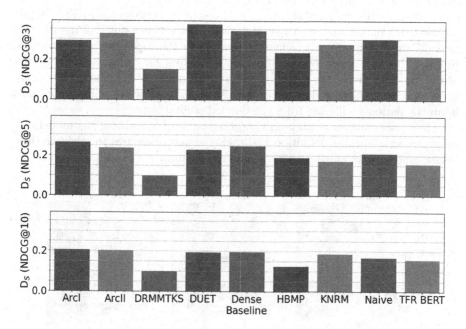

Fig. 2. D_S, the average pairwise absolute difference between utility values, measured on the rankings provided for each psychological topic at different relevance levels. Lower values are fairer.

5.2 RQ2: Unfairness Levels Across Topics

In our evaluation protocol, a query represents a psychological disease, which directly reflects the patients that suffer from it and that look for support to treat it. Hence, the decision-making process that generates a ranked list of therapeutical content affects all the patients that could be helped by the retrieved information. To ensure that therapeutic content is accessible and effective for patients with diverse mental health needs, it is crucial to investigate whether ranking algorithms exhibit bias towards specific psychological diseases. Such bias may result in negative impacts on the reliability of ranking outcomes, and limit the quality of therapeutical content provided to patients.

The operationalized fairness notion in Sect. 3.3 is then used to measure the extent to which the ranking utility for each topic differs from the others in a pairwise fashion. Figure 2 shows the unfairness level of each ranker in terms of NDCG disparity at different k of relevance. *DRMMTKS, TFR BERT, HBMP* report the best fairness degree for each top-k, while *DUET, ArcI* trade places as the unfairest model at different relevance levels.

Even though these rankers are suitable to be applied to psychological data in terms of utility, they do not seem to be reliable to provide fair rankings. Among all the models, *DRMMTKS* reports the lowest and most stable D_S across the different relevance levels. Still, the NDCG disparity between each pair of topics is close to 0.1 on average, which systematically highlights a different distribution of high- and low-quality therapeutical content in the top-k lists across queries. Besides, the unfairness levels of the top-3 ranking lists uncover a significant utility variance. Being the relevance binary, this means that some queries result in at least 1 low-quality document out of 3 in the list, which could potentially harm the patients suffering from the queried mental issue.

These observations remark on the importance of examining the model outcomes under a fairness definition and taking countermeasures to mitigate these issues, especially in domains with such sensitive data.

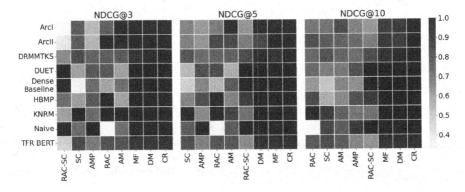

Fig. 3. Each cell represents the NDCG measured on the ranking generated for any queried topic (column) and any ranker (row) at different relevance levels. The columns are sorted by NDCG average over the columns. Darker values denote higher utility.

5.3   RQ3: Systematic Negative Impact

The previous research question uncovered a significant unfairness issue, reporting most of the rankers as not being able to provide similar utility values for all the topics. However, we have no insights into the utility of the rankings provided for each individual topic and we do not know whether querying specific psychological diseases leads to higher utility rankings w.r.t. to other ones. It is then important to conduct individualized analyses of each query to uncover potential factors that may be correlated with ranking performance.

Figure 3 aggregates all the models and psychological topics in three heatmaps (one for each relevance degree), where each cell represents the NDCG measured on the ranked list provided by a ranker (row) for an individual queried topic (column). Being the columns sorted in ascending order from left to right by NDCG average across models, it is straightforward to notice how the darker cells concentrate on the few topics at the right of each heatmap. In particular, the high-quality therapeutical content retrieved for the queried topics *Compliance with Rules (CR)*, *Diabetes Management (DM)*, and *Managing Life (MF)* is systematically ranked higher compared to the other models.

Such observation is probably related to the higher representation of high-quality utterances for the just mentioned topics. However, what seems to affect the ranking utility the most is the high representation of low-quality utterances. Indeed, the topics *SC*, *RAC*, *AMP* are composed of more than 1% of low-quality documents and the related columns are closer to the left side of the heatmap for each relevance level. A balanced representation of low- and high-quality utterances, as for the *RAC-SC* mental health issue, results in models with ranking utility divergent from each other.

Though these results are affected by the representation of *MI quality* classes, it does not seem evident a systematic impact on specific diseases. At least one model is able to provide optimal utility for a query and different models exhibit high and low-ranking utility for the same topics, except for the ones with an over-representation of high-quality utterances.

6   Conclusions and Future Work

In this paper, we investigated whether IR could be instrumental in supporting patients with their own mental health issues. Our methodology was based on a ranking task to provide high-quality therapeutic content in higher positions than low-quality ones. For such purpose, we used nine ranking models of a wide diversity of network complexities, and our results are indicative that conversational therapeutic data is suitable for ranking tasks, reporting high average utility.

Conversely, the fairness assessment uncovered a relevant utility disparity across topics for most of the models, remarking on the importance of addressing such issues in the psychology domain and taking countermeasures to mitigate them. Based on further analysis, these unfair outcomes were associated with the distribution of low-quality utterances for the related topic, hence, no systematic negative impact was reported toward specific mental issues.

However, the observations resulting from the performed experiments are limited by the size of AnnoMI in terms of therapy sessions and utterances for each psychological topic. Given that the *MI quality* is uniquely dependent on the therapist's utterances, the dataset was split by about half its size, which significantly condensed the corpora and negatively impacted the generalizability of our findings. Other than that, the mental issues not representing both of the MI classes were removed in order to evaluate the model's ability to rank high-quality therapists' utterances in higher positions than low-quality ones. This pre-processing step further reduced the number of utterances to just 3984, but AnnoMI still remains the first publicly available dataset in the psychology domain, hence the sole resource to study this type of data under IR tasks.

Another limitation associated with data scarcity in psychology research is the forced decision to treat individual therapist's utterances as documents instead of the whole therapy sessions, as depicted by our motivation. Providing a ranked list of therapy counseling sessions to support patients with the queried psychological disease would perfectly reflect the end goal envisioned by this study. However, such a setting would also require to use rankers of higher complexity, since treating a whole session as a single document would not respect the order of the conversation between the therapist and the patient. Nonetheless, if larger corpora had been available, our methodology could have been extended to entire therapy sessions, where each query would result in several dialogues between therapists and patients organized in a list ranked by estimated relevance. Given that each query represents a mental health issue, users could leverage therapeutical content autonomously to evaluate the extent to which they see themselves in the patients of the retrieved dialogues and whether the respective therapy could help them too. Such corpora should then require each dialogue to be labeled based on the psychological issue the patient suffers from, but other attributes could assist future research, such as the treatment duration, the therapists' experience, and the patients' sensitive information.

Future works will focus on augmentation techniques to extend AnnoMI to generate a higher number of therapy sessions per topic to work with. New relabeling techniques will be taken into account to shape broader topic grouping to leverage a higher number of dialogues for each mental health issue. Unfairness mitigation procedures will also be employed to reduce the ranking utility disparity reported across psychological topics. We also aim to incorporate world knowledge in the form of triples to address the domain adaptation challenges in mental health [18]. Additionally, by exploring factors such as the length of the therapeutic dialogues or the complexity of the patient's conditions, we could gain deeper insights into the specific challenges and opportunities presented by each mental health issue and inform the development of more effective ranking algorithms for therapeutical data.

References

1. Abd-Alrazaq, A.A., Alajlani, M., Ali, N., Denecke, K., Bewick, B.M., Househ, M.: Perceptions and opinions of patients about mental health chatbots: scoping review. J. Med. Internet Res. **23**(1), e17828 (2021)
2. Balloccu, G., Boratto, L., Fenu, G., Marras, M.: Post processing recommender systems with knowledge graphs for recency, popularity, and diversity of explanations. In: Amigó, E., Castells, P., Gonzalo, J., Carterette, B., Culpepper, J.S., Kazai, G. (eds.) SIGIR '22: The 45th International ACM SIGIR Conference on Research and Development in Information Retrieval, Madrid, Spain, 11–15 July 2022, pp. 646–656. ACM (2022). https://doi.org/10.1145/3477495.3532041
3. Bhandari, A., Kumar, V., Thien Huong, P.T., Thanh, D.N.: Sentiment analysis of covid-19 tweets: Leveraging stacked word embedding representation for identifying distinct classes within a sentiment. In: Artificial Intelligence in Data and Big Data Processing: Proceedings of ICABDE 2021, pp. 341–352. Springer (2022). https://doi.org/10.1007/978-3-030-97610-1_27

4. Boratto, L., Fenu, G., Marras, M., Medda, G.: Consumer fairness in recommender systems: contextualizing definitions and mitigations. In: Hagen, M., Verberne, S., Macdonald, C., Seifert, C., Balog, K., Nørvåg, K., Setty, V. (eds.) ECIR 2022. LNCS, vol. 13185, pp. 552–566. Springer, Cham (2022). https://doi.org/10.1007/978-3-030-99736-6_37

5. Boratto, L., Fenu, G., Marras, M., Medda, G.: Practical perspectives of consumer fairness in recommendation. Inf. Process. Manage. **60**(2), 103208 (2023). https://doi.org/10.1016/j.ipm.2022.103208. https://www.sciencedirect.com/science/article/pii/S0306457322003090

6. Buechel, S., Buffone, A., Slaff, B., Ungar, L., Sedoc, J.: Modeling empathy and distress in reaction to news stories. In: Proceedings of the 2018 Conference on Empirical Methods in Natural Language Processing, pp. 4758–4765 (2018)

7. Cabitza, F., Ciucci, D., Pasi, G., Viviani, M.: Responsible AI in healthcare. CoRR abs/2203.03616 (2022). https://doi.org/10.48550/arXiv.2203.03616

8. Chen, R.J., et al.: Algorithm fairness in AI for medicine and healthcare. CoRR abs/2110.00603 (2021). https://arxiv.org/abs/2110.00603

9. Currie, G., Hawk, K.E.: Ethical and legal challenges of artificial intelligence in nuclear medicine. Semin. Nucl. Med. **51**(2), 120–125 (2020)

10. Dessì, D., Helaoui, R., Kumar, V., Recupero, D.R., Riboni, D.: TF-IDF vs word embeddings for morbidity identification in clinical notes: An initial study. In: Consoli, S., ecupero, D.R., Riboni, D. (eds.) Proceedings of the First Workshop on Smart Personal Health Interfaces co-located with 25th International Conference on Intelligent User Interfaces, SmartPhil@IUI 2020, Cagliari, Italy, March 17, 2020. CEUR Workshop Proceedings, vol. 2596, pp. 1–12. CEUR-WS.org (2020), http://ceur-ws.org/Vol-2596/paper1.pdf

11. Diao, J.A., et al.: Clinical implications of removing race from estimates of kidney function. JAMA **325**(2), 184–186 (2021)

12. Gómez, E., Zhang, C.S., Boratto, L., Salamó, M., Marras, M.: The winner takes it all: Geographic imbalance and provider (un)fairness in educational recommender systems. In: Diaz, F., Shah, C., Suel, T., Castells, P., Jones, R., Sakai, T. (eds.) SIGIR '21: The 44th International ACM SIGIR Conference on Research and Development in Information Retrieval, Virtual Event, Canada, 11–15 July 2021, pp. 1808–1812. ACM (2021). https://doi.org/10.1145/3404835.3463235,https://doi.org/10.1145/3404835.3463235

13. Gómez, E., Zhang, C.S., Boratto, L., Salamó, M., Ramos, G.: Enabling cross-continent provider fairness in educational recommender systems. Future Gener. Comput. Syst. **127**, 435–447 (2022). https://doi.org/10.1016/j.future.2021.08.025

14. Guo, J., Fan, Y., Ji, X., Cheng, X.: Matchzoo: A learning, practicing, and developing system for neural text matching. In: Piwowarski, B., Chevalier, M., Gaussier, É., Maarek, Y., Nie, J., Scholer, F. (eds.) Proceedings of the 42nd International ACM SIGIR Conference on Research and Development in Information Retrieval, SIGIR 2019, Paris, France, 21–25 July 2019, pp. 1297–1300. ACM (2019). https://doi.org/10.1145/3331184.3331403

15. Han, S., Wang, X., Bendersky, M., Najork, M.: Learning-to-rank with BERT in tf-ranking. CoRR abs/2004.08476 (2020). https://arxiv.org/abs/2004.08476

16. Hu, B., Lu, Z., Li, H., Chen, Q.: Convolutional neural network architectures for matching natural language sentences. In: Ghahramani, Z., Welling, M., Cortes, C., Lawrence, N.D., einberger, K.Q. (eds.) Advances in Neural Information Processing Systems 27: Annual Conference on Neural Information Processing Systems 2014(December), pp. 8–13, 2014. Montreal, Quebec, Canada, pp. 2042–2050 (2014). https://proceedings.neurips.cc/paper/2014/hash/b9d487a30398d42ecff55c228ed5652b-Abstract.html

17. Kumar, V., Mishra, B.K., Mazzara, M., Thanh, D.N., Verma, A.: Prediction of malignant and benign breast cancer: a data mining approach in healthcare applications. In: Advances in data science and management. Springer (2020)

18. Kumar, V., Recupero, D.R., Helaoui, R., Riboni, D.: K-lm: knowledge augmenting in language models within the scholarly domain. IEEE Access **10**, 91802–91815 (2022)

19. Kumar, V., Recupero, D.R., Riboni, D., Helaoui, R.: Ensembling classical machine learning and deep learning approaches for morbidity identification from clinical notes. IEEE Access **9**, 7107–7126 (2020)

20. Le Glaz, A., Haralambous, Y., Kim-Dufor, D.H., Lenca, P., Billot, R., Ryan, T.C., Marsh, J., Devylder, J., Walter, M., Berrouiguet, S., et al.: Machine learning and natural language processing in mental health: systematic review. J. Med. Internet Res. **23**(5), e15708 (2021)

21. Locke, S., Bashall, A., Al-Adely, S., Moore, J., Wilson, A., Kitchen, G.B.: Natural language processing in medicine: a review. Trends in Anaesthesia and Critical Care **38**, 4–9 (2021)

22. Lopez, Leo, I., Hart, Louis H., I., Katz, M.H.: Racial and ethnic health disparities related to COVID-19. JAMA **325**(8), 719–720 (2021). https://doi.org/10.1001/jama.2020.26443

23. Luo, M., Mitra, A., Gokhale, T., Baral, C.: Improving biomedical information retrieval with neural retrievers. In: Thirty-Sixth AAAI Conference on Artificial Intelligence, AAAI 2022, Thirty-Fourth Conference on Innovative Applications of Artificial Intelligence, IAAI 2022, The Twelveth Symposium on Educational Advances in Artificial Intelligence, EAAI 2022 Virtual Event, 22 February–1 March 2022, pp. 11038–11046. AAAI Press (2022). https://ojs.aaai.org/index.php/AAAI/article/view/21352

24. Marras, M., Boratto, L., Ramos, G., Fenu, G.: Equality of learning opportunity via individual fairness in personalized recommendations. Int. J. Artif. Intell. Educ. **32**(3), 636–684 (2022). https://doi.org/10.1007/s40593-021-00271-1

25. Mhasawade, V., Zhao, Y., Chunara, R.: Machine learning and algorithmic fairness in public and population health. Nat. Mach. Intell. **3**(8), 659–666 (2021). https://doi.org/10.1038/s42256-021-00373-4

26. D Mitra, B., Diaz, F., Craswell, N.: Learning to match using local and distributed representations of text for web search. In: Barrett, R., Cummings, R., Agichtein, E., Gabrilovich, E. (eds.) Proceedings of the 26th International Conference on World Wide Web, WWW 2017, Perth, Australia, 3–7 April 2017, pp. 1291–1299. ACM (2017). https://doi.org/10.1145/3038912.3052579

27. Morahan-Martin, J.: How internet users find, evaluate, and use online health information: A cross-cultural review. Cyberpsychology Behav. Soc. Netw. **7**(5), 497–510 (2004). https://doi.org/10.1089/cpb.2004.7.497

28. Morahan-Martin, J., Anderson, C.D.: Information and misinformation online: recommendations for facilitating accurate mental health information retrieval and evaluation. Cyberpsychology Behav. Soc. Netw. **3**(5), 731–746 (2000). https://doi.org/10.1089/10949310050191737

29. Patel, D., Msosa, Y., Wang, T., Mustafa, O.G., Gee, S., Williams, J., Roberts, A., Dobson, R.J.B., Gaughran, F.: An implementation framework and a feasibility evaluation of a clinical decision support system for diabetes management in secondary mental healthcare using cogstack. BMC Medical Informatics Decis. Mak. **22**(1), 100 (2022). https://doi.org/10.1186/s12911-022-01842-5

30. Progga, F.T., Rubya, S.: "just like therapy!": Investigating the potential of storytelling in online postpartum depression communities. In: Fiesler, C., de Carvalho, A.F.P. (eds.) The 2023 ACM International Conference on Supporting Group Work, GROUP '23, Companion, Hilton Head, SC, USA, 8–11 January 2023, pp. 18–20. ACM (2023). https://doi.org/10.1145/3565967.3570977
31. Raj, A., Ekstrand, M.D.: Measuring fairness in ranked results: An analytical and empirical comparison. In: Amigó, E., Castells, P., Gonzalo, J., Carterette, B., Culpepper, J.S., Kazai, G. (eds.) SIGIR '22: The 45th International ACM SIGIR Conference on Research and Development in Information Retrieval, Madrid, Spain, 11–15 July 2022, pp. 726–736. ACM (2022). https://doi.org/10.1145/3477495.3532018,https://doi.org/10.1145/3477495.3532018
32. Rashkin, H., Smith, E.M., Li, M., Boureau, Y.L.: Towards empathetic open-domain conversation models: a new benchmark and dataset. In: Proceedings of the 57th Annual Meeting of the Association for Computational Linguistics (2019)
33. Snowden, L.R.: Bias in mental health assessment and intervention: theory and evidence. Am. J. Public Health 93(2), 239–243 (2003). https://doi.org/10.2105/AJPH.93.2.239,pMID: 12554576
34. Talman, A., Yli-Jyrä, A., Tiedemann, J.: Sentence embeddings in NLI with iterative refinement encoders. Nat. Lang. Eng. 25(4), 467–482 (2019). https://doi.org/10.1017/S1351324919000202
35. Wells, K., Klap, R., Koike, A., Sherbourne, C.: Ethnic disparities in unmet need for alcoholism, drug abuse, and mental health care. Am. J. Psychiatry 158(12), 2027–2032 (2001)
36. Wu, H., Ma, C., Mitra, B., Diaz, F., Liu, X.: A multi-objective optimization framework for multi-stakeholder fairness-aware recommendation. ACM Trans. Inf. Syst. 41(2) (2022). https://doi.org/10.1145/3564285
37. Wu, Z., Balloccu, S., Kumar, V., Helaoui, R., Reiter, E., Recupero, D.R., Riboni, D.: Anno-mi: a dataset of expert-annotated counselling dialogues. In: ICASSP 2022–2022 IEEE International Conference on Acoustics, Speech and Signal Processing (ICASSP), pp. 6177–6181. IEEE (2022)
38. Wu, Z., Helaoui, R., Kumar, V., Reforgiato Recupero, D., Riboni, D.: Towards detecting need for empathetic response in motivational interviewing. In: Companion Publication of the 2020 International Conference on Multimodal Interaction, pp. 497–502 (2020)
39. Xiong, C., Dai, Z., Callan, J., Liu, Z., Power, R.: End-to-end neural ad-hoc ranking with kernel pooling. In: Kando, N., Sakai, T., Joho, H., Li, H., de Vries, A.P., White, R.W. (eds.) Proceedings of the 40th International ACM SIGIR Conference on Research and Development in Information Retrieval, Shinjuku, Tokyo, Japan, 7–11 August 2017, pp. 55–64. ACM (2017). https://doi.org/10.1145/3077136.3080809
40. Yang, Z., Lan, Q., Guo, J., Fan, Y., Zhu, X., Lan, Y., Wang, Y., Cheng, X.: A deep Top-K relevance matching model for ad-hoc retrieval. In: Zhang, S., Liu, T.-Y., Li, X., Guo, J., Li, C. (eds.) CCIR 2018. LNCS, vol. 11168, pp. 16–27. Springer, Cham (2018). https://doi.org/10.1007/978-3-030-01012-6_2

Understanding Search Behavior Bias in Wikipedia

Bruno Scarone[1]($\boxtimes$), Ricardo Baeza-Yates[1,2], and Erik Bernhardson[3]

[1] Khoury College of Computer Sciences, Northeastern University, Boston, USA
scarone.b@northeastern.edu
[2] Institute for Experiential AI, Northeastern University, Boston, USA
rbaeza@acm.org
[3] Wikimedia Foundation, San Francisco, USA
ebernhardson@wikimedia.org

Abstract. As Wikipedia is one of the most visited sites on the Web, providing content to millions of readers daily from across the globe in more than 300 actively edited languages, it is relevant to understand the search behavior of its users. Extensive research over recent years has also highlighted the importance of studying the existence and potential impact of biases on the search process. Thus, based on Wikipedia's server logs we generate data sets containing millions of search sessions to characterize its website search and compare it to generic web search. We segment the studied quantities by the type of client being used and analyze whether there is a relation between the time a user spends on a page and its length, as well as between the time it takes a user to click on a result and the position of the selected page in the ranking. We rediscover known results in the context of web search that also apply to website search, along with new results in the context of website search.

Keywords: Search behavior · Search biases · Website search · Wikipedia

1 Introduction

Over recent years, the existence and impact of human bias[1] on the Web has been extensively acknowledged by the computer science community. By recognizing the Web as one of today's most prominent communication channels, [2] remarks that the first challenge in addressing bias in this context, is how to define and measure it. This work introduces different types of web biases and classifies them, highlighting that the first step to mitigate bias is being aware of it, also pointing at the fact that not all biases are negative. In particular, user interaction is outlined as a significant bias source, not only on the Web, but in general when making use of a user interface (*presentation or engagement bias*) as well as

---

[1] Bias is a systematic deviation with respect to a predefined expected reference value.

This paper was partially funded by NSF Grant 1956096 and the Wikimedia Foundation.

L. Boratto et al. (Eds.): BIAS 2023, CCIS 1840, pp. 134–146, 2023.
https://doi.org/10.1007/978-3-031-37249-0_11

from the user's own self-selected biased interaction (*position bias*). A relevant instance of the last type is *ranking bias*, particularly important in the context of any type of web search. Thus, understanding and analyzing search together with the behavior of users on the Web is a crucial activity to cope with bias.

On the other hand, Wikipedia is the world's largest and most widely used open encyclopedia on the Web, providing content to millions of readers daily from across the globe in more than 300 actively edited languages, being the 7th most visited site on the Web according to Similarweb.[2] Considering that in the top-6 of the previous ranking there are two search engines and three social networks, we could say that Wikipedia is the second most visited content-oriented website, as social networks include content but it is not their main goal. For this reason, understanding how people search using its website search tool, provides insights into several dimensions including language and devices used, as well as time spent on the platform.

Hence, in this work we focus on three research questions (RQ) to see if there are biases in the search behavior of users:

- **RQ1**: How is the search behavior affected (biased) by the client type used (desktop vs mobile interface)?
- **RQ2**: What is the relation between the time a user spends on a page and its length, *i.e.*, does page length bias the time a user spends on the page?
- **RQ3**: What is the relation between the time it takes a user to click on a result and the position of the page in the ranking, *i.e.*, does the ranking of a page bias the time it takes a user to click on the link to it?

We report the following findings:

RQ1: No significant differences are observed in the quantities studied when segmenting them by client type used, which is not the case in web search.

The distribution of dwell times, the time spent in the answer page, has two modes, with the first one in less than a second and the second in around 7 s. The former has been reported previously for mobile ads [8, 22] as *accidental clicks*. As also happens in search, this should be a generic phenomenon when interacting with a finger on a small screen. What is surprising in this context is to observe the same behavior occurring for desktop too.

RQ2: The time a user spends on Wikipedia pages is in general independent of the size of the answer link clicked, irrespective of the client being used, for dwell times larger than a minute. This behavior was known for a small sample of 25 users, but in this work we use logs containing millions of sessions.

RQ3: We found that the ranking position a user clicks on has no significant impact on the time it takes the user to perform the first click. Given that users rarely view more than 10-20 results [7] (in particular, not the entire list of results), we hypothesize they may skip results without really reading them, otherwise the time should be linear.

The rest of this paper is structured as follows: Sect. 2 discusses related work, while Sect. 3 delves into the data and methods used. In Sect. 4, we present and discuss all the results, finishing with our conclusions in Section 5.

---

[2] https://www.similarweb.com/top-websites/.

2   Related Work

We cover three related areas: bias in web search behavior, proxies for search behavior, and search/navigation in Wikipedia.

Bias in Web Search Behavior: User behavior on the Web has been empirically studied in the past. Through a user study [23] found that web browsing is a rapid activity even for pages with substantial content and links, which calls for page designs that allow for cursory reading. The study was conducted in 2004/2005 with 25 unpaid volunteers and considered the browsing activities performed by them over a period of two to four months. Our study expands the sample size to millions of search sessions. Other works have analyzed the relationship of various types of bias and the web search behavior of users. The case of *confirmation bias* in several web search contexts was analyzed by [10,17,20]. The term *domain bias*, *i.e.*, the tendency of a user to believe that a page is more relevant just because it comes from a particular domain, was introduced by [6], which detected it both in click activity and user judgments. As reported in [2], there are other relevant biases, like *ranking bias*, that have also been extensively studied. In this work, we focus on other potential sources of bias, namely type of device, page length and ranking position of a page.

Proxies for Search Behavior: As noted by [9], clicks on search results are one of the most widely used behavioral signals for predicting search satisfaction. However, clicks are affected by several factors (including position and caption bias) and thus dwell time (*i.e.*, how much time readers actually spend on a given page) is often incorporated into the analysis of user search behavior. Examples of this usage can be found in [24], where item-level dwell time is used as a proxy to quantify how likely a content item is relevant to a particular user or in [11], where it is analyzed as part of the factors that influence donations on Wikipedia. Other works have focused on analyzing user dwell times in different contexts like news [19] and non-news pages [5]. Our analysis is based on clickstream data and the dwell times derived from it, as will be discussed in Sect. 4.

Search and Navigation in Wikipedia: Due to its relevance across a diverse variety of topics [14], several efforts have been made to characterize and understand the behavior of Wikipedia users. The first systematic large-scale analysis of how readers browse Wikipedia was done in [15] based on page requests from Wikipedia's server logs, which found that navigation behavior is characterized by highly diverse structures. Additionally, they show that Wikipedia navigation is interleaved by navigation done in external sites, frequently via search engines. This work also points at the intuitive fact that navigation is abandoned when readers reach low-quality pages. Navigation paths followed by Wikipedia readers that lead them to long explorations (*rabbit holes*) were analyzed by [16]. Methods to approximate Wikipedia readers' navigation using publicly available resources

Table 1. Data sources used for this work.

Name	Data retention
Search logs[a]	90 days
discovery.query_clicks_daily (dqcd) table	90 days
wmf.mediawiki_wikitext_current table[b]	–

[a]https://github.com/wikimedia/schemas-event-primary/blob/
master/jsonschema/mediawiki/cirrussearch/request/0.0.1.yaml
[b]https://wikitech.wikimedia.org/wiki/Analytics/Data_Lake/
Content/Mediawiki_wikitext_current

was studied by [1], most notably the Wikipedia clickstream data. Dwell-time on Wikipedia pages was measured by [21], who found substantial differences across geographic regions. As remarked by [1], only few studies have characterized the navigation of readers on Wikipedia since data from web request logs is not public to protect readers' privacy. Large-scale article access data of the English Wikipedia was analyzed in [3] to compare articles with respect to the relative amount of views it received by search and the ability to relay traffic to other Wikipedia articles. Based on the English Wikipedia clickstream, [18] discovered that readers' navigation paths tend to start from semantically broad pages and become incrementally more specific with every step. Other studies have looked into how a diverse global readership assigns trust to Wikipedia articles and the strategies they use to assess Wikipedia's credibility [4], as well as into identifying why users read Wikipedia's various language editions [12]. Based on Wikipedia's private clickstream data, we focus on its website search and evaluate the previously mentioned sources of bias. These have to the best of our knowledge not been previously studied.

3 Data and Methodology

In this section we introduce the data sources used, as well as the general methodology employed for computing the results. All datasets used in this paper consist of data from the server logs of the Wikimedia Foundation. The different data sources utilized in the analysis are listed in Table 1, together with their description pages as well as the data retention policy that applies to them.

The main data source used is the dqcd table, which contains sessionized click-through for full text (*i.e.*, non autocomplete) searches made by the users (*i.e.*, non-bots), both for mobile and desktop access. The table only contains searches that have a non empty set of click-throughs, *i.e.*, searches that have at least one click, and considers all Wikipedias in the available languages[3]. The top-10 most frequent languages that account for 89% of the total traffic are shown in Table 2. The Search logs table is used to reconstruct the access method in dqcd, which was not natively available. The size of pages, used in Sect. 4.3, was obtained from the wmf.mediawiki_wikitext_current table.

---

[3] The full list can be found at https://meta.wikimedia.org/wiki/Special:SiteMatrix.

Table 2. Language distribution (top-10) `dqcd` table.

Language	Percentage	Language	Percentage
English	52.7	Spanish	3.6
German	10.6	Chinese	2.9
Japanese	4.9	Italian	2.9
Russian	4.2	Persian	1.8
French	4.1	Polish	1.3

The quantities analyzed have been computed for 2 one-week time ranges. All time ranges span the first complete week (from Monday to Sunday) of a month. The use of two different time ranges was done as an additional validation of the results. When results are considered to be similar for both time ranges only one set of results is referenced for brevity.

The client type characterization used is the one given in the web request logs' description page[4] by the `access_method` field. It uses the following criteria:

– Mobile app requests are identified by the user agent including `WikipediaApp` or `Wikipedia/5.0`.
– Mobile web requests are identified by the host name containing a subdomain of `m`, `zero`, `wap` or `mobile`.
– Any other request is classified as desktop.

Mobile app access method was excluded from the analysis, since its order of magnitude was significantly smaller than the one from the remaining 2.

When one of the data sources did not include the `access_method` field, it was reconstructed using the `getAccessMethod` function, implemented in the refinery-source code repository[5].

4   Search Behavior and Client Type

This section details the results obtained as part of the analysis when aggregating the data by client (*i.e.*, platform) type. As explained in Sect. 3 we consider two access methods: desktop and mobile web. Along the presentation, we discuss the answers to the research questions posed in Sect. 1.

4.1   Characterizing Sessions

For both datasets, approximately 60% of the sessions are desktop, while the remaining 40% are mobile web. The datasets contain 4,087,262 and 3,605,793

---

[4] https://wikitech.wikimedia.org/wiki/Analytics/Data_Lake/Traffic/Webrequest.
[5] https://github.com/wikimedia/analytics-refinery-source/blob/master/refinery-core/src/main/java/org/wikimedia/analytics/refinery/core/Webrequest.java# L277.

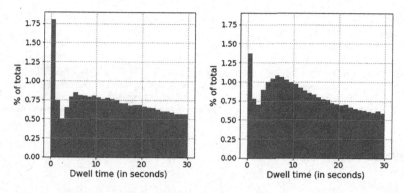

Fig. 1. Dwell times histograms for 4-10/July/2022 (subrange $[0\,s, 30\,s]$) using one second bins for desktop (left) and mobile web devices (right).

sessions. The majority ($\sim 60\%$) of sessions with 1 click are desktop sessions. The difference evens out when considering the number of clicks in $\{2, \ldots, 10\}$. The top 5 values for the number of clicks within a session lie in the interval $[268, 405]$ for desktop and $[179, 364]$ for mobile web. The majority of sessions have a number of clicks whose size lies within $[1, 5]$.

4.2 Dwell Time

Based on the clicks collected per session we computed the associated *dwell times*. Dwell time on web pages, defined as the length of time a user spends on a given document is considered, as noted in Sect. 2, a significant indicator of document relevance besides clickthrough [13]. For 2 consecutive clicks c, c' within a session, we define the associated dwell time as

$$\mathrm{dw}(c, c') = c'.\mathtt{timestamp} - c.\mathtt{timestamp}.$$

Dwell times whose duration lies in the time range $[0s, 30s]$ using one-second bins are plotted for the 2 access methods in the histograms displayed in Fig. 1.

Two modes can be observed in the histograms, the first one is hypnotized to correspond to *accidental clicks* [8, 22]. This was inspired by the fact that multiple consecutive clicks to the same page and from the same referrer were being made among several sessions. In order to validate this, consecutive requests to the same page and from the same referrer were filtered from the sessions. After the filtering the first mode vanishes, confirming the previously formulated hypothesis. By analyzing the data we also confirmed that when segmenting by access method, a dwell time can be computed for a minority of the clicks (between 26% - 30%). More "mobile web" clicks have a dwell time compared to "desktop" clicks ($\sim$ 6% difference).

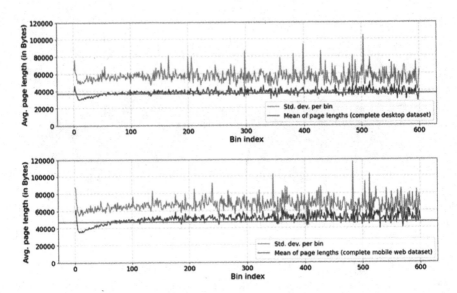

Fig. 2. Average page length per dwell time bin (subrange $[0\,s, 600\,s]$).

4.3   Page Length and Dwell Time

An additional element of interest is to evaluate the relation between the duration of dwell times and the size of the pages where these were measured. For a dwell time given by $\mathrm{dw}(c, c')$, we compute the associated page length as

$$\texttt{page\_length}(\mathrm{dw}(c, c')) = \texttt{size}(\text{page pointed by } c)$$

where the size of the page is measured in Bytes. The results obtained are shown in Fig. 2. To generate the plots, first we computed the pairs consisting of a dwell time and the corresponding page length for all dwell times measured across the sessions. Later, we classified the dwell times in bins and calculated the average of the associated page lengths. The mean plotted on the graphs corresponds to the mean computed considering all pages (*i.e.*, not restricted to the interval plotted on the charts).

By observing the plots, we note that both access methods exhibit the same general pattern: An initial peak is found closely after $0s$, due to *accidental clicks* as noted before in Sect. 4.2. Following it, there is a steady increase which indicates that for dwell times shorter than a minute (precisely lying in the interval $[5s, 48s]$ for desktop and $[5\,s, 57\,s]$ for mobile web) the longer the dwell time, the bigger in size are the pages being accessed. After this point in time, the pattern changes and the page length oscillates. Intuitively, one could assume that a user would spend more time on a longer Wikipedia page, particularly on desktop platforms. According to our data, this would only be the case for dwell times shorter than a minute irrespective of the platform type.

The relation between these two variables, this time without binning dwell times (and thus not averaging page lengths), can also be assessed by observing

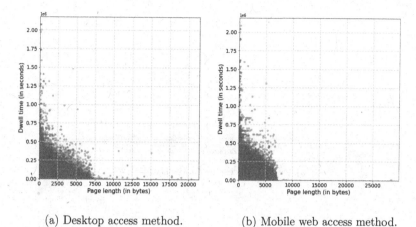

(a) Desktop access method.   (b) Mobile web access method.

Fig. 3. Dwell time vs Page length - linear scale.

Fig. 3. The figure contains two scatter plots, one for each access method. Again, no correlation can be observed in the charts. The Pearson correlation coefficient of the 2 data series is 0.029 without segmentation ($p < 0.001$), 0.023 for desktop ($p < 0.001$) and 0.036 ($p < 0.001$) for mobile devices, analytically supporting the hypothesis.

4.4 Rank Position Clicked and Time to First Click

We further evaluated the relation between the ranking position of the search result a user clicks on and the time it takes the user to first click on one (commonly known as *Time To First Click* or TTFC for short). This was done both at the search-level, as well as at the session-level by averaging over the different searches within a session. Results computed, both at the search and session levels are displayed in Fig. 4.

The two aggregation levels show similar results, meaning that the search behavior tends to be uniform within a session. In terms of access methods, TTFCs are similarly spread for the first 10 ranking positions. For the rest of the positions, points corresponding to a mobile client tend to concentrate more at the bottom of the chart. The associated Pearson correlation coefficients together with their p-values are shown in Table 3, all entries confirming the uncorrelation.

Based on these facts, we conclude that the ranking position a user clicks on has no significant impact on the time it takes the user to perform the first click. This finding, considering that users rarely view more than 10-20 results [7] (in particular, not the entire list of results), could be explained by the fact that users skip results without fully reading them, otherwise a linear time increase should be observed.

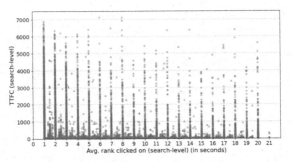

(a) Desktop access method - search-level.

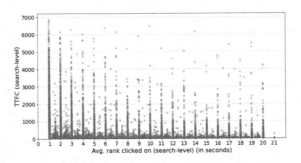

(b) Mobile web access method - search-level.

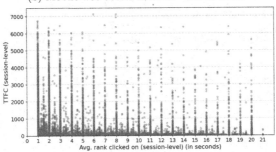

(c) Desktop access method - session-level.

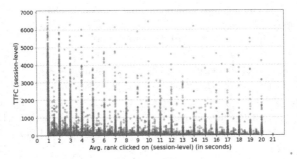

(d) Mobile web access method - session-level.

Fig. 4. Avg. rank clicked on vs TTFC.

Table 3. Rank Position vs TTFC - correlation coefficients and p-values.

Device type	Agg. level	Correlation	p-value
All	search	0.081	< 0.001
Desktop	search	0.079	< 0.001
Mobile web	search	0.090	< 0.001
All	session	0.091	< 0.001
Desktop	session	0.084	< 0.001
Mobile web	session	0.105	< 0.001

Table 4. Summary of contributions.

Group	Result	Novel for Wikipedia users seg. by client types (abbr. c.t.)	Rediscovered to be valid in (website) search	Novel for website search
C_1	*Accidental clicks phenomenon*	✓ [Ind. of c.t.]	✓ [Prev. context: mobile ads]	✓
C_2	Time a user spends on a Wikipedia page is ind. from page length	✓ [Ind. of c.t.]	✓ [Prev. context: web search, we expand sample size]	✓
C_3	Ranking pos. clicked on is ind. from TTFC	✓ [Ind. of c.t.]	-	✓

5   Conclusions

We have presented several new results regarding the search behavior of Wikipedia users for the two main client types, desktop and mobile. Additionally, we have rediscovered known results in other contexts to be also valid in search, along with new results in the context of website search. Our contributions categorized across these dimensions are listed in Table 4.

Future work includes providing further insights into what factors produce the observed behavior. Particularly, given the in general transient nature of the search behavior, it would be interesting to explore either measures that encourage a more in-depth reading of the articles (and thus longer page stay times) or alternatively others which ensure that the essential information of the articles is located at the beginning of the pages. It would also be valuable to segment the users further and see if other behavioral patterns emerge from the data. Additional future work directions include extending our new results to generic web search and exploring new research questions that should also address the semantics of the queries being issued. This includes most popular languages, most popular contents, and queries that are not well satisfied by the underlying system.

Acknowledgments. The authors would like to thank Leila Zia, Martin Gerlach, Fabian Kaelin, and Mike Pham for their valuable comments and insightful discussions, as well as the anonymous reviewers for their helpful comments.

The content of this paper is based on a technical report (Available at https://meta.wikimedia.org/wiki/Research:Understanding_search_behavior_of_users.) that summarizes the work of the first author while being a Ph.D. intern at the Wikimedia Foundation in 2022. (The source code for computing the results can be found at https://gitlab.wikimedia.org/bscarone/search-metrics/.)

References

1. Arora, A., Gerlach, M., Piccardi, T., García-Durán, A., West, R.: Wikipedia reader navigation: when synthetic data is enough. In: Proceedings of the Fifteenth ACM International Conference on Web Search and Data Mining, pp. 16–26. WSDM 2022, Association for Computing Machinery, New York, NY, USA (2022). https://doi.org/10.1145/3488560.3498496
2. Baeza-Yates, R.: Bias on the web. Commun. ACM **61**(6), 54–61 (2018). https://doi.org/10.1145/3209581
3. Dimitrov, D., Lemmerich, F., Flöck, F., Strohmaier, M.: Query for architecture, click through military: comparing the roles of search and navigation on wikipedia. In: Proceedings of the 10th ACM Conference on Web Science, pp. 371–380. WebSci 2018, Association for Computing Machinery, New York, NY, USA (2018). https://doi.org/10.1145/3201064.3201092
4. Elmimouni, H., Forte, A., Morgan, J.: Why people trust wikipedia articles: Credibility assessment strategies used by readers. In: Proceedings of the 18th International Symposium on Open Collaboration. OpenSym 2022, Association for Computing Machinery, New York, NY, USA (2022). https://doi.org/10.1145/3555051.3555052
5. Homma, R., Soejima, K., Yoshida, M., Umemura, K.: Analysis of user dwell time on non-news pages. In: 2018 IEEE International Conference on Big Data (Big Data), pp. 4333–4338 (2018). https://doi.org/10.1109/BigData.2018.8621950
6. Ieong, S., Mishra, N., Sadikov, E., Zhang, L.: Domain bias in web search. In: Proceedings of the Fifth ACM International Conference on Web Search and Data Mining, pp. 413–422. WSDM 2012, Association for Computing Machinery, New York, NY, USA (2012). https://doi.org/10.1145/2124295.2124345
7. Jansen, B.J., Spink, A.: An analysis of web searching by European alltheweb.com users. Inf. Process. Manage. **41**(2), 361–381 (2005). https://doi.org/10.1016/S0306-4573(03)00067-0. https://www.sciencedirect.com/science/article/pii/S0306457303000670
8. Kaplan, Y., Krasne, N., Shtoff, A., Somekh, O.: Unbiased filtering of accidental clicks in verizon media native advertising. In: Proceedings of the 30th ACM International Conference on Information & Knowledge Management, pp. 3878–3887. CIKM 2021, Association for Computing Machinery, New York, NY, USA (2021). https://doi.org/10.1145/3459637.3481958

9. Kim, Y., Hassan, A., White, R.W., Zitouni, I.: Modeling dwell time to predict click-level satisfaction. In: Proceedings of the 7th ACM International Conference on Web Search and Data Mining, pp. 193–202. WSDM 2014, Association for Computing Machinery, New York, NY, USA (2014). https://doi.org/10.1145/2556195.2556220

10. Knobloch-Westerwick, S., Johnson, B.K., Westerwick, A.: Confirmation bias in online searches: impacts of selective exposure before an election on political attitude strength and shifts. J. Comput.-Mediated Commun. **20**(2), 171–187 (2014). https://doi.org/10.1111/jcc4.12105

11. Kocielnik, R., Keyes, O., Morgan, J.T., Taraborelli, D., McDonald, D.W., Hsieh, G.: Reciprocity and donation: how article topic, quality and dwell time predict banner donation on wikipedia. Proc. ACM Hum.-Comput. Interact. **2**(CSCW), 3274360 (2018). https://doi.org/10.1145/3274360

12. Lemmerich, F., Sáez-Trumper, D., West, R., Zia, L.: Why the world reads wikipedia: Beyond English speakers. In: Proceedings of the Twelfth ACM International Conference on Web Search and Data Mining, pp. 618–626. WSDM 2019, Association for Computing Machinery, New York, NY, USA (2019). https://doi.org/10.1145/3289600.3291021

13. Liu, C., White, R.W., Dumais, S.: Understanding web browsing behaviors through weibull analysis of dwell time. In: Proceedings of the 33rd International ACM SIGIR Conference on Research and Development in Information Retrieval, pp. 379–386. SIGIR 2010, Association for Computing Machinery, New York, NY, USA (2010). https://doi.org/10.1145/1835449.1835513

14. Okoli, C., Mehdi, M., Mesgari, M., Nielsen, F.Å., Lanamäki, A.: Wikipedia in the eyes of its beholders: a systematic review of scholarly research on wikipedia readers and readership. J. Am. Soc. Inf. Sci. **65**(12), 2381–2403 (2014)

15. Piccardi, T., Gerlach, M., Arora, A., West, R.: A large-scale characterization of how readers browse wikipedia. ACM Trans. Web **17**, 1–22 (2023). https://doi.org/10.1145/3580318, https://doi.org/10.1145/3580318, just Accepted

16. Piccardi, T., Gerlach, M., West, R.: Going down the rabbit hole: characterizing the long tail of wikipedia reading sessions. In: Companion Proceedings of the Web Conference 2022, pp. 1324–1330. WWW 2022, Association for Computing Machinery, New York, NY, USA (2022). https://doi.org/10.1145/3487553.3524930

17. Rieger, A., Draws, T., Theune, M., Tintarev, N.: This item might reinforce your opinion: Obfuscation and labeling of search results to mitigate confirmation bias. In: Proceedings of the 32nd ACM Conference on Hypertext and Social Media, pp. 189–199. HT 2021, Association for Computing Machinery, New York, NY, USA (2021). https://doi.org/10.1145/3465336.3475101

18. Rodi, G.C., Loreto, V., Tria, F.: Search strategies of wikipedia readers. PLOS ONE **12**(2), 1–15 (2017). https://doi.org/10.1371/journal.pone.0170746

19. Seki, Y., Yoshida, M.: Analysis of user dwell time by category in news application. In: 2018 IEEE/WIC/ACM International Conference on Web Intelligence (WI), pp. 732–735 (2018). https://doi.org/10.1109/WI.2018.000-3

20. Suzuki, M., Yamamoto, Y.: Analysis of relationship between confirmation bias and web search behavior. In: Proceedings of the 22nd International Conference on Information Integration and Web-Based Applications & ; Services, pp. 184–191. iiWAS 2020, Association for Computing Machinery, New York, NY, USA (2021). https://doi.org/10.1145/3428757.3429086

21. TeBlunthuis, N., Bayer, T., Vasileva, O.: Dwelling on wikipedia: investigating time spent by global encyclopedia readers. In: Proceedings of the 15th International Symposium on Open Collaboration. OpenSym 2019, Association for Computing Machinery, New York, NY, USA (2019). https://doi.org/10.1145/3306446.3340829

22. Tolomei, G., Lalmas, M., Farahat, A., Haines, A.: You must have clicked on this ad by mistake! data-driven identification of accidental clicks on mobile ads with applications to advertiser cost discounting and click-through rate prediction. Int. J. Data Sci. Anal. **7**(1), 53–66 (2019)
23. Weinreich, H., Obendorf, H., Herder, E., Mayer, M.: Not quite the average: An empirical study of web use. ACM Trans. Web **2**(1), 1326566 (2008). https://doi.org/10.1145/1326561.1326566
24. Yi, X., Hong, L., Zhong, E., Liu, N.N., Rajan, S.: Beyond clicks: Dwell time for personalization. In: Proceedings of the 8th ACM Conference on Recommender Systems, pp. 113–120. RecSys 2014, Association for Computing Machinery, New York, NY, USA (2014). https://doi.org/10.1145/2645710.2645724

Do You MIND? Reflections on the MIND Dataset for Research on Diversity in News Recommendations

Sanne Vrijenhoek[(⊠)]

Institute for Information Law, University of Amsterdam, Amsterdam,
The Netherlands
s.vrijenhoek@uva.nl

Abstract. The MIND dataset is at the moment of writing the most extensive dataset available for the research and development of news recommender systems. This work analyzes the suitability of the dataset for research on diverse news recommendations. On the one hand we analyze the effect the different steps in the recommendation pipeline have on the distribution of article categories, and on the other hand we check whether the supplied data would be sufficient for more sophisticated diversity analysis. We conclude that while MIND is a great step forward, there is still a lot of room for improvement.

Keywords: news recommendation · dataset analysis · diversity

1 Introduction

Engagement with the news has dropped drastically over the last years, with interest dropping from 63% in 2017 to 51% in 2022, and a significant number of people avoiding news altogether [5]. News recommender systems may have a role to play in alleviating these issues by correctly identifying a reader's interest and bringing the right content to the right people. An often-heard criticism on news recommender systems is that they increase the risk of locking users in so-called 'filter bubbles', where users are consistently presented with items similar to their preferences or items they have interacted with before. The presence of these filter bubbles and their effects has been hard to prove or disprove, exacerbated by the lack of an exact definition [4]. The in 2020 published MIND dataset [12] is at the moment of writing the largest open source dataset for training and evaluating news recommender systems. It also comes with a set of state-of-the-art news recommender systems that can be trained to predict the articles users will click, and can as such be used to investigate the influence news recommender systems have on the distribution of news content and its diversity, often quoted as the antidote for filter bubbles. Recent work has argued for a normative interpretation of diversity that reflects the role news plays in democratic society [9,10]. The normative diversity metrics proposed here rely on complex metadata that is not

© The Author(s), under exclusive license to Springer Nature Switzerland AG 2023
L. Boratto et al. (Eds.): BIAS 2023, CCIS 1840, pp. 147–154, 2023.
https://doi.org/10.1007/978-3-031-37249-0_12

readily available without sophisticated analysis of article content. Furthermore, they are mostly tailored towards so-called 'hard' news. In general, *"[F]oreign and domestic politics, economy and finance are usually regarded as hard news. News about sports, celebrities, royal families, crime, scandals and service are regarded as soft news."* [6]. In this regard the MIND dataset comes with a number of caveats. MSN News (rebranded Microsoft Start in September 2021) is a news aggregator, and there is very little information available on what news content makes it onto the platform, and how values such as diversity and inclusivity are balanced with financial gains[1]. As the MIND dataset is expected to contain a significant amount of soft news, it may not be directly useful for research into normative diversity, and experiments run on it may come back skewed. To investigate this we study the overall content present in MIND, using the article category, which is directly available in the dataset, as the relevant unit of analysis. By comparing the presence of article categories at different stages of the recommendation pipeline we can analyze both the influence the recommender system has on the distribution of content and the datasets' suitability for more in-depth news diversity research.

2   Method

MIND contains the interactions of 1 million randomly sampled and anonymized users with the news items on MSN News between October 12 and November 22 of 2019. Each datapoint contains an anonymized user id, the user's reading history at that point in time, a list of which items were presented to the user (which we here refer to as the 'candidate list'), and which of these items the user ended up clicking. [12] describe the performance of several news recommender algorithms when trained on this dataset, including news-specific recommendation methods NPA, NAML, LSTUR and NRMS. The recommenders rank each candidate based on the likeliness a user will click on it. Unfortunately, how the items for the candidate list are chosen is not discussed in the paper. The data is split among training-, validation- and test sets. We generate the recommendations by running the code in the supplied notebooks[2] with the large dataset. In total, 376.471 interactions with the system are recorded, and on average each candidate list consisted of 37 items. 25% of all interactions had 10 items or less in the candidate list. Close to half (179.383) of the anonymized user ids are unique, with roughly 50.000 and 16.000 ids occurring respectively 2 and 3 times, and 10.000 ids returning more frequently. We assume that user ids are static, and that this means that half of the users only access the site once, and roughly 48.000 visits are from recurring users (>4 times). The average time difference between a user id's first- and last recording in the system is 6 h and 22 min, and the maximum 23 h and 20 min. We calculate the overlap between the generated recommendations using Rank-Biased Overlap (RBO) [11], reported in Table 1. This shows a strong overlap in the results of the neural recommenders of $0.61 - 0.63$

---

[1] according to its Support page *"[...] the content we show aligns with our values and [...] crucial information features prominently in our experiences"*).

[2] https://github.com/microsoft/recommenders/tree/main/examples/00_quick_start.

Table 1. Rank-biased Overlap (RBO) between different neural recommender strategies. The calculation encompasses the complete ranking list.

	LSTUR	NPA	NAML
NRMS	0,614	0,626	0,746
NAML	0,616	0,639	–
NPA	0,635	–	–

between most recommenders, with a much higher score of 0.746 between NRMS and NAML. As Rank Biased Overlap weighs matches at the beginning of the lists more heavily than those at the end, the recommendations should be divergent enough to observe differences in their outcomes. Interestingly, LSTUR and NRMS are reported by [12] to perform best in terms of accuracy, and show comparatively little overlap in Table 1. To avoid redundancy we will only include LSTUR and NRMS in further analysis and comparison with the content in the dataset.

3   Results

The different article categories present at different stages of the recommendation pipeline are counted and averaged, the results of which are displayed in Table 2. For the recommended items, only the top 8 are considered.[3] As the goal of the neural recommenders is to predict which items have been clicked, the category distributions for the neural recommenders often resembles the distribution in the 'clicked' column.

Table 2 shows a general overview of the distribution of article categories among all the articles that were in the dataset, the result after the first candidate selection, what was in users' history, and in the set of articles recommended by LSTUR and NRMS. Furthermore, we aggregate the categories present into *hard* and *soft* news following the distinction described in the Introduction. In this dataset, this means that the categories 'news' and 'finance' are considered hard news, whereas the rest is soft. One major discrepancy can already be observed after candidate selection: the 'lifestyle' category, which in the complete dataset only accounts for 4.4% of the articles, has a comparatively big representation (17%) in the set of candidates. The news and sport categories are the most inversely affected, with a 30% and 31% representation in the overall dataset and 23% and 16% after candidate selection. Because the recommender strategies evaluated here have no influence over the candidate selection, this is an important observation to take into account.

In general, the two news-specific recommender strategies seem to behave largely similar. Given that the neural recommenders take the items in users'

---

[3] The dataset also contains a few items with categories 'kids', 'middleeast' and 'games', but as these appear less than 0.1% in the full dataset and never in the recommendations they are left out of the analysis.

Table 2. Distribution of the different article categories (the whole dataset, what was in the users' reading history, the dataset after candidate selection, and what the user clicked), and the recommender approaches. For the recommendations the top 8 items are selected. The distribution shown does not account for ranking.

	MIND				Recommendations	
	all	candidate	history	clicked	LSTUR	NRMS
hard	0,363	0,302	0,348	0,269	0,261	0,253
soft	0,636	0,698	0,622	0,730	0,739	0,747
news	0,305	0,233	0,279	0,235	0,215	0,224
sports	0,314	0,163	0,142	0,245	0,209	0,207
finance	0,058	0,069	0,069	0,034	0,046	0,029
travel	0,049	0,027	0,030	0,020	0,024	0,021
video	0,045	0,020	0,019	0,021	0,021	0,016
lifestyle	0,044	0,171	0,105	0,178	0,174	0,185
foodanddrink	0,043	0,068	0,050	0,057	0,078	0,077
weather	0,040	0,028	0,012	0,015	0,028	0,021
autos	0,030	0,030	0,036	0,024	0,019	0,019
health	0,028	0,034	0,047	0,034	0,047	0,041
music	0,013	0,044	0,027	0,035	0,042	0,057
tv	0,013	0,047	0,082	0,048	0,046	0,041
entertainment	0,008	0,029	0,034	0,024	0,029	0,034
movies	0,008	0,038	0,038	0,030	0,024	0,028

reading history into account, we would expect the recommenders to reflect similar patterns as the history; however, this does not seem to be the case. On the contrary, while the list of candidate items consisted of 23% news items, and the reading history almost 28%, the neural recommenders are further downplaying the share of news items in the recommendations, containing only about 22% news. The opposite happens for the sport and lifestyle category: where the candidate selection contains 16% sport and 17% lifestyle, and the reading history respectively 14% and 10%, the LSTUR recommender is increasing the presence of these categories to 21% and 17%. It does, however, very closely resemble the distribution of items that users have clicked, which is also not surprising given that this is what the recommender is optimized on.

More interesting patterns can be observed when considering the length of the recommendation, as shown in Table 3. At 1, only the item with the highest predicted relevance is included, continuing on until all items in the recommendations are. At this point, the recommendation is equal to the full candidate list, as ordering is not taken into account in this analysis. The table is ordered on the category's share in position 1, which is of extra importance given an average user's tendency towards position bias [2]. Both LSTUR and NRMS are very likely to recommend sports and news at the beginning of a recommendation. Finance only appears much later: despite it's relatively large presence in both the overall dataset and the candidate list (7% and 6%), finance does not even appear among NRMS' top 10 categories. They also both prominently feature category 'foodanddrink' in first position (10% and 15%, versus only 7% in the candidate list). But we see also more distinct differences: NRMS comparatively often recommends items from it's top categories in first place, whereas for LSTUR this is more spread out. At the first position, NRMS recommends more than 83% of the content out of 4 most frequently occurring categories, whereas for LSTUR this is around 74%. NRMS is also much more likely than LSTUR to recommend news in the first position (28% vs. 22%). At position 10, both recommenders actually list *less* news than in the overall dataset. It seems here that news either gets recommended in the top positions, or not at all.

Table 3. Distribution of the top 8 article categories at different recommendation lengths, ordered by frequency at recommendation length 1. Category 'food' is short for category 'foodanddrink'.

		1	2	5	10	20	∞
LSTUR	sports	0,24	0,25	0,23	0,20	0,18	0,16
	news	0,22	0,21	0,21	0,22	0,22	0,23
	lifestyle	0,17	0,17	0,17	0,17	0,17	0,17
	food	0,10	0,09	0,08	0,08	0,07	0,07
	health	0,04	0,05	0,05	0,05	0,04	0,03
	travel	0,04	0,03	0,03	0,02	0,02	0,03
	enter	0,03	0,03	0,03	0,03	0,03	0,03
	finance	0,03	0,04	0,04	0,05	0,06	0,07
NRMS	news	0,28	0,26	0,23	0,22	0,22	0,23
	sports	0,22	0,22	0,22	0,20	0,18	0,16
	lifestyle	0,17	0,18	0,18	0,18	0,18	0,17
	food	0,15	0,13	0,09	0,07	0,07	0,07
	music	0,04	0,06	0,06	0,06	0,05	0,04
	enter	0,03	0,03	0,03	0,03	0,03	0,03
	health	0,02	0,03	0,04	0,04	0,04	0,03
	tv	0,02	0,02	0,03	0,04	0,05	0,05

4 Conclusion

Analyzing the results of the different recommendation strategies reveals characteristics of the recommendations that are not visible when purely reporting on performance statistics such as NDCG or AUC. The neural recommenders have a distinct impact on the dissemination of content, especially considering what content is present in the overall dataset and the type of content users have clicked in the past. As expected, the neural recommenders largely reflect the types of clicks that have been recorded. The candidate list reduces the presence of frequently occurring categories while inflating that of less frequent ones. However, this behavior is to be expected; the candidate selection ought to contain a wide range of content, so that the recommender system can correctly identify content that is specifically relevant to that particular user. It does however raise questions about the granularity of the categories chosen. In the design of MIND the choice was made to distinguish between 'movies', 'music', 'tv' and 'entertainment', even though these account for less than 10% of all items in the dataset. A dataset that is more focused on news content could instead split this top-level category into subcategories such as 'local news', 'global news' or 'politics'. MIND does contain subcategories, such as 'newsus', 'newspolitics', and 'newsworld' (respectively 47%, 17% and 8% of all news items), which could be more relevant for future research.

The neural recommenders also behave differently when compared to each other, with NRMS prominently recommending news and food in top positions, and LSTUR favoring sports and other, less common categories. With the neural recommenders largely focusing on lifestyle and entertainment, and downplaying news and finance, one could argue they mostly promote soft news. This is not to say these personalized recommendations are bad; there can be value in bringing the right soft news to the right people, as [1] notes that consuming soft news may serve as a stepping stone to more active participation and engagement. This does warrant a more in-depth discussion about the purpose of the recommender system, a thorough investigation into the mismatch between produced content, user reading history and user clicking behavior, and an editorial decision on the balance between 'quality' and 'fun' [8].

In terms of research into normative diversity, MIND leaves a few things to be desired. With only 20% of articles in the recommendations being news articles, there is only little information to determine whether users receive a balanced overview of the news. This is strengthened by the lack of metadata that is present in the dataset: only the article title, (sub)category and url are directly supplied. Automatic stance- or viewpoint detection based on article fulltext, which could be retrieved by following the url to the MSN News website, may be a direction for future research [7]. For example, [3] published a detailed annotation of different stances and emotions present in German news articles. They do, however, lack the scale and user interactions that MIND has.

The majority of interactions recorded in MIND are (assumed to be) unique visits, though it does contain a considerable amount of returning users: almost 10.000 access the system 4 times or more, resulting in a total of 48.000 visits from recurring users. If we combine this with the average length of the candidate list of 37 items, and the fact that 22% of recommended items is news, this yields us about 400.000 news items shown. However, even when the users return to the system more frequently, there are on average only six hours between a user's first and last interaction with the system, and no user id appears again after more than 24 h pass. This implies that user ids are reset, making it impossible to see how the users and the recommender's behavior towards those users change over time [4]. Ideally, if one were to research the effect of a recommender system on the diversity of consumed news, they would want to do this based on a system with 1) a large number of frequently returning users (though a smaller number of unique users compared to MIND would be acceptable), 2) a focus on hard news, and 3) over a longer period of time, allowing for both the users and the recommender system to evolve over time. In conclusion: the MIND dataset is, especially given the fact that it is open source, a great step forward in the research on news recommender systems and their effects. However, when to goal is to move the discussion beyond recommender accuracy and towards news recommender diversity, there are still several points of improvement necessary.

Acknowledgements. I thank Mateo Gutierrez Granada for his help in generating the recommendations used in this analysis. I also thank Savvina Daniil, Lien Michiels and an anonymous reviewer for their critical comments on earlier versions of this work, and in doing so their contributions to improving the end product.

References

1. Andersen, K.: An entrance for the uninterested: who watches soft news and how does it affect their political participation? Mass Commun. Soc. **22**(4), 487–507 (2019)
2. Craswell, N., Zoeter, O., Taylor, M., Ramsey, B.: An experimental comparison of click position-bias models. In: Proceedings of the 2008 International Conference on Web Search and Data Mining, pp. 87–94, WSDM 2008, Association for Computing Machinery, New York, NY, USA (2008). ISBN 9781595939272, https://doi.org/10.1145/1341531.1341545
3. Mascarell, L., et al.: Stance detection in German news articles. In: Proceedings of the Fourth Workshop on Fact Extraction and VERification (FEVER), pp. 66–77, Association for Computational Linguistics (2021)
4. Michiels, L., Leysen, J., Smets, A., Goethals, B.: What are filter bubbles really? a review of the conceptual and empirical work. In: Adjunct Proceedings of the 30th ACM Conference on User Modeling, Adaptation and Personalization, pp. 274–279 (2022)
5. Newman, N., Fletcher, R., Robertson, C.T., Eddy, K., Nielsen, R.K.: Reuters institute digital news report 2022. Reuters Institute for the study of Journalism (2022)
6. Reinemann, C., Stanyer, J., Scherr, S., Legnante, G.: Hard and soft news: A review of concepts, operationalizations and key findings. Journalism **13**(2), 221–239 (2012)
7. Reuver, M., Mattis, N., Sax, M., Verberne, S., Tintarev, N., Helberger, N., Moeller, J., Vrijenhoek, S., Fokkens, A., van Atteveldt, W.: Are we human, or are we users? the role of natural language processing in human-centric news recommenders that nudge users to diverse content. In: Proceedings of the 1st Workshop on NLP for Positive Impact, pp. 47–59, Association for Computational Linguistics, Online (Aug 2021). https://doi.org/10.18653/v1/2021.nlp4posimpact-1.6. https://aclanthology.org/2021.nlp4posimpact-1.6
8. Smets, A., Hendrickx, J., Ballon, P.: We're in this together: a multi-stakeholder approach for news recommenders. Digital Journalism, pp. 1–19 (2022)

9. Vrijenhoek, S., Bénédict, G., Gutierrez Granada, M., Odijk, D., De Rijke, M.: Radio-rank-aware divergence metrics to measure normative diversity in news recommendations. In: Proceedings of the 16th ACM Conference on Recommender Systems, pp. 208–219 (2022)

10. Vrijenhoek, S., Kaya, M., Metoui, N., Möller, J., Odijk, D., Helberger, N.: Recommenders with a mission: assessing diversity in news recommendations. In: Proceedings of the 2021 Conference on Human Information Interaction and Retrieval, pp. 173–183 (2021)

11. Webber, W., Moffat, A., Zobel, J.: A similarity measure for indefinite rankings. ACM Trans. Inf. Syst. (TOIS) **28**(4), 1–38 (2010)

12. Wu, F., et al.: Mind: a large-scale dataset for news recommendation. ACL (2020)

Detecting and Measuring Social Bias of Arabic Generative Models in the Context of Search and Recommendation

Fouzi Harrag$^{(\boxtimes)}$ ⓘ, Chaima Mahdadi, and Amina Nourhane Ziad

Ferhat Abbas University, Setif, Algeria
fharrag@acm.org, {chaima.mahdadi,amina.ziad}@univ-setif.dz

Abstract. Pre-training large language models on vast amounts of web-scraped texts is a current trend in natural language processing. While the resulting models are capable of generating convincing text, they also reproduce harmful social biases. Several modern studies have demonstrated that societal biases have a significant impact on the outcome of information retrieval systems. Our study is among the recent studies aimed at developing methods for quantifying and mitigating bias in search results and applying them to retrieval and recommendation systems based on transformer-based language models. This paper explores expressions of bias in Arabic text generation. Analyses will be performed on samples produced by the generative model AraGPT2 (a GPT-2 fine-tuned for Arabic). An Arabic bias classifier (Regard Classifier) based on new transformer model AraBERT (a BERT fine-tuned for Arabic) will be used to captures the social Bias of an Arabic-generated sentence or text. For the development of this classifier, a dataset will be crowd-sourced, cleaned, and independently annotated. AraGPT2 will be used to generate more biased descriptions from the standard prompts. Our Bias Detection Model (BDM) will be based on the combination of the two transformers (AraGPT2-AraBERT) models. In addition to our quantitative evaluation study, we will also conduct a qualitative study to understand how our system would compare to others approaches where users try to find bias in Arabic texts generated using AraGPT2 model. Our proposed model has achieved very encouraging results by reaching an accuracy percentage of 81%.

Keywords: Bias detection · Arabic Generative Models · Transformers · AraBERT · AraGPT2 · Arabic Natural Language Understanding (NLU) · Search · Recommendation Systems

1 Introduction

Nowadays, the presence of Artificial Intelligence (AI) and ML (Machine Learning) is deeply rooted in our daily lives. We have become almost entirely dependent on intelligent algorithms to make many decisions on our behalf, from the news feeds we receive, to filtering spam email, in addition to ads, language translation, and image classification, to controlling traffic, to determining who has priority get a loan, the list goes on.

L. Boratto et al. (Eds.): BIAS 2023, CCIS 1840, pp. 155–168, 2023.
https://doi.org/10.1007/978-3-031-37249-0_13

While human biases are inevitable due to the human nature, algorithmic bias must be manageable. Whereas, artificial intelligence (AI) systems are essentially intelligent systems capable of simulating human intelligence in carrying out the tasks assigned to them. Autonomous software systems are also artificial intelligence systems that have complete autonomy in their operation. Thus, they are able to make complex decisions without human intervention. It seems that without any convincing or clear reasons, artificial intelligence systems made headlines for being biased, after a series of problems caused by these systems. The approximate beginning of this series of news was in 2017, when Facebook apologized for an error in the posts translation service that caused the Israeli police to arrest a Palestinian man after he published a post in Arabic containing the word "good morning" on his Facebook page, and the Facebook service translated the sentence into "kill them". AIs also tend to unfairly associate certain words with a specific set of topics, which is why FaceApp apologized for building an AI that was racist by associating hotness feature with being white. When the user taps the hotness button on FaceApp to make the picture hot, the application automatically makes the face in the image white. Thus, creating the impression that only a white face is hot regardless of other skin tone [1]. In this context, Caliskan et., al [2] warned, "AI has the potential to reinforce existing biases because, unlike humans, algorithms may be unequipped to consciously counteract learned biases". Referring to the results of [3], it turns out that the percentage of female "CEO" is only 11% in Google Images, while the US has more than 27% of female CEOs, the same remarks for "Doctors" images, which are predominantly male; while the most of the images of "nurses" are female. In fact, this data never reflects the reality. Another example that we can address, is the error in the accuracy of the COMPAS system of recidivism in the field of crime, as it was found that this system is very lenient with regard to white people and very harsh with black people. In [4], it was explained that ML algorithms are "black boxes" that are protected by industrial secret protocols and legal protections, in addition to deliberate obfuscation by large companies. Thus, distinguishing bias becomes invisible while mitigating it becomes almost impossible. While most researches focuses mainly on detecting or measuring biases in algorithms, only a few works to date have devoted attention to understanding the causes of bias detected in generation algorithms and models. On the other hand, many recent studies have shown that although recommendation algorithms achieve good and high prediction accuracy, many of them suffer from societal biases. These influences have been extensively analyzed for English, but studies for Arabic are almost nonexistent. In this work, we proposed a transfer learning based framework for bias detection in Arabic language generation model. We also proposed a New AraBERT [5] based classifier for bias detection, which allows bias checks in Social media textual data. Here, we focused on measuring and mitigating biases reproduced by large-scale language models used for Arabic text generation AraGPT2 [6]. The impact of large language models makes them a specific point of interest. Our motivation is to deal with this topic specifically for the Arabic language. Thus far, most researches on bias in natural language generation has been focusing on English [7], although German variants of models like GPT-2 do exist [13] moreover, GPT-3 [8]. European institutions are working to develop their multilingual equivalents. In consequence, research on the evaluation and mitigation of biases in Arabic language models is overdue. The idea of a bias classifier is similar to that of a sentiment classifier. However, as opposed to sentiment, regard does not capture the polarity of a sentence in general, but specifically the social perception that it reinforces. Consequently, one of the goals of this paper was the development of an Arabic bias classifier. For this end, a dedicated dataset was crowd-sourced, cleaned, and annotated. The remaining of this paper is organized as follows: Sect. 2 gives an overview of related research on measuring and mitigating bias in natural language generation. In Sect. 3, we propose conceptual approach for bias detection in Arabic generative models. Section 4 is devoted to the presentation of the results obtained from the different experiments. Section 5 concludes the paper.

2 Literature Review

Several studies have been conducted in the field of measurement and mitigation of bias in natural language processing. In the following paragraphs, we will present a series of scientific studies and researches in this field. Zhou in [3] said that "biased associations faced a challenge to detect the toxic language and develop classifiers, and what makes it difficult is fairness accuracy". To solve this problem, some methods have been created and applied to toxic detection, focusing on lexical and dialect. Those methods were capacity limited, so another strategy has been proposed to correct them, this strategy reduced the toxicity in dialect. In the end, the author discover that de-biasing a model prepared on toxic data is not as successful as just relabeling data to eliminate biases. Liang et al., in [9] discussed the impact of machine learning technologies and their utilization in our recent life in different contexts. They also mentioned different real cases of bias where pre-trained models could present very dangerous biases including sexual, religious, racist and lot of other stereotypes of bias. They defined precisely few sources of bias before creating or thinking about new standards and metrics. Using these technologies, they offered strategies to mitigate social biases during the text produc-tion. Their result after human and empirical evaluation shows the effectiveness of their experiments in mitigating bias. The work of Xu et al., [10] proposed some techniques to mitigate toxic language model (LM) generation. First, they diminish the usefulness of LM used on language by marginalized groups. Specifically, they did some automatic & human evaluations of the text generation quality when LM is conditioned by inputs in different dialects & identifiers groups. They observed that the LM become more sensitive to the changes of distribution, principally on marginalized group language. As result, they found that these breakdowns came from detoxification methods. Vaidya et al., in [11] studied the problem of models that have learned incorrectly to associate non-toxic comments as toxic comments. Their goal was to reduce identity bias in toxic comment. They used a multi-task learning model with an attention layer and get a good accuracy of 71% compared to other state of art models. As result, they found that multi-task learning models significantly improve classification performance when the comments are related to the following identities: Homosexual, Muslim, Black, and Jewish. Dathathri et al., in [12] addressed the problem of difficulty of large transformer-based language models for controlling attributes of the generative language model. They discussed the idea of using the Plug and Play Language Mode. They confirmed that Plug and Play model is more flex-ible and easy for constructing attributes. The paper of Sheng et al., in [7] covered many aspects of natural language generation models and their rapid developments. These models can generate scripts fluently and efficiently, but the researchers said that bias could appear in all stages of building of these complex software from systems deployment, to evaluation, to decoding, to data, to model architecture. Kraft in [13] presented many algorithms for detecting and mitigating bias in the German language generation using variants of GPT2 and GPT3. The work of Gururangan et al., in [14] focuses on language models pretrained on text from a model to the domain of a target task. They confirmed that unlabeled data improves performance even after domain-adaptive Pretraining. They also showed that corpus augmented using simple data selection strategies is an effective alternative, especially when resources for domain-adaptive Pretraining might be unavailable. Schick et al., in [15] presented a new technique called self-diagnosis for decoding textual description. This method reduces the probability of producing toxic text. The self-debiasing technique does not require any training data or manually crafted word list.

3   Model Architecture

This section illustrates the steps followed to investigate the main contributions of our study. The developed model shown in Fig. 1 is composed of seven (7) major steps:

1. Collecting dataset
2. Cleaning dataset
3. Training collected data with AraBERT
4. Generating tweets using AraGPT2
5. Classifying generated tweets using The *Bias Detection Model (BDM)*
6. Qualitative evaluation of results
7. Quantitative evaluation of results

Table 1 below demonstrates the abbreviations of our proposed Model.

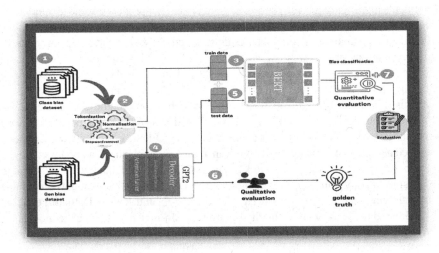

Fig. 1. Proposed Model Architecture.

Table 1. Model architecture abbreviations.

Abbreviation	Signification
E	Embedding token
CLS	[CLS] stands for classification its token should added at the beginning of every sentence
C	Class Label
T	Token

4 Experiments and Results

Different experiments have been carried out using our proposed model. This section shows the details of our work. Comparisons between experiments are also illustrated with tables and graphs.

4.1 Experiment Setup

Based on our model architecture presented in the previous section, we used Python programming language and its robust libraries to build the different modules of our system that can predict if a sentence is biased or not. Our system consists of four (4) main modules: The data Preprocessor, the AraBERT based classifier, The AraGPT2 Generator and the evaluation module. We divided the dataset into two parts. The first part will be reserved for the generation phase (about 200 tweets). The second part of our dataset, will be randomly separated into two parts, training set consisting of 70% of the initial dataset and 30% for the test set.

4.2 Research Questions

For analyzing the results, we mainly focus on the following research questions:

- RQ-1: How effective is our model under different data balancing techniques?
- RQ-2: How effective is our model by tuning some hyperparameters of our model?
- RQ-3: How effective is our model under a qualitative evaluation?

4.3 Dataset

We used the'Multilingual and Multi-Aspect Hate Speech Analysis dataset, available on *Github*[1] Published on Sep 27,2021, it consists of more than 13,000 tweet IDs related to detailed taxonomy with cross-cutting attributes, collected in 4 csv files. We have used the file named "ar dataset.csv" containing 3,353 Arabic tweets. As it is shown in Table 2, the attribute "Target" presents the cases when the tweet contains what its meaning leads to insults or discriminates against people. This represents a bias on five different cases namely origin, religious affiliation, gender, sexual orientation, special needs or other.

---

[1] https://github.com/HKUST-KnowComp/MLMA_hate_speech.

Table 2. Dataset description.

Attribute	Label	Statistic
Target	Race	877
	Gender	548
	Religion	145
	Other	1782
	Ethnicity	1

4.4 Data Pre-processing

The data pre-processing step is primordial to any successful model. It aims at preparing the data for further exploitation. After choosing our mains dataset, we started the cleansing step on our selected data. We first imported the 'NLTK' library for these operations and for every functionality we create a function to solve it. We have in total six (6) functions:

Remove Punctuations. Punctuations such as \ ؟ ( ) : !will be eliminated.

Remove Repeating Char. Using the "re" library and remove every characters repetition more than once successively.

Remove Diacritics. Remove the Arabic diacritics like *'Fatha','Dhamma','Sukun'* ... With 're' library too then turn our result into string.

Remove Numbers. Delete all the Arabic and the numeric numbers inside the data.

Remove Tag. Always removing tags from different sentences using 're' library u"@ user" # emoticons u"@ url" # symbols & pictographs.

Normalize Arabic. Replace "ة" by "ه" and " ا or إ to ا for example.

After applying different preprocessing operations, we get our dataset prepared for the coming steps of our model architecture. Noted that we have previously kept about 6% of our data to be used in the generation step.

4.5 Experiment I (RQ-1: Different Data Balancing Techniques)

This experiment provides the experimental results to the first investigated research question Q1 raised in Sect. 4.2. We proposed a model configuration built on the basic structure of AraBERT. The hyper-parameters of this architecture are described in Table 3 below.

Table 3. First Experiment Hyper-parameters.

Parameter	Value
Max Length	64
Learning Rate	0.00006
Batch Size	6
Epochs	4

As it was described in Table 3, we can easily note a huge class imbalance in the dataset that would certainly affect the system performance. To resolve the imbalanced data problem, we test four (4) different configuration of our dataset.

a) Original data.

After removing the 6% of the data for the generation step, we kept 3153 tweets; we divide them into 2207 tweets (70%) for the train data, consisting of 1720 biased sentences and 487 non-biased sentences. The remaining 30% of our data is used for testing purpose.

b) Balanced Data.

We would like to know what will happen if we changed our data distribution. Since our initial data was not balanced, we then decided to run the same experiments on new versions of the data. We applied three different balancing techniques on our initial data.

• Manually balanced data:

As we previously mentioned, our data has 3153 tweets, 715 of them are normal tweets without any type of bias compared to 2438 tweets classed as biased. Therefore, we decided to keep the same size for biased and normal sets. We removed 1723 tweets from the second set and we just kept 715 normal tweets & 715 biased tweets. Our new balanced data is next divided into 70% for training and 30% for a testing.

• SMOT balanced data:

SMOT is a method used to make data balanced by taking the minority class and making equal to the majority class [16]. We used the SMOT technique with the parameter "Sampling Strategy = Minority". The data of the minority class has been amplified from 512 to 1695.

• Augmented data:

Data augmentation describes a set of algorithms that create synthetic data from the available datasets. These synthetic data usually contain small changes to the data that require the model's predictions to be invariant. In our case of text augmentation, we tried to apply the data augmentation through the generation. Our data has biased tweet, size is twice more than the normal data. We used the normal tweets as inputs for the AraGPT2 algorithm to generate the double using two different output max length 64 and 128. We appended the new resulted tweets to the original set of normal tweets, so our new dataset contains as much biased as normal tweets.

Table 4 presents the experimental results. To better visualize the trend, we also plot the results in Fig. 3.

Table 4. First Experiment Results.

Balancing Technique	Accuracy	Precision	Recall	F1 score
Raw Data	0.80	0.77	0.60	**0.75**
Manual Balanced Data	0.61	0.61	0.61	**0.61**
SMOT Balanced Data	0.70	0.79	0.70	**0.73**
Augmented Data	0.67	0.75	0.67	**0.75**

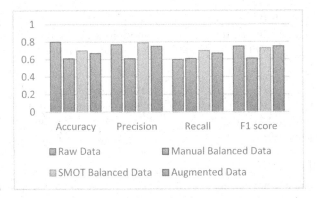

Fig. 2. Perfomances of Experiment I.

As seen in Fig. 2, the configuration of our model using the original distribution of data got the best accuracy and Macro F1 scores. Precision as well as recall show an improvement for the SMOT and augmented techniques.

From this experiment, we obtained an F1 score of 75% for the first technique, 61% for the second, 73% for the SMOT and 75% for the Augmentation technique. In the next experiment, we will add some regularization to our model and see if the performances metrics will be enhanced.

4.6 Experiment II (RQ-2: Different Hyperparameters)

In this experiment, we provide the experimental results to the second investigated research question Q2. We tested different configurations using 4 values for the parameter "Max length", 2 values for the parameter "Batch size" and 2 values for the parameter "Epochs". The hyper-parameters used to compile and run the model are illustrated in Table 5.

Table 5. Second Experiment Hyper-parameters.

Parameter	Value
Max Length	64/128/256/512
Learning Rate	0.00006
Batch Size	6/32
Epochs	4/10

Table 6 presents the experimental results of our model using the following parameters Max_length = 512, Batch_size = 6 and Epochs = 4.

Table 6. Second Experiment results.

Max Length	Accuracy	Precision	Recall	F1 score
64	0.80	0.77	0.60	**0.75**
128	0.78	0.72	0.77	**0.69**
256	0.78	0.74	0.78	**0.74**
512	0.81	0.78	0.81	**0.78**

Figure 3 below is showing the approximated training and validation loss obtained by our model based on the hyper-parameters of experiment II.

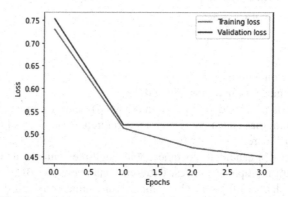

Fig. 3. Training and validation loss for best hyperparameters.

The results of this experiment clearly show us the ability of transformer learning models to detect bias in Arabic texts with a high degree of accuracy. Through this experiment, we can also realize the importance of the hyperparameters' impact on the performance of these classifiers. The AraBERT model using the parameter "Max_Length" = 512 significantly outperformed all other models.

4.7   Experiment III (RQ-3: Qualitative Evaluation of Generation Process)

This experiment provides the experimental results to the third investigated research question RQ3 raised in Sect. 4.2. We proposed a model configuration built on the basic structure of AraGPT2. The maximum length of generated texts is 80 words. For the generation process, we used the set of 6% that was initially kept, which is about 200 tweets. Table 7 shows the hyper-parameters of our generation model.

Table 7. Third Experiment Hyper-parametres.

Parameter	Value
Return Tensor	PT
Input Max Length	80
Skip Special Tokens	True
Output Max Length	80

Table 8. ROUGE & BLEU Evaluation Statistics.

Metric	Value
BLEU Score	1.107090
BLUE-1 Score	0.069522
ROUGE-1 Score "r"	0.008020
ROUGE-1 Score "p"	0.000839
ROUGE-1 Score "f"	0.000465

a) Model evaluation with Bleu & Rouge.
- BLEU (BiLingual Evaluation Understudy).
  Bleu measure is interested on how much the words (and/or n-grams) in the machine generated summaries appeared in the human reference summaries [17].
- BLEU Corpus Score.
  Compares one (1) candidate document with multiple sentence and 1 + reference document with multiple sentences. Different than averaging BLEU scores of each sentence, it calculates the score by summing the numerators and denominators for each hypothesis-reference(s) pairs before the division [17].
- ROUGE (Recall Oriented Understudy for Gisting Evaluation).
  It includes measures to automatically determine the quality of a summary by comparing it to other (ideal) summaries created by humans. The measures count the number of overlapping units such as n_gram, word sequences, and word pairs between the computer-generated summary to be evaluated and the ideal summaries created

by humans [18]. Table 8 is showing the model evaluation results with BLEU and ROUGE. We can notice that our system gave acceptable results.

b) Human Annotation Evaluation.
Motivation: We are interested in investigating the question of how does the difference in annotation affect our model's evaluation? In this research, the annotation task is specifically focused on *Target Bias* to make comparison with automatic evaluation easy.

Approach: We perform a limited scale qualitative analysis to understand to what extent human are able to detect bias in generated text. In this experiment, each of the 200 samples are annotated by two annotators for *Target Bias* in generated tweets. We conducted a user experience study of our system with two annotators (*E1, E2*), where the participants judge our system reporting biased or unbiased for each generated text. In an annotation, the annotators will not always agree: for instance, some may be more severe in their judgments than others. *E1, E2* discussed also the results that were obtained by our system to resolve any disagreements until reaching a consensus.

• Kappa
In the context of test–retest or annotators agreement in our case, Cohen's Kappa coefficient [19] is often used to measure inter-rater reliability. The Kappa coefficient in test–retest represents the degree of agreement between two sets of data obtained on two distinct occasions or more.

We organized our two annotator's results in the Table 9 below.

Table 9. Annotation Results.

	Feature	Annotator 2		
		Absent or 1	Present or 0	Total
Annotator 1	Absent or 1	A = 75	B = 11	A + B = 86
	Present or 0	C = 32	D = 82	C + D = 114
	Total	A + C = 107	B + D = 93	A + B + C + D = 200

Our annotators agreed that 75 tweet are biased and 82 tweet are normal, so they agreed on 157 tweet and disagreed on 43 between normal and biased from the total of 200 tweets. The percentage of agreement is $p_0 = 0.79$ calculated with the following formula:

$$P_0 = \frac{A \text{ expected value} + D \text{ expected}}{(A + B + C + D)} * 100\% \tag{1}$$

We could not take this percentage as a reference because one of the annotators or both could evaluate a tweet by a chance. The kappa value take this chance into count. It is calculated based on the Observed Agreement p_0 compared to how much this agreement would be expected by chance called Expected Agreement $p_e = 0.27$.

The final Kappa coefficient is calculated based on the following formula:

$$\text{Kappa} = \frac{p_0 - p_e}{1 - p_e} = \frac{0.79 - 0.27}{1 - 0.27} = 0.72 \tag{2}$$

- Automatic evaluation.
  The automatic evaluation step is technically done before the comparison between annotators and the model prediction. Currently, after the training phase of our model, we used our generated Arabic tweets as inputs to test our model. We asked the system to predict the biasness in the generated tweets based on what the model have already learned from the previous experiments. Our system is used as a *Regard Classifier* for the detection of bias introduced by the generative model. The result of the prediction phase are used with the previous annotator's results (*Ground Truth*) to finalize the global evaluation process.
- Final evaluation.
  This phase is putting a spotlight on every case between the prediction and the annotators result. Table 10 presents the final evaluation results of RQ-3. The system agreed with the annotators in 96 tweet, 69 of them are biased while the rest are normal tweets. The percentage of agreement is 48%.

Table 10. Final Evaluation Statistics.

	Normal tweet	Biased tweet
Annotator 1	115	85
Annotator 2	95	105
The system	43	157

As Findings for Experiment III, we can say that now, we could know how much our annotators agreed in their vote from the kappa result. As it is 72% leads us to know that their agreement level is **Substantial** and they are reliable in [61%–80%] of the data.

The system agreed with the annotators in 96 tweet, 69 of them are biased while the rest are normal tweets. The percentage of agreement with system is of 48%, which means that the annotators still contradict the system in more than 50% of the results. This also means that the research field of studying bias, detecting and mitigating it, still needs great efforts, especially with regard to low resourced languages such as Arabic Language and Arabic dialects.

5 Conclusion

In this paper, we propose a new transfer-learning-based paradigm consisting of seven (7) major steps. We designed a regard classifier or bias detection model based on a modified version of AraBERT to achieve the goal of detecting whether an Arabic sentence or tweet is biased or not. The Arabic generation model was built on top of AraGPT2 to allow us to generate a set of sentences using normal, unbiased Arabic tweets as input. We tested the ability of AraGPT2 to generate different types of bias stereotypes. In order to obtain the best result associated with detecting bias using AraBERT, we conducted several experiments by changing different Hyperparameters. We achieved the best result, which was close to 81% for the accuracy metric, by using the following parameters: Max_Length = 512, batch_size = 6, and Epochs = 4. In the generation step, our experiment consists of recruiting two annotators to compare their evaluation and the results of their work on the generative model evaluation process. We measured the agreement between them using the Kappa measure and then compared the results with the AraBERT predictions. Ultimately, the methods described in this paper yielded promising results, as described in the last section. However, we can consider improving our system by training the model on a larger data set, and doing more experiments. Furthermore, we can invest in using our model to serve other Arabic NLP applications. In fact, social bias can potentially influence on search and recommendation systems' decisions, which align with many recent studies that rise the risk of unfairness and social bias in the data used to train and test those systems. In this direction, our bias detection model can be effective in catching appropriate hate speech keywords that have direct impact on the results of search and recommender systems.

References

1. Hern, A., Facebook translates' good morning'into'attack them', leading to arrest. The Guardian, 24 (2017)
2. Caliskan, A., Bryson, J.J., Narayanan, A.: Semantics derived automatically from language corpora contain human-like biases. Science **356**(6334), 183–186 (2017)
3. Zhou, X: Challenges in automated debiasing for toxic language detection. University of Washington (2021)
4. Pasquale, F.: The Black Box Society: The Secret Algorithms that Control Money and Information. Harvard University Press (2015). https://doi.org/10.4159/harvard.978067473 6061
5. Antoun, W., Baly, F., Hajj, H.: AraBERT: transformer-based model for Arabic language understanding. arXiv preprint arXiv:2003.00104 (2020)
6. Antoun, W., Baly, F., Hajj, H., Aragpt2: pre-trained transformer for Arabic language generation. arXiv preprint arXiv:2012.15520 (2020)
7. Sheng, E., Chang, K.W., Natarajan, P., Peng, N.: Societal biases in language generation: progress and challenges. arXiv preprint arXiv:2105.04054 (2021)
8. Brown, T., et al.: Language models are few-shot learners. Adv. Neural. Inf. Process. Syst. **33**, 1877–1901 (2020)
9. Liang, P.P., Wu, C., Morency, L.P., Salakhutdinov, R.: Towards understanding and mitigating social biases in language models. In: International Conference on Machine Learning, pp. 6565–6576. PMLR (2021)
10. Xu, A., Pathak, E., Wallace, E., Gururangan, S., Sap, M., Klein, D.: Detoxifying language models risks marginalizing minority voices. arXiv preprint arXiv:2104.06390 (2021)
11. Vaidya, A., Mai, F., Ning, Y.: Empirical analysis of multi-task learning for reducing identity bias in toxic comment detection. In: Proceedings of the International AAAI Conference on Web and Social Media, vol. 14, pp. 683–693 (2020)
12. Dathathri, S.: Plug and play language models: a simple approach to controlled text generation. arXiv preprint arXiv:1912.02164 (2019)

13. Kraft, A.: Triggering models: measuring and mitigating bias in German language generation, Doctoral dissertation, Master's thesis, University of Hamburg (2021)

14. Gururangan, S., Marasović, A., Swayamdipta, S., Lo, K., Beltagy, I., Downey, D., Smith, N.A.: Don't stop pretraining: adapt language models to domains and tasks. arXiv preprint arXiv:2004.10964 (2020)

15. Schick, T., Udupa, S., Schütze, H.: Self-diagnosis and self-debiasing: a proposal for reducing corpus-based bias in NLP. Trans. Assoc. Comput. Linguist. **9**, 1408–1424 (2021)

16. SMOTE for Imbalanced Classification with Python - MachineLearningMastery.com. Accessed 09 Jan 2023

17. Papineni, K., Roukos, S., Ward, T., Zhu, W.J.: BLEU: a method for automatic evaluation of machine translation. In: Proceedings of the 40th Annual Meeting of the Association for Computational Linguistics, pp. 311–318 (2002)

18. Lin, C.Y.: ROUGE: a package for automatic evaluation of summaries. In: Text Summarization Branches Out, pp. 74–81 (2004)

19. Wang, J., Xia, B.: Relationships of Cohen's Kappa, sensitivity, and specificity for unbiased annotations. In: Proceedings of the 4th International Conference on Biomedical Signal and Image Processing (ICBIP 2019), pp. 98–101 (2019)

What Are We Missing in Algorithmic Fairness? Discussing Open Challenges for Fairness Analysis in User Profiling with Graph Neural Networks

Erasmo Purificato[1,2](✉) [ID] and Ernesto William De Luca[1,2] [ID]

[1] Otto von Guericke University Magdeburg, Magdeburg, Germany
{erasmo.purificato,ernesto.deluca}@ovgu.de
[2] Leibniz Institute for Educational Media | Georg Eckert Institute, Brunswick,
Germany
{erasmo.purificato,deluca}@gei.de

Abstract. Due to the rising importance of human-centred perspectives in artificial intelligence and all related fields, *algorithmic fairness* is currently a key topic when dealing with research on novel machine learning models and applications. However, in most cases, in the context of fairness analysis, we are commonly facing situations in which the fairness metrics are applied only in binary classification scenarios, and the capability of a model to produce fair results is evaluated considering the *absolute difference* of the scores of the two sensitive groups considered. In this paper, we aim to discuss these two open challenges and illustrate our position from an ethical perspective. To support our arguments, we present a case study on two recent scientific contributions exploiting Graph Neural Networks models for user profiling, which are considered state-of-the-art technologies in many domains. With the presented work, our goal is also to create a valuable debate in the community about the raised questions.

Keywords: Algorithmic Fairness · AI Ethics · Graph Neural Networks

1 Background and Motivation

As the use of automated decision-making systems has massively increased lately, **algorithmic fairness** [18,21] has become a crucial research topic, mainly due to the social impact such systems are having on people's life. There is a significant amount of literature on methods to detect and address bias in machine learning (ML) and deep learning (DL) models [2,4,30], notably in user-related scenarios [24], information retrieval (IR) [9,11,26,28] and recommendation systems [12,19,27]. A number of studies have also been conducted to figure out the potential roots of unfairness in automated systems [20,22], which are commonly identified in two main categories: (1) biased *data* and (2) *algorithms* receptive to the biases already present in the datasets used for training.

L. Boratto et al. (Eds.): BIAS 2023, CCIS 1840, pp. 169–175, 2023.
https://doi.org/10.1007/978-3-031-37249-0_14

Among the most powerful technologies falling in the latter category, there are **Graph Neural Networks** (GNNs) [13, 17, 29, 33, 34], recently emerged as an effective solution for dealing with graph data structures in many domains, such as recommenders [15], natural language processing [32], and user profiling [5, 31]. Like any ML system, GNNs are susceptible to learning biases from the historical data they are trained on, and this can manifest in their output. This is primarily due to the unique structure of graphs and the GNNs' message-passing procedure, which can exacerbate discrimination as nodes with similar sensitive attributes are more likely to be connected to each other than those with different attributes [25]. In the last couple of years, several works have been published about the analysis and evaluation of fairness in GNNs [1, 6, 7, 20, 23]. Most of them (especially all those cited) show, in their fairness assessment, two crucial characteristics we aim to highlight and argue in this position paper from an ethical perspective:

1. the fairness metrics are applied in classification scenarios where both the target class and the sensitive attribute (e.g. gender, age, race) are *binary*;
2. the capability of a model to produce fair results is evaluated considering the *absolute difference* of the scores of the two sensitive groups considered.

It is worth noting that these aspects are not specific to the fairness analysis of GNN-based models, but they reflect broader issues in bias detection studies for general automated decision-making systems.

To address the open challenges, in the rest of this paper, we first focus on two publications related to GNN-based models for user profiling (i.e. [6, 23]) in order to present the two publications and illustrate how the fairness analysis has been performed in both cases. Finally, we present the results of the experiments carried out on the two analysed contributions to concretely discuss our position. In particular, the case study presented in Sect. 3 aims to provide quantitative motivations to the above challenges by running two types of analysis on the considered models, re-adapting the experiments conducted in the original publications. In the first one, we focus on the use of the *absolute difference* of the computed fairness metrics, while in the second one, we consider a specific combination of model and dataset in [23] and run the experiment with the original multiclass distribution of the sensitive attribute investigated.

One of the main purposes of the proposed case study is to create a valuable debate in the community about the raised questions.

2   Analysed Contributions

The scientific works we selected for our case study (Sect. 3) to examine and discuss the posed open challenges are illustrated below and belong to the field of **user profiling**, which primarily aims to generate an efficient user representation, namely a *user model* by gleaning individuals' personal characteristics [16].

Dai and Wang [6] proposed *FairGNN*, a novel framework for fair node classification that employs an adversarial debiasing mechanism for dealing with the shortage of sensitive attributes and producing unbiased results. The authors conducted the experiments in a common binary classification scenario on three different datasets[1] and adopted two standard fairness metrics in their analysis: *statistical parity* [8,10] and *equal opportunity* [14]. For both metrics, they quantitatively evaluated the absolute difference of the probabilities computed for the single sensitive attributes, reported as Δ_{SP} and Δ_{EO}, respectively.

In one of our previous works (hereinafter formally referred to as Purificato et al.) [23], we presented the fairness assessment of two state-of-the-art GNN-based models for user profiling, i.e. *CatGCN* [5] and *RHGN* [31] on two real-world use cases, in order to derive potential correlations between the different profiling paradigms of the analysed architectures and the fairness scores they produce. The authors considered a binary scenario performing a fairness analysis on two datasets and leveraging four metrics: *statistical parity, equal opportunity, overall accuracy equality* [3] and *disparate mistreatment* [3]. Similar to the previous work, the evaluation is made by exploiting the absolute difference of the probabilities computed for the single sensitive attributes, namely Δ_{SP}, Δ_{EO}, Δ_{OAE} and Δ_{TE}.

Table 1. Fairness metrics computation without absolute value for Dai and Wang [6] (in particular, we exploited the *FairGCN* version).

Dataset	Δ_{SP}	Δ_{EO}
Pokec-z	0.024 ± 0.007	0.012 ± 0.003
NBA	−0.021 ± 0.007	0.018 ± 0.001

Table 2. Fairness metrics computation without absolute value for Purificato et al. [23].

Dataset	Model	Δ_{SP}	Δ_{EO}
Alibaba	CatGCN	−0.045 ± 0.021	0.139 ± 0.074
	RHGN	0.019 ± 0.012	−0.133 ± 0.086
JD	CatGCN	0.033 ± 0.013	−0.052 ± 0.016
	RHGN	.009 ± 0.007	−0.042 ± 0.017

3 Case Study

We run two types of experiments for the open challenges presented in Sect. 1. In the first one, we focused on the use of the *absolute difference* of the computed fairness metrics. The setting is straightforward: we remove the absolute value from the fairness computation of the analysed models and execute the same experiments presented in the original papers with the default parameters, computing Δ_{SP} and Δ_{EO}. The results are displayed in Table 1 and Table 2. In

---

[1] Due to the page limit constraint, the details of the experiments carried out in the original paper are not discussed.

the results, it is evident the alternation of positive and negative scores, meaning that for a given combination of model and dataset, the unfairness (regardless of the specific value) might be directed towards one sensitive group or the other.

Concerning the issue related to fairness analysis in binary scenarios, we conducted an experiment only for a specific model and dataset, because the derived implications can be easily extended. In particular, we focused on RHGN model and Alibaba dataset from Purificato et al. [23] work, adopting the original binary classification task, but with the following setting for the sensitive attribute: on the one hand, we considered its original multiclass distribution (seven groups, named as s_0-s_6) and calculated every single *statistical parity* (SP) probability; on the other hand, we binarised the attribute, as done in the original paper, and again computed the single probabilities for the binary groups. The resulting binary sensitive attribute groups are composed as follows: $A = \{s_0, s_1, s_2, s_3\}$, $B = \{s_4, s_5, s_6\}$. The results are shown in Table 3.

Table 3. Statistical parity scores for binary and multiclass sensitive attribute groups for Purificato et al. [23] (RHGN model and Alibaba dataset).

Binary group	SP	Multiclass group	SP
A	0.887 ± 0.015	s_0	0.81 ± 0.02
		s_1	0.91 ± 0.02
		s_2	0.91 ± 0.01
		s_3	0.92 ± 0.01
B	0.797 ± 0.055	s_4	0.89 ± 0.01
		s_5	0.72 ± 0.03
		s_6	0.78 ± 0.07

The observation derived from these results is that binarisation can lead to misleading evaluation of a specific subgroup. In this specific experiment, the group s_0 should be treated as a disadvantaged group if considered in the fine-grained assessment, but it would be treated as an advantaged group when included in the binary group A. The opposite applies to group s_4.

4   Ethical Implications of the Open Challenges

From an ethical perspective, there are several implications from the presented results which led us to argue the following positions regarding the challenges we open with this paper:

1. In many of the current works about fairness evaluation of automated systems, the sensitive attributes, that are natively multiclass, are made binary to meet the standard fairness metrics definitions. From our point of view, there are two crucial reasons why it is essential to evaluate fairness by examining the

actual distribution of sensitive groups. Firstly, if the system at hand is not as effective for certain groups, they will end up receiving less effective services, such as targeted advertisements or recommendations. Secondly, reducing the different classes and groups into a binary representation can lead to an incorrect evaluation of the fairness of models, potentially distorting the original data conditions.

2. In the same context, considering the absolute difference score in the fairness analysis can be hazardous for other motivations. In particular, from both a system and user perspective, with this practice, we cannot figure out the disadvantaged groups for every specific combination of model, dataset and fairness metrics, and thus unable to make in place any tailored intervention to mitigate the issue in a real-world scenario.

5   Conclusion

In this paper, we posed and discussed two potential open challenges in recent studies on algorithmic fairness, namely the common practices of performing the assessment only in classification scenarios where both the target class and the sensitive attribute are binary, and the use of the absolute difference of the fairness metrics scores in the evaluation to deem a model as fair or not. With a case study on GNN-based models for user profiling, we presented our position arguing in favour of a multiclass assessment with a clear understanding of the disadvantaged groups, exposing also some ethical implications which derive from the experimental results displayed. Our aim is to foster discussion in the community around these topics and continue to deepen into them with even more detailed future analysis.

References

1. Agarwal, C., Lakkaraju, H., Zitnik, M.: Towards a unified framework for fair and stable graph representation learning. In: Uncertainty in Artificial Intelligence, pp. 2114–2124. PMLR (2021)
2. Barocas, S., Hardt, M., Narayanan, A.: Fairness and Machine Learning. fairmlbook.org (2019). http://www.fairmlbook.org
3. Berk, R., Heidari, H., Jabbari, S., Kearns, M., Roth, A.: Fairness in criminal justice risk assessments: the state of the art. Sociol. Methods Res. 50(1), 3–44 (2021)
4. Caton, S., Haas, C.: Fairness in machine learning: a survey (2020). arXiv preprint arXiv:2010.04053
5. Chen, W., et al.: CatGCN: graph convolutional networks with categorical node features. IEEE Trans. Knowl. Data Eng. (2021)
6. Dai, E., Wang, S.: Say no to the discrimination: learning fair graph neural networks with limited sensitive attribute information. In: Proceed. of the 14th ACM International Conference on Web Search and Data Mining, pp. 680–688 (2021)
7. Dong, Y., Kang, J., Tong, H., Li, J.: Individual fairness for graph neural networks: a ranking based approach. In: Proceedings of the 27th ACM SIGKDD Conference on Knowledge Discovery & Data Mining, pp. 300–310 (2021)

8. Dwork, C., Hardt, M., Pitassi, T., Reingold, O., Zemel, R.: Fairness through aware-
    ness. In: Proceedings of the 3rd Innovations in Theoretical Computer Science Con-
    ference, pp. 214–226 (2012)
9. Ekstrand, M.D., Das, A., Burke, R., Diaz, F., et al.: Fairness in information access
    systems. Found. Trends® Inf. Retrieval 16(1–2), 1–177 (2022)
10. Feldman, M., Friedler, S.A., Moeller, J., Scheidegger, C., Venkatasubramanian,
    S.: Certifying and removing disparate impact. In: Proceedings of the 21th ACM
    SIGKDD International Conference on Knowledge Discovery and Data Mining, pp.
    259–268 (2015)
11. Gao, R., Shah, C.: How fair can we go: detecting the boundaries of fairness opti-
    mization in information retrieval. In: Proceedings of the 2019 ACM SIGIR inter-
    national conference on theory of information retrieval, pp. 229–236 (2019)
12. Gómez, E., Zhang, C.S., Boratto, L., Salamó, M., Ramos, G.: Enabling cross-
    continent provider fairness in educational recommender systems. Future Gener.
    Comput. Syst. 127, 435–447 (2022). https://doi.org/10.1016/j.future.2021.08.025
13. Hamilton, W., Ying, Z., Leskovec, J.: Inductive representation learning on large
    graphs. In: Advances in Neural Information Processing Systems, vol. 30 (2017)
14. Hardt, M., Price, E., Srebro, N.: Equality of opportunity in supervised learning.
    In: Advances in Neural Information Processing Systems, vol. 29 (2016)
15. He, X., Deng, K., Wang, X., Li, Y., Zhang, Y., Wang, M.: LightGCN: simplifying
    and powering graph convolution network for recommendation. In: Proceedings of
    the 43rd International ACM SIGIR Conference on Research and Development in
    Information Retrieval, pp. 639–648 (2020)
16. Kanoje, S., Girase, S., Mukhopadhyay, D.: User profiling trends, techniques and
    applications. arXiv preprint arXiv:1503.07474 (2015)
17. Kipf, T.N., Welling, M.: Semi-supervised classification with graph convolutional
    networks. In: 5th International Conference on Learning Representations, ICLR
    2017, Conference Track Proceedings (2017)
18. Kleinberg, J., Ludwig, J., Mullainathan, S., Rambachan, A.: Algorithmic fairness.
    In: AEA Papers and Proceedings, vol. 108, pp. 22–27 (2018)
19. Leonhardt, J., Anand, A., Khosla, M.: User fairness in recommender systems. In:
    Companion Proceedings of the Web Conference 2018, pp. 101–102 (2018)
20. Loveland, D., Pan, J., Bhathena, A.F., Lu, Y.: FairEdit: preserving fair-
    ness in graph neural networks through greedy graph editing. arXiv preprint
    arXiv:2201.03681 (2022)
21. Mitchell, S., Potash, E., Barocas, S., D'Amour, A., Lum, K.: Algorithmic fairness:
    choices, assumptions, and definitions. Ann. Rev. Statist. Appl. 8, 141–163 (2021)
22. Pessach, D., Shmueli, E.: Algorithmic fairness. arXiv preprint arXiv:2001.09784
    (2020)
23. Purificato, E., Boratto, L., De Luca, E.W.: Do graph neural networks build fair
    user models? assessing disparate impact and mistreatment in behavioural user
    profiling. In: Proceedings of the 31st ACM International Conference on Information
    & Knowledge Management, pp. 4399–4403 (2022)
24. Purificato, E., Lorenzo, F., Fallucchi, F., De Luca, E.W.: The use of responsible
    artificial intelligence techniques in the context of loan approval processes. Int. J.
    Hum.-Comput. Interact. 1–20 (2022)
25. Rahman, T., Surma, B., Backes, M., Zhang, Y.: Fairwalk: towards fair graph
    embedding. In: Proceedings of the 28th International Joint Conference on Arti-
    ficial Intelligence, pp. 3289–3295 (2019)

26. Ramos, G., Boratto, L.: Reputation (in)dependence in ranking systems: Demographics influence over output disparities. In: Proceedings of the 43rd International ACM SIGIR conference on research and development in Information Retrieval, SIGIR 2020, pp. 2061–2064. ACM (2020). https://doi.org/10.1145/3397271.3401278

27. Ramos, G., Boratto, L., Caleiro, C.: On the negative impact of social influence in recommender systems: a study of bribery in collaborative hybrid algorithms. Inf. Process. Manag. **57**(2), 102058 (2020). https://doi.org/10.1016/j.ipm.2019.102058

28. Saúde, J., Ramos, G., Boratto, L., Caleiro, C.: A robust reputation-based group ranking system and its resistance to bribery. ACM Trans. Knowl. Discov. Data **16**(2), 26:1-26:35 (2022). https://doi.org/10.1145/3462210

29. Veličković, P., Cucurull, G., Casanova, A., Romero, A., Lio, P., Bengio, Y.: Graph attention networks. arXiv preprint arXiv:1710.10903 (2017)

30. Verma, S., Rubin, J.: Fairness definitions explained. In: IEEE/ACM International Workshop on Software Fairness (FairWare 2018), pp. 1–7. IEEE (2018)

31. Yan, Q., Zhang, Y., Liu, Q., Wu, S., Wang, L.: Relation-aware heterogeneous graph for user profiling. In: Proceedings of the 30th ACM International Conference on Information & Knowledge Management, pp. 3573–3577. Association for Computing Machinery, New York, NY, USA (Oct 2021)

32. Yao, L., Mao, C., Luo, Y.: Graph convolutional networks for text classification. In: Proceedings of the AAAI Conference on Artificial Intelligence, vol. 33, pp. 7370–7377 (2019)

33. Zhang, C., Song, D., Huang, C., Swami, A., Chawla, N.V.: Heterogeneous graph neural network. In: Proceedings of the 25th ACM SIGKDD International Conference on Knowledge Discovery & Data Mining, pp. 793–803 (2019)

34. Zhang, Z., Cui, P., Zhu, W.: Deep learning on graphs: a survey. IEEE Trans. Knowl. Data Eng. **34**(1), 249–270 (2022)

Author Index

L. Boratto et al. (Eds.): BIAS 2023, CCIS 1840, p. 177, 2023.
https://doi.org/10.1007/978-3-031-37249-0

Printed in the United States
by Baker & Taylor Publisher Services